MW01059271

irreverent guides

Boston

other Irreverent titles: **Amsterdam, Chicago, London, Manhattan, Miami, New Orleans, Paris, San Francisco, Santa Fe, Virgin Islands (U.S.), Washington, D.C.**

irreverent guides

Boston

BY

JEANNE COOPER

AND

ANNE MEREWOOD

A BALLIETT & FITZGERALD BOOK

MACMILLAN • USA

Where to monitor Christian Science...

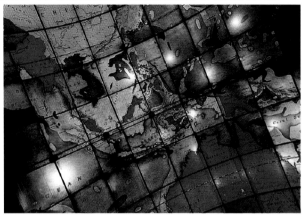

The First Church of Christ, Scientist, see Diversions

Take on "The Godfather Platter"...

La Piccola Venezia, see Dining

Walk the bridges of Middlesex County...

Charles River, see Getting Outside

Observe marine tactical operations...

New England Aquarium, see Diversions

Visit the real-life Hester Prynne...

Kings Chapel Burial Ground, see Diversions

Never utter the name "Babe Ruth"...

Fenway Park, see Entertainment

Kick around the seat of government...

State House, see Diversions

Book a Shaker–modern room...

Charles Hotel, see Accomodations

Blow a small fortune on a fine meal...

La Meridien, see Dining

Enjoy the gospel brunch, buy a T-shirt...

House of Blues, see Entertainment

Eat where they serve up global cuisine...

The Small Planet restaurant, see Dining

Entertain even crabby kids...

Children's Museum, see Diversions

Get stewed with the pols in Beantown.

Doyle's Pub, see Dining

what's so irreverent?

It's up to you.

You can buy a traditional guidebook with its fluff, its promotional hype, its let's-find-something-nice-to-say-about-everything point of view. Or you can buy an Irreverent guide.

What the Irreverents give you is the lowdown, the inside story. They have nothing to sell but the truth, which includes a balance of good and bad. They praise, they trash, they weigh, and leave the final decisions up to you. No tourist board, no chamber of commerce will ever recommend them.

Our writers are insiders, who feel passionate about the cities they live in, and have strong opinions they want to share with you. They take a special pleasure leading you where other guides fear to tread.

How irreverent are they? One of our authors insisted on writing under a pseudonym. "I couldn't show my face in town again if I used my own name," she told me. "My friends would never speak to me." Such is the price of honesty. She, like you, should know she'll always have a friend at Frommer's.

Warm regards,

Michael Spring

Michael Spring
Publisher

a disclaimer

Prices fluctuate in the course of time, and travel information changes under the impact of the varied and volatile factors that influence the travel industry. Neither the author nor the publisher can be held responsible for the experiences of readers while traveling. Readers are invited to write to the publisher with ideas, comments, and suggestions for future editions.

about the author

Except for 22 humid years in Houston, **Jeanne Cooper** has always lived where she can play tour guide to friends and family: the San Francisco Bay Area, Washington, D.C., and more recently, Boston. She has been a writer and editor for the *Daily Californian*, the *Washington Post*, and the *Boston Globe*, where she currently reviews theater and pop music. She wishes to thank colleagues Clea Simon and Michelle McPhee for their respective assistance on the Diversions and Nightlife chapters.

Anne Merewood, who contributed the Accommodations and Dining chapters, is a British-born writer who has lived in Boston for eight years. She has three sons, and her work has appeared in British *Vogue*, *Islands*, and *Glamour*.

photo credits

Page i, Page iv top, Page v top, Page vi top, Page viii middle: © f-stop Fitzgerald Inc.; Page ii, Page iv middle, Page v bottom, Page vii top, middle, and bottom, Page viii top and bottom: by Richard McCaffrey; Page iv bottom courtesy of Greater Boston Convention & Visitors Bureau Inc.; Page vi bottom courtesy of Massachusetts Office of Travel and Tourism.

Balliett & Fitzgerald, Inc.
Series editor: Holly Hughes / Executive editor: Tom Dyja / Managing editor: Duncan Bock / Production editor: Howard Slatkin / Photo editor: Maria Fernandez / Editorial assistants: Jennifer Lebin, Iain McDonald
Macmillan Travel art director: Michele Laseau

Design by Tsang Seymour Design Studio

All maps © Simon & Schuster, Inc.

Air travel assistance courtesy of Continental Airlines

MACMILLAN TRAVEL
A Simon & Schuster Macmillan Company
1633 Broadway
New York, NY 10019

ISBN 0-02-860885-2
ISSN 1085-4746

special sales

Bulk purchases (10+ copies) of Frommer's Travel Guides are available to corporations at special discounts. The Special Sales Department can produce custom editions to be used as premiums and/or for sales promotions to suit individual needs. Existing editions can be produced with custom cover imprints such as corporate logos. For more information write to: Special Sales, Simon & Schuster, 1633 Broadway, New York, NY 10019.

Manufactured in the United States of America

contents

introduction

Boston is a place you think you know. But you don't. Whatever your expectations of the city are, you'll discover that half the time they were wrong. Take the famous "Cheers" bar—please. Its real name is the Bull & Finch, the interior looks nothing like the TV version, and if everybody knows your name, it's because you forgot to remove your name badge. In a perverse way, that's a quintessential Boston tourist experience: confusing, surprising, and souvenir-ready.

But the other half of the time, you'll be right. Just across the street from the Bull & Finch, there's the Public Garden, which looks just as inviting as it did 100 years ago. You can just imagine Henry James's Bostonians or William Dean Howells' Silas Lapham taking an evening constitutional here. The Swan Boats serenely ply its lagoon, just as they did in *Make Way for Ducklings*. And up the street, the gold-domed Massachusetts State House beams benignly over the Boston Common, established more than 360 years ago. Even with today's Italian-ice stands, homeless people, and trolley-ticket booths, you can walk through the Common's open spaces and feel connected to colonial times. And you don't have to take home a Styrofoam beer-can holder to remember it by.

You think Boston, and you think tradition: conservative, hidebound, downright boring. But what do 200,000 college students know about tradition? That's how many pour into the greater Boston area (including Cambridge, a narrow river away) every year. Their traditions include body piercing, intemperate drinking, nightclub hopping, and stage diving. Ride the city's Green Line trolleys from Grunge Central (a k a Kenmore Square) toward Boston University and Boston College at night, and you'll hardly see a soul over 30. In this part of town, Aerosmith is considered as much an old-guard institution as the Boston Symphony Orchestra, and the local pantheon of alternative-rock heroes that includes Letters to Cleo and Juliana Hatfield is constantly filling up with new idols. And forget traditional Yankee thrift—an influx of wealthy European, Middle Eastern, and Japanese students fuel plenty of money-burning establishments here, from Newbury Street's designer boutiques to Lansdowne Street's dance spots.

Then there's the other side of the equation. Although parishes are merging and churches are closing, Catholicism still holds sway. The Monsignor O'Brien Highway through Cambridge and Somerville is *never* called just the O'Brien Highway. Once I rode with a cabbie—a devout Muslim who had converted to Islam many years ago—who was shocked to hear that I'd been in Boston two months and still not seen the Cathedral of the Holy Cross. He switched off the meter, drove to the South End edifice, and proudly announced, "I was an altar boy there! That's where the Pope celebrated Mass!" The Paulist Fathers' chapel across from the Boston Common on Park Street normally fades into the wall, but around 1pm on Ash Wednesday every year a tide of well-dressed office workers surges out, sporting smudged foreheads. One of the city's chief holidays is March 17—officially Evacuation Day, commemorating the British decampment during the Revolution, but everyone knows it's really St. Patrick's Day. It's been tarnished in recent years by the refusal of parade organizers to let gays and lesbians identify themselves in the traditional march through South Boston, known as "Southie," home to fifth-generation Irish-Americans. Not to worry: liberal Cambridge has countered with an even larger, multicultural St. Patrick's Day parade.

In a town where the city's elite WASPs are still called Brahmins, you'd expect a fair amount of sacred cows: The Kennedys and the Celtics are two such revered home teams, and Red Sox fans still blame Bill Buckner for losing the 1986 World Series. But things do change: Republicans are elected, the Boston Garden is demolished, and the Sox want to leave darling Fenway Park for a new stadium. Boston has a collective history of impassioned oratory, from Cotton Mather to Daniel Webster to John F. Kennedy, but the area has also spawned plenty of wisecrackers, including Jay Leno, Steven Wright, Denis Leary, Paula Poundstone, and Jonathan Katz. It's no wonder. Before the immigrant Irish and Italian underclass became the ruling class, it measured its strength in words. "Cheers" had Boston right in one respect: For every refined, snooty Diane, there's a loudmouthed, down-to-earth Karla taking her down a peg.

On the tour boats and trolleys, it's easy to tell the local guides from the college kids: The true Bostonians rarely stop talking. They're proud of their city and they're happy to tell you why, in their unique accent: "You can walk heah. There's plenty of culchah. The nicest season may be summah, when hahf the city hangs out along the Chahles River, listening to free concerts at the Hatch Shell. Wintah—a real pissah, and wicked cold." Boston has constantly had to reinvent itself, from a Colonial hamlet to a metropolitan center, from an industrial port to a high-tech center. The residents have adapted in their own fashion, most notably behind the wheels of their cars. A speeding auto runs a red light, makes an illegal U-turn at the next intersection, and runs the same red light coming the other way. In the cradle of liberty, it's every driver for him- or herself. On the tangled skein of old colonial streets, Yankee ingenuity triumphs over anachronistic inefficiency: The one-way street is driven one way—but sometimes, in reverse. The few street signs that exist seem geared to the people who know where they're going, which, given the constant influx of students, visitors, and new residents, means only about 50 percent of the people on the road. If you're lost, Bostonians will be happy to give you directions—using Dunkin Donuts stores as landmarks.

People here like being approached for help by the hopelessly lost; it reinforces their belief that they have something others don't. So don't come here expecting to get to know the place like a local. No two locals know the same city, anyway—but don't ever tell them that. Another cabdriver once told me, "Of all the cities in the world to live in, Boston is definitely the best." When I asked where else he had lived, he crowed, "No place but here!" In Boston, that's the equivalent of "Case closed."

Boston Neighborhoods

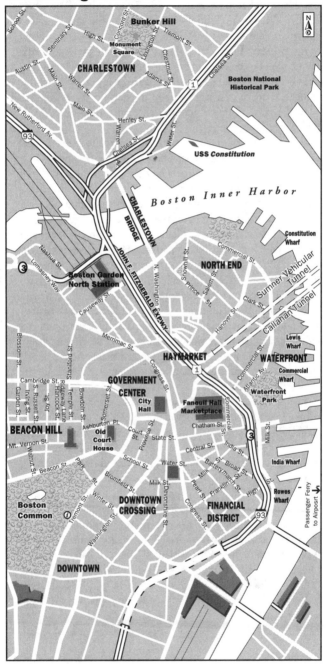

you probably didn't know

Why they call it the Hub... For one thing, it sounds better than "Beantown." Nineteenth-century author Oliver Wendell Holmes referred to the Massachusetts State House as "the hub of the solar system," and Bostonians quickly took up and shortened the phrase. Local newspapers like to use "Hub," a nice small word for headline writers and an easy way to refer to Boston and Cambridge, both founded in 1630 and still not fond of being lumped together. Holmes also came up with the term "Boston Brahmins" for members of the upper caste of local society, who over the last century have retained prestige and their seats at the symphony while losing power and money.

The meaning of a Smoot... When you walk across Harvard Bridge to get one of the best views of the Boston skyline available, look down for a moment and you'll notice the hatch marks known as Smoots. They've been repainted over the years but still reflect the exact length of a 1958 MIT student named Smoot who was painstakingly laid end to end over the bridge to officially measure it at 364.4 Smoots (and one ear).

T-line colors (chaos or cabal?)... The seemingly mad train system in the Hub (known as the T) actually follows an abstruse logic—sort of. It's like memorizing the periodic table. You don't *need* to know all the elements, but it can be helpful—particularly if you want to impress your friends. The Red Line, which stretches from Alewife in Cambridge to spurs in Mattapan and Braintree, originally ended at Harvard Square, home of the Harvard *Crimson*…. The Blue Line, which runs from Bowdoin (during weekday work hours) or Government Center (all other times) out to Wonderland, goes underneath Boston Harbor between the Aquarium stop near Long Wharf and Maverick Square in East Boston. It then runs to Logan Airport and through the oceanside communities in Revere. Get it? Water, water everywhere, hence blue. The Green Line, which has now extended its route from the Boston Common to start in Lechmere, across the Charles in Cambridge, diverges along four lettered spurs, one of which used to connect most of landscape architect Frederick Law Olmsted's "Emerald Necklace" of parks—inspiring the green tint. As for the formerly elevated Orange Line, which runs from Malden north of the city to Forest Hills, it follows Washington Street for most of its Boston route. Washington Street got its name after a visit by the first U.S. president in 1789, but, typical of New England, it had four names for different stretches before that: Cornhill, Newbury, Essex, and, you guessed it, Orange.

A Green Line is a Green Line… There are four Green Lines in Boston. Don't panic. Take a deep breath…. It's a piece of Boston arcana worth mastering. Between Lechmere and Copley Square, all four trolleys run the same route. The E trolleys diverge at Copley to head to Huntington Avenue, where many hotels are clustered, continuing to stops at tourist attractions like the Prudential Center, Symphony Hall, and the Museum of Fine Arts. (Sharp-eyed passengers will note the E on the front of some cars has a red slash through it; that's trolleyspeak for a line that doesn't run its entire route. Many travel guides still show T maps with the E leg ending at the Arborway in Jamaica Plain, but after Heath Street the route is served by buses.) At Kenmore Square, two stops after Copley, the B, C, and D spurs diverge. Try these mnemonics on for size: The B trolleys run along Commonwealth Avenue through Brighton to Boston College, the C trolleys along Beacon Street to Cleveland

Circle, and the D runs parallel to Boylston Street to Riverside (well, at least there's a *d* in it).

You can't get there from here... Just because Boston subway nomenclature makes a little sense, expect no mercy from the street names. If you insist on driving, you will get lost. Take Washington Street, for example. (You can take it all the way to Rhode Island if you want, but that's another story.) As a special way of honoring good old George, all but three Boston city streets change names when they cross Washington. While the transitions from West Something to East Something in the South End aren't that surprising, downtown you'll find Winter turns into Summer, Court into State, and, completely inexplicably, Stuart into Kneeland, among others. The only exceptions are Massachusetts Avenue ("Mass. Ave." to locals), Columbus Avenue, and Roxbury's Melnea Cass Boulevard, the last a relatively new thoroughfare named after the neighborhood's famous civil rights activist and suffragist. Other downtown streets are tortuous, since they're basically paved-over footpaths that wind around vanished Colonial-era obstacles. The Big Dig has only added to a sense of being punished for original sin as you cross downtown. By contrast, most of the Back Bay is a blissfully straightforward grid, with alphabetical cross streets (Arlington to Hereford) from Beacon to Boylston Streets. But there's a catch for drivers: As in most of the city core, streets are one way, and almost all parking spaces are *(a)* for residents only and *(b)* filled. So, count your blessings when Boston's street labyrinth has you turned

Traffic rules
Warning: Bostonians consider driving a blood sport. If you think Hub motorists are not incompetent but blatantly criminal, you're right. Here are the rules:
1. Don't give away your strategy—never use turn signals.
2. Pass other cars on either side. Passing on the right is actually preferable, since it carries the element of surprise (though not to other Boston drivers).
3. Rest one hand on the horn.
4. Wave the other angrily out the window.
5. Avoid eye contact and courtesy—you might lose. (Lose what? Who the hell cares.) Here are the rules for Boston's undaunted pedestrians:
1. Jaywalk.
2. Jaywalk fast.
3. Jaywalk en masse— it's safer.

BOSTON | YOU PROBABLY DIDN'T KNOW

upside down and inside out. The winding, one-way passageways force Boston drivers to slow down—they are the only thing standing between you and mayhem. If Boston driving (see the "Traffic rules" sidebar) took place in a city with wide-open boulevards and freeways like Los Angeles, it would make *The Road Warrior* look tame. For pedestrians, who usually don't bother with the interminable wait for a "walk" light, the catch is the frustrated driver who just navigates in reverse. As a tourist, you may be tempted to keep your head buried in a map, but unless the nape of your neck has 20/20 vision, don't.

Where the hell can you park... If you were dumb enough to bring a car, and still dumber not to book a hotel with parking (however much it costs), here's one last-ditch scam for finding a space for your wheels. In much of Beacon Hill, the Back Bay, and Cambridge, curbside parking is limited to residents who have the right sticker on their windshields. Park here and you'll be fined, but the fine is often cheaper than a garage, especially if you just don't pay it. *(Note: We do not endorse this strategy.)* Think of a parking ticket as a garage fee, good for about 24 hours. Or find one of the Back Bay cross streets that allow parking after 6pm. At about 5:45, start cruising them. When the driver in front of you swings over to the curb to park, do likewise. The street will be full within moments. There's no way the tow truck will get there before 6, so you'll all have nice free overnight parking.

What's the Head of the Charles... The former estuary known as the Charles River divides Boston from Cambridge; you will hear some people refer to it as "the Chuck," but these people are preppies—they talk like that sober. The annual Head of the Charles Regatta, a daylong event traditionally held the second Sunday in October, pits college teams against those of prep schools, older masters—including several former Olympians—and independent rowing clubs in a series of races, involving more than 800 boats and 3,000 rowers (women as well as men). An estimated quarter-million spectators swarm over the banks of the Charles to watch, lining the 3-mile course from the John Weeks Footbridge near Harvard to Watertown. Until recent years, heavy drinking seemed an inseparable part of the event, turning the river into a giant urinal, which gave new meaning to the term "Head of the Charles." The park police have cracked down on this part of the festivities, however, and the last few Heads have become much more family friendly. To sound conversant with the regatta, know these terms: The teams aren't "rowing," they're "sculling"; the vessels they're in aren't "boats," they're "shells," and they're more often made of fiberglass than of wood these days; and the short fellow or lady barking orders in the front is a "coxswain," or "cox."

Who serves the best ice cream cone... Not a joking matter in Boston. Rival ice cream makers have cultish followings here, and Bostonians, among the country's most voracious cone heads, should know from ice cream. Nothing bad can be said about Steve's though it has lost some its lustre since the heady seventies when visionary owner Steve Herrell brought chop-ins like Heath Bars and Oreos to the masses. After selling Steve's (now found in Somerville, Brookline, and Faneuil Hall), the ice cream guru opened Herrell's (Harvard Square, Longwood Galleria, Allston). But his supremacy is challenged by competitors such as Christina's (Inman Square) and Toscanini's (Central Square), who vie for titles in best sorbets and most intriguing flavors. Guinness ice cream, anyone? J.P. Licks draws families to its store on Jamaica Plain's Centre Street, where an attractive plastic cow adorns the roof, and draws heavily pierced youth to its Newbury store. Try a cone from each of the contenders and decide which is the best yourself. It's a Boston tradition.

What the Big Dig means to you... The Big Dig was supposed to unloose a hoard of foot-long scavenging rats on Boston. Nobody has seen the rats to date, so for now the Big Dig just means unpredictable construction obstacles around prime tourist areas. Rivaling WPA-era dams in epic scale and costing billions of dollars, the Big Dig is the largest U.S. public works project going. It aims to move the downtown stretch of I-93 underground. Currently, the highway travels on an elevated expressway named the Central (clogged) Artery, where you are often lucky to break 5 miles per hour thanks to traffic. Finish date: 2004 (or thereabouts). Once the roads are underground, parks will be built above them, and the isolated North End and Waterfront will be reconnected to downtown. In an already-finished phase, the project built a new underwater link to Logan Airport, the Ted Williams Tunnel from South Boston, which for the time being is open to commercial traffic only. That has made airport taxi fares to and from points south of the city cheaper but, when your destination is the North End, not necessarily faster than the Sumner and Callahan Tunnels.

Do they ban art in Boston anymore... Nope. The last city censor left office in the early 1970s, and since then, all hell has broken loose. The People's Republic of Cambridge has long had a progressive reputation, but today even Beantown proper has a cutting-edge cultural scene. The Theater Offensive in Boston and the American Repertory Theatre in Cambridge sponsor fall festivals of provocative work that make the National Endowment for the Arts granters look like Puritans. The Institute for Contemporary Arts in Back Bay and the multimedia Mobius center near South Station are hip venues for the latest in visual and performance art. The three performance spaces of the Middle East Club in Cambridge's Central Square showcase a mind-boggling array of musical innovators.

Where the hills of John Winthrop's city went... After deserting Charlestown for the Shawmut Peninsula (today's Boston), the leader of the Massachusetts Bay Colony, John Winthrop, instructed his followers to see themselves as a "city on a hill." You may notice the hills are gone today. Instead we have landfill. Tremont Street, heart of the Theater District, gets its name from the three original peaks ("Trimountaine") around the Boston Common. They were leveled to make one shorter mound, today's quaint Beacon Hill, in the late 18th and early 19th centuries, and the dirt now supports several neighborhoods: Charles Street, where antique stores cater to the elegant households on "the flat of the hill"; the West End, once a colorful, ethnically integrated tenement district and now a sterile hospital and high-rise apartment complex; and North Station, home of the new Fleet Center arena (as well as sports bars galore) and the grubby gateway to the North End. Another former peak was nicknamed "Mount Whoredom," thanks to its bordellos that catered to sailors. But if you're looking for that kind of activity today, you're better off checking the Combat Zone, which flows into Chinatown, or Bay Village, another landfill project. Among the skyscrapers in the busy-by-day, slow-at-night Financial District,

High Street isn't very high anymore; its remains may sit over the original site of the Boston Tea Party ship.

Where you shouldn't go in Boston... Some parts of the staunch Irish-American neighborhoods of South Boston and Charlestown can still be less than welcoming to "outsiders," meaning if you're not white, if you look too fancy, if you're gay, or if you have out-of-state license plates. The 1970s wounds from enforced school busing and gentrification are still raw. Many Bostonians will go out of their way to avoid driving through parts of the South End and Roxbury, prone to drug-related violence. Resentment still lingers over the notorious 1987 Charles Stuart case, in which a white man claimed a black man shot him and his pregnant wife, who died. Virtually all black males were considered suspect for several days, until eventually a family member tipped police off that Stuart was the culprit. (Stuart jumped off the Tobin Bridge to his death.) You generally don't have to worry about interpreting what's bias and what's common sense: You're not likely to go to any of those neighborhoods. More important, pedestrians after dark should avoid Washington Street south of Downtown Crossing; stick to well-lit streets in Chinatown, the South End, and Back Bay (Newbury has the busiest foot traffic); and resist cutting across Boston Common or the Public Garden. Although the T stations' malfunctioning escalators (particularly at Aquarium) have caused more injuries than subway crime has, in the wee hours it may make sense to take a cab instead. If you can't find one on the street to hail, head to the nearest hotel or grocery store for a cab stand. But don't spend a lot of time worrying; this is still a very civilized town—despite the way people drive.

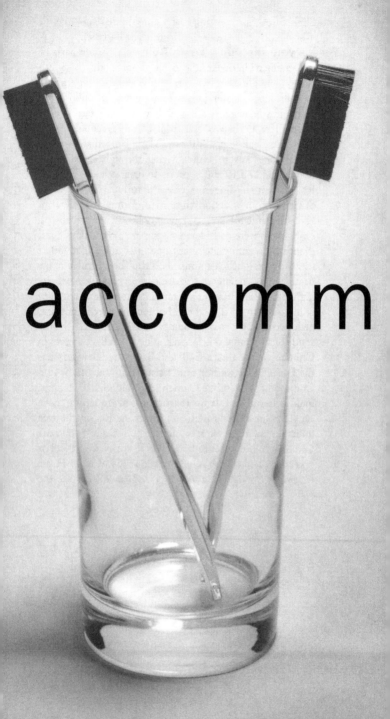

accomm

1
odations

To quote a check-
in clerk at one of
Boston's biggest
hotels, "We can't
tell you our rates.
I charge whatever
I feel like, within

a certain range." Capricious? Maybe. But this is a city where hotels tend to fill up, at least during the summer and fall peak seasons. There may be a throng of deluxe hotels in the Back Bay, but they all seem to be doing very nicely, thank you. Competition keeps things lively, but few hurt for business.

Yankee hoteliers are too sharp to give anything away for nothing, and in this cobbled-together city, crammed onto its narrow peninsula, space is at a premium. That's why the Back Bay, which once was an honest-to-god body of water, was filled in during the 19th century: to create more real estate. In the 20th century, folks started building upward instead, hemming in the Common, the Public Garden, and Copley Square with looming skyscrapers. In today's Boston, Paul Revere wouldn't have been able to see the spire of North Church, let alone know how many lanterns were hanging there.

So reserve in advance if you don't want to get left out in the cold—or out in the sweltering heat (forget that New England is in a northern clime; summers here are HOT). Whatever you're paying, make sure you explore your options. Views vary from a city skyline to the Public Garden to panoramas of the Charles or the Atlantic—but not all rooms in a hotel may have that prize view. Be explicit when you make your reservations if you want a newly refurbished room; with hotels constantly updating, often half the hotel has been made over while the other half still has shabby carpets. And always think "high up": You'll get great views from the upper floors of the high-rises, and even if the hotel has only five floors, top floors will be quieter.

One more word of advice: Parking costs can add $20 a day onto your bill, so scope out the situation in advance if you're bringing a car (god forbid you should *rent* a car while you're here—but more on that later). The Howard Johnson hotels here may be glorified motor inns, but *they provide free parking*, which is more significant than you might think.

Winning the Reservations Game

Just call the hotel, reserve the dates you want, and give a credit card number, right? Wrong! Paying the asking price is like paying full fare on an airplane: strictly for chumps. Of course, some smaller hotels, bed-and-breakfasts, and hostels do have fixed tariffs, but most big hotels do not. This is great money-saving news for guests.

Happily for vacationers, some of the best deals happen on weekends, when executives on expenses go home (though even executives can save by asking for a corporate). Be sure to ask about weekend rates when you first call; they can save you as much as $100 per night. Weekend packages might include meals, show or nightclub tickets, health club "extras," and free parking. In addition, some hotels run romantic vacation packages for couples, others offer family discounts, and many hotels allow kids to sleep for free in their parents' room—though the age limit varies from 12 to 18, so ask. Check out the Boston Travel Planner, available from the Greater Boston Convention and Visitors Bureau (tel 800/374–7400 or 617/536–4100), for many advertised packages.

One big factor in pricing is "availability." That means hotels would rather rent an empty room cheap than not at all, so you can find major discounts out of season, or by waiting until the last minute. Don't assume that everything will be booked up: A spot-check on a Friday night in mid-July found vacancies in more than half the hotels: The Bostonian, the Colonnade, the Copley Plaza, the Copley Square, 57 Park Plaza, and the Milner all had space, while the Boston Marriott at Copley Place, the Westin at Copley Place, and the Newbury Guest House were filled. Watch out for graduation season (late spring), though. If you don't want to shop around yourself, try the **Hotel Reservations Network** (tel 800/964–6835): It offers discounted rates on a limited number of hotels, and claims to be able to get rooms when everything else is sold out.

If you prefer a bed-and-breakfast, reservations services can do the footwork for you. Try **Bed and Breakfast Associates Bay Colony Ltd.** (tel 617/449–5302 or 800/347–5088, fax 617/449–5958), **Bed and Breakfast Agency of Boston** (tel 617/720–3540 or 800/248–9262, fax 617/523–5761), or **Bed and Breakfast Cambridge and Greater Boston** (tel 617/576–1492 or 800/888–0178, fax 617/576–1430). Maybe you'd like to go native and have the use of an apartment during your stay? Try **AAA Corporate Rentals** (tel 617/357–6900 or 800/487–5020, fax 617/357–7330) for short-term rentals and **The Greenhouse** (tel 617/267–6777 or 800/330–4020, fax 617/267–0075) for longer-term rentals.

Is There a Right Address?

Beacon Hill, home to the Brahmins, has always been the city's Best Address. Even today, Bostonians happily pay $1,500 per month for tiny studios on these picturesque gaslit streets with no place to park at night. There's no hotel on Beacon Hill, but if you want to stay here, you can choose between select bed-and-breakfasts or a couple of self-catering options. Besides the snob value, the location is perfect, with Boston Common and the Public Garden on one side, and the Charles River on the other. If you prefer a proper hotel, go where the Brahmins went after they outgrew The Hill: **Back Bay**, now the heart and soul of Boston, with the Public Garden, the city's best shopping streets and malls, the Convention Center, and Symphony Hall. The **South End**, with shady streets of Victorian row houses built by nouveau riche tradesmen, was once abandoned to waves of unwealthy immigrants; now, the revitalized neighborhood is "nouveau Boston"—a colorful mishmash of blacks, whites, Hispanics, gays, and trendy young professionals—with a couple of intimate lodging alternatives.

Stay downtown in some cities and you'll see nothing but sterile streets and tall, empty buildings after dark; in Boston, however, the **Financial District** has plenty of life after 5:00, mainly because it's on the ocean and beside the cheerful, touristy area around Faneuil Hall. Cross the Charles and you're in **Cambridge**, where accommodations cater to Harvard University business, or take advantage of prime riverside locations there. There's no obvious reason to choose Cambridge over Boston—prices and quality are the same in both—but no reason to avoid it, either. Cambridge is well-served by the T, and you just might find free, on-street, overnight parking.

Prices do start to drop once you move out to the suburbs. **Brookline**, easily accessible to Boston by the T, is close to the Harvard Medical School area and hospitals. It is populated by wealthy doctors and is a safe, pleasant place to stay (note that snobby bylaws forbid overnight parking on Brookline's streets). **Newton**, another upscale suburb, is further out but still on the T, and offers a Marriott and several other hotels.

The Lowdown

Beds for Brahmin wannabes... Straighten your tie, press your pants, and head for the **Beacon Hill Bed and Breakfast**, a six-story brick Victorian row house in the heart of Brahmin territory on The Hill. The rooms are big, full of period antiques, and have details like fireplaces (nonworking, alas) and cunning little oriel windows. Host Susan Butterworth has lived in this house since 1967, "But that's not long enough," she sighs. "You're never a Brahmin unless you're born to it." The self-catering **Eliot and Pickett Houses**, right beside the State House on Beacon Hill, are decent options as well—they're not the real thing, but their bedrooms are well enough furnished, with four-poster and canopy beds as well as Colonial antique reproductions (they're adjacent buildings under one management). A Boston stalwart since 1854, though not always in the same building, the Parker House—excuse us, the **Omni Parker House**— isn't strictly on the Hill (it's just across the Common), but it's the oldest continuously operating hotel in the nation, which confers a certain Brahmin cachet. With its staid, wood-paneled look and smallish rooms, it has always catered to conservative businessmen and politicians— though when Irish upstart John F. Kennedy came here to announce his first campaign for public office, some of the older clients must have spun in their graves.

Beds for Brahmin never-would-be's... The B&B **82 Chandler St.**, a five-story brick row house with mansard roof, fits right in with its countercultural South End location: stylish but hip, with brass-bedded rooms in yellow, green, red, and blue opening off a central staircase, and a trendy penthouse suite with exposed brick and hanging plants.

For travelers with old money... Where else but **The Ritz-Carlton Boston**. Built in 1927, the Ritz-Carlton overlooks the elegant Public Garden; rooms are furnished in French provincial style, with floral fabrics and chandeliers, and some have working fireplaces. The cast of characters here includes society matrons, white-gloved elevator operators, personal butlers (on the Club floor), and the kind of business travelers who take for granted the free weekday limo service to downtown. Also consider the grande dame **Copley Plaza**, built in 1912 in the last gasp of the Gilded Age, with tons of marble, gold, and crystal chandeliers downstairs and ornate guest rooms to match. Or go for the male of the species, the **Omni Parker House**, where dark red carpets, wood-paneled walls, brass elevator doors, and handsome crests in the lobby breathe conservative masculinity.

For travelers with modern tastes... The Ritz-Carlton's number one competitor is the **Four Seasons Hotel**, built in 1985 around the corner on the south edge of the Common. (The rivalry intensified when the Ritz was demoted in 1993 to an AAA four-diamond hotel, while the Four Seasons retained its five-diamond rating.)

You can't beat the Ritz for romance and old world charm, but you can beat it for service (sometimes), business amenities, fitness facilities, and room quality, in all of which the Four Seasons shines. As you approach, two doormen sweep open the glass doors in smooth synchrony; the lobby's loaded with marble, handmade carpets, blond woods, and exotic flowers. Rooms are large, light, and luxurious, with king-size beds. Gazillionaires will be happy to know that for around $2,000 per night you can rent the Presidential Suite, where the mahogany dining table seats 14 and the marble bathtub is bordered by a miniature garden. While Ritz-Carlton guests have to trek off-site for pool and sauna, the Four Seasons has an excellent on-site facility, with a 51-foot pool, a sauna, and massage; they'll also provide jogging shoes and a map of routes near the hotel. The less fit can use the free town-car service to downtown. The Four Seasons even offers a pets' room-service menu with low-fat entrees (no kidding). In a slightly lower price range, the **Harborside Hyatt Conference Center and Hotel** is another temple to modernity, in glass and red brick. Jet-setters may appreciate its airport location, from which you can whisk across the Inner Harbor on the water shuttle to downtown. Elevators glide up and down the futuristic glass tower designed to look like a lighthouse (the lamp is controlled by Logan Airport so it won't confuse pilots); the low lobby is topped by a zodiac ceiling mural with fiber-optic stars, some of which hang down on little (visible) wires. Rooms have modern furnishings with geometric patterns, voice mail, two phones (one line), big bathrooms, and for $15 extra a fax machine (though none in the bathroom, yet).

For travelers with money, period... Old, new, who cares—if you have enough money, stay at the sparkling **Boston Harbor Hotel**, where luxury power yachts moor dockside. A constant fresh breeze blows by the copper-domed oceanside rotunda and on through the magnificent 80-foot archway, a gateway to Boston from the sea. A museum-quality art collection and Chippendale-style furniture in the rooms gives the interior a refined spin. The hotel and adjoining buildings (shops, offices, and condominiums) at the 15-story Rowes Wharf complex are an architectural dream and a tourist attraction in themselves. With one foot in the Financial District, one in the tourist mecca around Faneuil Hall, and another in the ocean, this is the most inspired and inspiring hotel in the city. Splurge on a Spa Retreat one-night package: deluxe room, lunch, dinner, herbal body wrap, and facial, for around $450 per night.

For travelers with no money (or not much)... Don't believe the brochure—the **Midtown Hotel** is not "Boston's most convenient hotel," but it is reasonably priced and reasonably close to Copley Square, though it's on a particularly busy stretch of Huntington Avenue. It's more of a motel than a hotel, really, but the rooms are a decent size and there's a pool. The **Milner Hotel** markets itself as "Boston's Best Value," and it might be right. Quaintly, The Milner claims to be "European style"— read: old-fashioned, with small rooms and a Continental breakfast thrown in. The Theater District location is convenient, but hardly charming. Another central, low-cost hotel is the newly refurbished—well, at least recarpeted and repainted—**Chandler Inn**, an eight-story anomaly amid the town houses of the South End. A tad further out is the **Boylston Street Howard Johnson**—an absolutely run-of-the-mill HoJo, but convenient to Red Sox games, and with a pool. Of course, it's always cheaper to stay out of town: The **Beacon Inns**, a pair of strictly basic bed-and-breakfast spots, are located in suburban Brookline, right on the Green Line T.

Overrated... Dare we say it—the **Ritz**? Surely it's Boston's most overpriced place to stay. Why do the smallest rooms with no view cost $50 more than standard rooms at the Copley Plaza? And why are rooms with views $150 more? I guess those who stay here wouldn't be seen dead anywhere else, but to some the standard overnight rate of $285 to $385 just seems too steep. As for all those business giants downtown, from the **Westin** to the **Sheraton**, they are not so much overrated as indistinguishable: big rooms, big windows, and big bills.

Somewhat hostile hostels.... Between Copley Square and Fenway and not really convenient to anything, the **YMCA's Central Branch** has a grand, carved lobby with flags hanging from the gallery. Is this really the Y? you ask. Not to worry—the grim, non-air-conditioned rooms with heavy wooden furniture, well-worn sheets, and regulation-style folded blankets soon bring you down to earth. A major overhaul, begun in September 1995, should bring much-needed improvements. The usual Y recreational facilities are a big plus, though; *Boston* magazine named it the best gym in town in 1993 and '94. Convenient to Symphony Hall and the Museum of Fine Arts, the **Boston International Youth Hostel** provides slightly more cheerful accommodations in three- to five-person dormitories, but check ahead in summer, when American Youth Hostel members may have the whole place booked up. In the true hosteling "move along now" spirit, this place kicks you out after five nights in summer, two weeks in winter. One of a dying breed, the **Berkeley Residence YWCA** on the edge of Back Bay is one of those women-only hotels—shades of "Bosom Buddies"—with nun-like single and double rooms with shared bathrooms. Ask for a room overlooking the pleasant gardens.

Homes away from home... B&Bs offer some of the most economical rates in Boston, as well as local savvy, personal assistance, homey charm, and all that. On the upper end of the scale, there's the **Beacon Hill Bed and Breakfast**, which offers three large antique-furnished rooms on, where else? Beacon Hill; the larger **Newbury Guest House**, which lives up to its stylish Back Bay address with a beautifully carved central staircase, polished wood floors, and reproduction Victorian furniture; and, across the river in North Cambridge, **A Cambridge House Bed and Breakfast**, which has enough antiques and Victorian primness to make you feel positively transcendentalist. (Ask for the main building—rooms in the neighboring carriage house are tiny, cunning floor-to-ceiling wall mirrors and all.). In the very unstuffy South End, brass beds, fireplaces, and bay windows lend Victorian grace notes at **82 Chandler St.**, in an 1853 red-brick row house. Its spacious rooms have discreetly placed microwaves and refrigerators, but the South End has so many neat cafes you probably won't use a kitchenette. **The Beacon Inns**, at two Brookline locations, are clean but slightly shabby, low-budget B&Bs (you collect your coffee and muffins downstairs and eat them in your room), just a short T ride out of Boston. If you don't like cozy chats or "family style" breakfasts, opt for do-it-yourself beds and make-your-own breakfasts. Back Bay's **Beacon Inn Guest Houses** (not to be confused with the Beacon Inns above) are pristine, self-contained studio apartments with wall-to-wall carpeting, some with refrigerators, others with complete kitchenettes. The **Eliot and Pickett Houses** on Beacon Hill have full kitchens downstairs, always stocked with eggs, muffins, cereals, milk, and other items, so you can cook your own breakfast in a shared kitchen and then eat it in the privacy of your room. Tote in your own groceries and you can use the kitchen to whip up other meals as well.

Anonymous giants... Sometimes you just want to close the soundproof door, flick a remote, and order room service. If you find anonymity more relaxing than friendly fuss, head for the **Westin** or the **Boston Marriott Copley Place**, sleek modern towers erupting from opposite ends of Copley Place, Boston's premier in-town shopping mall, with upscale stores, cinemas, and restaurants on the doorstep, as it were. Their vast lobbies are great for people-watching; the Marriott's has a four-story chandelier, marble floors, full-size trees, and a waterfall, as well as a glitzy glass walkway leading straight into the Prudential Center (more shops). On entering the Westin, you glide up an escalator, past a thundering waterfall. Amid all the bars, lounges, restaurants, and shoppers, it takes half an hour to locate check-in. You could close your eyes and know what the guest rooms look like: plush Downtown Business Deluxe.

Big city, small hotel... If you break into a cold sweat at the mere thought of negotiating the Westin lobby, try the more personal service across the street at the **Copley Square Hotel**, where receptionists wear a genuine smile, you're served complimentary tea and cookies in the lounge every afternoon, and the hotel's seven floors are served by just one nice, old-fashioned elevator. Rooms may be long and narrow, and they may sport an entrance hall or large alcoves, but they'll always have plenty of character. Not to be confused with the ritzy big Copley Plaza, this 19th-century dowager is like the favorite family hotel you knew as a kid, with all modern conveniences on top (voice mail, electronic keys, modem hookups, blah, blah, blah…). Nearby, the **Lenox** also feels small despite

BOSTON | ACCOMMODATIONS

its 200-plus rooms; service is pleasant (receptionists and porters chat naturally rather than between their teeth), rooms have brass door knockers, brass chandeliers, and marble bathrooms, and some have fireplaces. Or slip down Huntington Avenue to the European-style **Colonnade**, with its L-shaped rooms, chocolates on the pillow, multilingual staff, friendly service, and a cheery yellow duck in the bathtub.

Convenient for conventioneers... Sheraton is Boston's native hotel chain, so perhaps it's fitting that the **Sheraton Boston Hotel and Towers** is connected by indoor walkway to the Hynes Convention Center, giving it an inside edge on booking those convention hordes. This 29-story charmer offers all the usual stuff, plus a tropical domed pool complex, Jacuzzi, health club, and extra phones in the bathrooms—can't let calls of nature interfere with those all-important business calls. Convention VIPs can get brownnosed on three executive-level floors. The **Back Bay Hilton** doesn't have the all-weather cattle chute, but it's also smack dab next to Hynes. Another modern high-rise, it's much smaller— 330 rooms as opposed to the Sheraton's 1,200—and many of the pastel-toned guest rooms have beautiful city views. Two other central Boston titans, the **Boston Marriott Copley Place** and the **Westin**, are also relatively close to the Hynes; both have their own conference facilities, too, and lobbies so big and busy you'll never notice how many folks are wearing the same plastic tags. The **Harborside Hyatt Conference Center and Hotel** is better for smaller working meetings, with a business level that has fully equipped work areas complete with "dataport" hookups, and its right-by-the-airport location makes it handy for delegates to zip in and out. Hey, you might never know you're in Boston at all.

Where to drop after you shop... The **Newbury Guest House** is right on Boston's best shopping street and is surrounded by boutiques, antiques shops, art galleries, trendy hairdressers, trendy neighborhood fruit stores, and trendy restaurants (yes, everything on Newbury Street is frightfully trendy). The look inside is totally Back Bay, with sleigh beds and four-posters, polished pine floorboards, and prints from the MFA. Of course, both the **Boston Marriott Copley Place** and the **Westin** at

Copley Place are deluxe cookie-cutter high-rises rooted in the city's flashiest mall; the Westin offers a "Shoppers's Package" with a low overnight room rate and a discount card for many mall stores. In Cambridge, the sleek, modern **Royal Sonesta** is next door to the brand-new Galleria shopping mall; when you drop after shopping, Charles River views and museum-quality artwork in the rooms should soothe your weary senses.

For people who hate conventioneers... How about an elegant Back Bay town house where you can pretend you live in Boston and you don't have to deal with elevators, bellhops, or conventioneers? The **Beacon Inn Guest Houses** (*not* the Beacon Hill Bed & Breakfast, *not* the Beacon Inns) provide anonymous self-catering studios in the Back Bay—just pick up the key from the realtor's office and let yourself in. It's a great price for a snooty area.

Grande dames... The grandest of them all is the **Copley Plaza**: Winston Churchill stayed here, so did Caruso, and if you like glamour and gold, so should you. Right on Copley Square, guests are greeted outside by golden lions and gloved doormen, swept beneath enormous Waterford crystal chandeliers, and deposited in a lobby of gleaming marble pillars, a mosaic floor, and a gilded ceiling painted with blue skies and scudding clouds. Ornate is the operative word, right through to the guest rooms with their English carpets, Italian furniture, and marble bathrooms. If you can't afford to stay here, you can sign up for a tour (every Sunday at 1pm) or pick up a self-guided-tour brochure from the concierge desk in the lobby. Far more subdued in style, the **Eliot Hotel** is the sole survivor of a gaggle of former grande dames on Commonwealth Avenue, which once included the Somerset, the Tuilerie, and the Vendôme, all of which have long gone to hotel heaven. Behind its iron-and-glass portico, handmade in Italy, the Eliot puttered on as a faded hotel with noisy plumbing and long-staying elderly residents until a massive restoration program in the early 1990s turned things around. Now all the rooms are suites—small luxury condos, really—with foyers, kitchenettes, and spacious living rooms separated from the bedrooms by French doors.

Landmark restoration... At the heart of the Financial District, **Le Meridien** is housed in the former Federal

Reserve Bank and modeled after a 16th-century Roman palazzo. Distinctive red awnings trim the outside of this historic landmark, curiously surrounded by some of the tallest skyscrapers in the city, and thousands of city workers picnic every lunchtime in the green, fountained Post Office Square in front. Think of how many quarries it took to make this gleaming interior: Low, vaultlike marble corridors lead to a cream-colored marble lobby with square marble pillars; a grand marble staircase sweeps up to the glass-roofed Café Fleuri and the posh Julien restaurant. Guest rooms, which vary in size and shape, have marble floors and tubs, with polished granite vanities (for a change of pace), and all have been recently refurbished, with formal striped upholsteries.

Luscious love nests... If Victorian decor, antiques, lush carpets and a rosy, well-ordered glow mean romance for you, try **A Cambridge House Bed and Breakfast** and rent the so-called suite (actually one room), with its canopy bed and fabric-covered walls. The plant-filled top floor of **82 Chandler St.**, in the South End, is also a great couple hideaway: When you tire of gazing into each other's eyes, there's a row of windows overlooking residential rooftops from the breakfast room, and wide bay windows overlook downtown from the bedroom. For Merchant Ivory–style romantic moods, try the Back Bay's older hotels. A welcoming fire burns in the lobby of the **Lenox**, where the guest rooms are outfitted in a curious variety of American, Oriental, and French provincial styles, all with marble bathrooms. The **Eliot Hotel** lets you and your lover sprawl in a plush suite; the glittering **Copley Plaza** lets you make a grand entrance in the ornate lobby, then hole away in your luxe room. For big hotel romance beside the ocean, try the **Boston Harbor Hotel**, a stunning modern hotel where yachts bob in the water right outside and the health spa offers all kinds of hedonistic delights. Farther up the waterfront, the **Boston Marriott Long Wharf** gives the Boston Harbor a respectable run for the money, with similarly dramatic architecture, dreamy harbor views, and a decent spa and pool. Weekend couples packages at the Marriott may clinch the deal for you.

Down by the sea... Ferries and small cruise ships come and go from the door, planes land every few minutes at

Logan across the water, great skyscrapers loom over you landward: Even the most jaded traveler can't help but catch the excitement at the spectacular **Boston Harbor Hotel** on Rowes Wharf. In any other lodging the city skyline would be breathtaking enough, but at this stunning contemporary hotel, you'll probably want a room with an ocean view. If you stay at the **Harborside Hyatt Conference Center and Hotel,** you'll have to take the airport water shuttle every day—quite pricey despite the hotel discount—to reach Boston from your room (driving into Boston via the airport tunnel on a daily basis would ruin your vacation). If that's your idea of fun, the Hyatt is a great oceanside hotel, sleek and futuristic but with properly maritime paintings of tall ships on the walls. While the Harborside Hyatt is built to resemble a lighthouse, the multitiered **Boston Marriott Long Wharf** is supposed to resemble a ship (a redbrick ship?), thrusting out into the sea from Long Wharf. Popular after-work bars, a public walkway, and an open-plan lobby (displaying a famed Rufus Porter fresco) make it a lively, integral part of the waterfront scene. Most guest rooms have sea views, and the breezy location makes this a pleasant spot even on the hottest summer afternoons.

On the river... The upscale **Royal Sonesta,** technically in Cambridge but so close to Boston you'd never notice, sits on the banks of the Charles and offers fabulous views of the city skyline. The Cambridge-side Galleria and the Museum of Science are both within easy walking distance, though for anything else you'll need a taxi or the T. On the other side of the MIT campus, the **Hyatt Regency**—a bronze-glass heap known locally as "the pyramid on the Charles"—offers excellent river views from many rooms, and Memorial Drive's riverside jogging and cycling paths are right outside the door, along with a flock of honking geese. The typically Hyatt atrium resonates with noise; the rooms are standard-issue deluxe, so demand a river-view balcony—it'll go a long way toward making your stay feel special.

Park your car in Harvard Yard... Close to Harvard Square, the **Charles Hotel** does a damn good job of blending past and present, just like this old university city, which produces some of the best high-tech in the world.

The Charles' modern exterior looks like a jumbled pile of rectangular blocks, but in traditional red brick that echoes the Harvard campus. Inside, big bright bedrooms contain reproduction Shaker furniture and simple four-poster beds draped with quilts, yet the quilts have snazzy geometric patterns in blues and browns. Need to cram for an exam? Room service will actually pop out to one of the 26 bookstores in Harvard Square and pick up the book of your choice. The Regatta Bar downstairs is one of the city's coolest jazz spots. **The Inn at Harvard** is actually on the University campus, a Georgian-style redbrick building (put up in 1991) with a stunning four-story, glass-roofed atrium lobby. Guest rooms with round, square, and arched windows overlook the lobby, which was designed to look like a Venetian piazza. Although **DoubleTree Guest Suites** is on the Boston side of the river, it's really handier to Cambridge: It's next door to the Harvard Business School and across the bridge from Harvard Square. Modern guest rooms in pink, gray, and gold surround a 15-story central atrium; many rooms have views over the river toward Cambridge.

Sweet suites... Boston's two all-suite hotels couldn't be more different: **DoubleTree Guest Suites** is a plush high-rise overlooking the Charles and the Mass. Pike; the **Eliot Hotel** is small and deluxe, with flowery balconies overlooking Commonwealth Avenue. The Eliot also has a small split-level lobby where the writing desk and fresh flowers call to mind an elegant private foyer, while glass elevators whiz up the DoubleTree's totally mod atrium. In both places, however, you basically get two top-quality rooms for the price of one room anywhere else.

For kids who whine for their own suite... There's only one place for these little darlings—**The Ritz-Carlton**, where pampered youngsters can enjoy the Junior Presidential Suite complete with TV, stereo, Nintendo, child-size bathroom, children's furniture and wall coverings, and a minibar crammed with the kind of treats kids like—all for only $495 a night.

For traveling families... You passed up the Ritz-Carlton's Junior Presidential Suite? Never mind—you can still bring the kids to an upscale, kid-friendly hotel without breaking the bank. The **Boston Park Plaza**'s "Cub

Club" package offers a fully childproofed room with two double beds and two bathrooms; kids can use the communal video/game den downstairs and attend the daily story hour, and their parents get free valet parking and discounted baby-sitting to boot. Otherwise, this is a staid, older hotel—the decor looks either stylish or dated, depending on how you feel about pastel colors, intricate moldings, and chandeliers. But what the hell, it's got an indoor pool and it's close to the Swan Boats and to FAO Schwarz. The modern high-rise **Westin Hotel** at Copley Place offers a competing "Kids Stay and Eat Free" package that includes room service; you can request bed rails, activity packs, night-lights, outlet covers, tippy cups, high chairs, and the like. Kids may be the only guests who are actually impressed by the waterfall in the chaotic Westin lobby. A package at the **Royal Sonesta** in Cambridge offers free accommodation for two children under 18 in their parents' room, free boat rides on the Charles, free use of bicycles and cameras, and all the free ice cream you can eat between 4 and 9:30pm each day. On top of this, the hotel has a great indoor/outdoor pool with retractable roof, and it's right next door to the Museum of Science and the new New England Sports Museum in the Galleria shopping mall. For budget family accommodation, the motelish **Midtown Hotel** has some of the cheapest regular rates in town (but check out family deals at other hotels first); kids stay free in their parents' rooms, which are actually large enough to hold everyone reasonably well, and there's an outdoor pool. The Copley Square area location means you can walk to lots of attractions kids like.

For students and their families... If you're in town for interviews, or to tour the Boston College or Boston University campuses, the no-frill **Beacon Inns** in Brookline make good, low-budget bases. At 1087 Beacon Street, a four-story Victorian town house, a glorious carved-oak staircase and floor-to-ceiling fireplace greet you in the lobby; guest rooms are large with high ceilings, period wallpapers, and desks and chairs. Rates and standards at 1750 Beacon Street are slightly lower: Big rooms have all the requisite charm, with fireplaces, wood paneling, and sloping attic ceilings, but they could do with a lick of paint. Both properties have streetcar T stops almost outside the door. Students interested in Northeastern University may find the **Central Branch YMCA**,

squeezed between campus buildings, most convenient—
hell, students are used to cramped rooms and shared
baths. In Cambridge, (wealthy) students and their parents could check into the smartly contemporary **Charles
Hotel**, right next door to Harvard's Kennedy School of
Government (where Streisand wowed 'em live), or try the
on-campus **Inn at Harvard**, which has a faux-Georgian
exterior (shades of Harvard Yard) but very un-studenty
cherry furniture and a dazzling atrium.

**For doctors, future doctors, patients, and their
families...** Location is everything for the **Inn at
Children's**: It may be just a standard **Best Western**, but
it's surrounded by the buildings of the Harvard Medical
School and by Harvard-affiliated hospitals (Children's,
Beth Israel, Brigham and Women's, The Deaconess,
Joslin's, and the Dana Faber Cancer Institute are all within two minutes' walk). The Inn opens into a small shopping mall, with a large food court where surgeons, physi-
cians, med students, nurses, and eminent Harvard
research scientists catch a quick lunch, just like the TV
docs on "ER" and "Chicago Hope."

For travelers who want to avoid families... No one
would dream of bringing the kids to **A Cambridge
House Bed and Breakfast**; anyway, the management at
this rather stuffy, Victorian-style B&B won't let them in
unless they're over six years old. The place is immaculate-
ly decorated, beautifully managed, and quiet—the ideal
place if you have three toddlers, and decided to leave
them home. Although the Omni part of the **Omni
Parker House** tries to do the usual chain thing to attract
families—goody packages when checking in and so on—
the old Parker House spirit prevails. I doubt you'll see
many kids at this starchy, old-fashioned hotel near the
Common and the State House.

Deals for solo travelers... The self-contained apartments known as the **Beacon Inn Guest Houses**, plunked
down in the thick of Newbury Street shopping, have attractive, single-bed studios for a very attractive rate. Or, if
you really must have a double bed, the small rooms of the
Milner, in the Theater District, are clean and dirt cheap.
Single women traveling alone might like the **Berkeley**

Residence YWCA. What with the small spartan rooms, the shared baths, and the dining hall downstairs, you'll feel transported to a Seven Sisters dorm circa 1962.

For gay couples who don't want to push the beds together... You can be sure no one will ask awkward questions at the small B&B town house **82 Chandler St.**, or at the budget low-rise **Chandler Inn**, both in the hip n' happy Boys Town of the South End. Rooms are bigger and more homey at 82 Chandler St., and you can do your own cooking there, but at least the down-market Chandler Inn has TVs in every room.

Hotels with a conscience... The century-old **Copley Square Hotel** is ahead of its brassy new competition in one respect: The folks here recycle almost everything, from paper and glass to porcelain toilets (potties make marvelous road gravel). Mattresses and old linen are donated to homeless shelters, toilets are of the water-conserving variety, and even guests can pitch in by opting to change their sheets and towels every second day instead of every night. Over at the **Boston Park Plaza**, too, the staff recycles, uses recycled paper, and has stopped using Styrofoam, disposable plastic, and aerosols. Rooms have water-saving showerheads, and a "Green Team" is constantly working to eliminate waste and minimize the hotel's environmental impact.

For writers... Considering its pretensions of being a "European-style hotel," it's no surprise that the **Colonnade**, in the Back Bay, recently opened an author's suite, complete with large writing desk, brass reading lamps, and inspiring floor-to-ceiling picture windows, for the use of "celebrated visiting authors." Writers are asked to leave a signed copy of their latest book for permanent display in the suite's library (aspiring authors need not apply...).

Front-row seats for theater lovers... You can walk to the Theater District from almost any hotel in town, but if you want to stay where the actin' is, you can't get closer than the **Tremont House**, across the street from the Wang Center and surrounded by theaters on all sides. The lobby, with its tremendous Czech crystal chandelier, Ionic and Doric columns, sculpted doors,

BOSTON | ACCOMMODATIONS

and lavish gold leaf, could be mistaken for a theater lobby itself—listening to the piped-in music, you can't help waiting for the curtain to rise. The staff's friendly and the elevators move at manageable speeds; rooms are smallish but pleasant, in grays and pinks, with writing desks. This place used to be the national headquarters of the Elks, of all things. Nearby **57 Park Plaza** is also convenient, but has a whole lot less character—it's a high-rise HoJo with private balconies, large rooms, and an up-to-date health club.

Back-of-the-house seats for theater lovers... If you can't afford the Tremont House, but still crave the Theater District, try the **Milner**, a one-elevator hotel where the low rate includes continental breakfast. Corridors have ugly exposed pipes; small rooms have plastic-covered lamp shades (what do they think we're going to do with them?), prints of flamingos, and flimsy pink-and-blue bedspreads; but the service is friendly and the place is clean.

For tourists... Faneuil Hall is the tourist hub of the Hub, and the only hotel right at Faneuil Hall is **The Bostonian**. Geraniums fill the window boxes, but it's not cutesy colonial—a stunning steel sculpture and fountain decorate the brick-cobbled rotary outside check-in, and the lobby/lounge sits beneath an atrium of glass and steel. Rooms in the older Harkness wing (converted from a warehouse built in 1824) have fireplaces, exposed brick, Jacuzzis, and oak ceiling beams; the new section's stunningly modern, with plush fawn and pink furnishings, brass fixtures, striped wallpapers, and big dressing rooms and bathrooms. The location may sound like an asset, but some rooms are noisy at night—think higher than the fourth floor when making reservations.

At the airport (or not?)... Ludicrously, the **Logan Airport Hilton** still claims to be "the only hotel at the airport," maintaining that the snazzy new **Harborside Hyatt Conference Center and Hotel** is "on Bird Island." Technically, it might be, but you wouldn't notice: Planes are parked right out back of the Hyatt, there's a free shuttle bus to all terminals, and the airport water shuttle into Boston leaves from the front door. You gotta understand, the airport location was the only thing that gave the bland box-like rooms at the Hilton any draw. But the Hilton's days are numbered anyway—it's slated to be demolished in a couple of years as part of the airport's remodeling, though a new hotel will be built to replace it.

My favorites... Which to pick from all the above? I like big rooms, the ocean, and modernity; I'd choose **The Boston Harbor Hotel**, **The Boston Marriott Long Wharf**, and (for snob value) **The Four Seasons**.

The Index

$$$$$	over $180
$$$$	$130–$180
$$$	$80–$130
$$	$55–$80
$	under $55

Back Bay Hilton. Convenient for Back Bay business, the high-rise Hilton has a health club and standard rooms—hell, you know what a Hilton's like. Check out the "Boston for Beans" package, available weekends and weeknights, which includes parking and breakfast at less than the regular room rate.... *Tel 617/236–1100, 800/874–0663, fax 617/267–8893. 40 Dalton St., 02115, Hynes or Prudential T. 330 rms, 2 suites. $$$$*

Beacon Hill Bed and Breakfast. Huge guest rooms here have oriel windows, nonworking fireplaces, and Victorian antiques. The loud navy-and-white-check wallpaper on the third floor comes as a bit of a shock, but is stylish, I suppose, in its own way.... *Tel 617/523–7376. 27 Brimmer St., 02108, Charles St. T stop. 3 rms. No credit cards. $$$*

Beacon Inn Guest Houses. These studio apartments in the Back Bay offer self-catering accommodation: Rooms have a

private bathroom and either a fridge or a kitchenette. They're
available for nightly or weekly rates.... *Tel 617/266–7142,
617/266–1771, fax 617/266–7276. 248 Newbury St.,
02116, Copley T stop. 25 rms. AE, D, DC not accepted. $$*

Beacon Inns. These budget guest houses are located on
Beacon Street in Brookline. Reserve your free parking spot
in advance; space is limited.... *Tel 617/566–0088, 800/
726–0088, fax 617/397–9267. 1087 Beacon St., Brook-
line 02146, St. Mary's T stop. 11 rms (3 share baths). $$.
1750 Beacon St., Brookline 02146, Tappan St. T stop. 13
rms (7 share baths). D, DC not accepted. $*

Berkeley Residence YWCA. This women-only facility offers
small, basic rooms (linens provided), and, for a one-time $2
fee when you check in, health-club facilities a couple of blocks
away, including pool, track, and gym. There's also a dining
room serving inexpensive meals.... *Tel 617/482–8850, fax
617/482–9692. 40 Berkeley St., 02116, Arlington T stop.
200 rms with shared baths. AE, D, DC not accepted. $*

The Best Western Boston/The Inn at Children's. A new Best
Western affiliate, handy to the Harvard hospitals. Some
rooms have queen-size beds, others have kings and kitchenettes. Guests can use a nearby health club for $12 per day.
The city center is 10 minutes away by T.... *Tel 617/731–
4700, 800/528–1234, fax 617/731–6273. 342 Longwood
Ave., Brookline 02115, Longwood T stop. 152 rms. $$–$$$*

Boston Harbor Hotel. Superb modern hotel on the wharf, complete with health spa and 60-foot lap pool.... *Tel 617/439–
7000, 800/752–7077, fax 617/330–9450. 70 Rowes
Wharf, 02110, Aquarium T stop. 230 rms, 24 suites. $$$$$*

Boston International Youth Hostel. Most rooms sleep three
to five; some private rooms for two or three guests are available. All have shared baths. Linen is rented. The hostel
requires summer guests to be full YHA members.... *Tel
617/536–9455. 12 Hemenway St., 02115, Hynes/ICA T
stop. 46 rms, 200 beds. AE, D, DC not accepted. $*

Boston Marriott Copley Place. Rooms in this skyscraping
hotel have individual mailboxes (saves ironing the morning
paper) and cleaners carry red feather dusters. The hotel,
which underwent a $7 million renovation in early 1995, has

all the glories of a deluxe downtown business-oriented hotel, including a fine health club.... *Tel 617/236–5800, 800/228–9290, fax 617/236–5885. 110 Huntington Ave., 02116, Prudential T stop. 1,139 rms, 77 suites. $$$$*

Boston Marriott Long Wharf. Super-convenient to waterfront attractions like the Aquarium, Faneuil Hall, and Boston Harbor boat trips, this bold and breezy hotel offers great packages. Concierge-level rooms come with complimentary Continental breakfast and private lounge. Spa with pool.... *Tel 617/227–0800, 800/228–9290, fax 617/227–2867. 296 State St., 02109, Aquarium T stop. 402 rms, 12 suites. $$$$$*

Boston Park Plaza Hotel and Towers. This older, well-heeled hotel overlooking the Public Garden has smallish bedrooms. Larger deluxe rooms in the Towers come with complimentary cocktails; private check-in; and business amenities, including dual-line phones. Indoor pool and spa.... *Tel 617/426–2000, 800/225–2008, fax 617/426 5545. 64 Arlington St., 02116, Arlington T stop. 966 rms, 10 suites. $$$*

Bostonian Hotel. This unusual small hotel combines the overtly modern with an oak-beamed 19th-century wing. Complimentary passes for a full-service health club three blocks away.... *Tel 617/523–3600, 800/343–0922, fax 617/523–2454. Faneuil Hall Marketplace, 02109, Government Center T stop. 152 rms, 16 suites. $$$$–$$$$$*

A Cambridge House Bed and Breakfast. Although this antique-filled B&B is on busy Mass. Ave., it's set well back from the road and quiet. A shopping center and the T are just one block away.... *Tel 617/491-6300, 800/232–9989, fax 617/868–2848. 2218 Massachusetts Ave., Cambridge 02140, Davis Square T stop. 14 rms, 4 with shared bath. D not accepted. $$$ $$$$*

Chandler Inn. This inexpensive, eight-story, South End hotel offers small, air-conditioned rooms with double or twin beds, TVs, and phones. Rooms were recently recarpeted and redecorated, and rates include complimentary Continental breakfast. It's a short walk to Amtrak's Back Bay station, the Greyhound bus, and downtown.... *Tel 617/482–3450, 800/842–3450, fax 617/542–3428. 26 Chandler St., 02115, Back Bay T stop. 56 rms. $$*

Charles Hotel. This contemporary luxury hotel near Harvard Square has a tri-level health club with machines, pool, and Jacuzzi.... *Tel 617/864–1200, 800/882–1818, fax 617/864–5715. 1 Bennett St., Cambridge 02138, Harvard Square T stop. 296 rms, 44 suites. $$$$$*

Colonnade Hotel. This friendly, centrally located hotel with big, elegant rooms offers a range of entertainment, from happy hour at the rooftop pool to live music and dancing in the bar on weekends.... *Tel 617/424–7000, 800/962–3030, fax 617/424–1717. 120 Huntington Ave., 02116, Prudential T stop. 285 rms, 10 suites. $$$$*

Copley Plaza Hotel. Right on Copley Square, this fancy grande dame built in 1912 glitters with crystal and shines with style. Guests may use a neighboring health club for free.... *Tel 617/267–5300, 800/996–3426, fax 617/267–7668. 138 St. James Ave., 02116, Copley T stop. 373 rms, 51 suites. $$$$*

Copley Square Hotel. Built in 1891, the Copley Square is friendly and reasonable, yet competitively modern. King-size beds, but no pool.... *Tel 617/536–9000, 800/225–7062, fax 617/267–3547. 47 Huntington Ave., 02116, Copley T stop. 143 rms, 12 suites. $$$*

DoubleTree Guest Suites. Across the bridge from Harvard Square, this suite hotel has modern guest rooms, a central atrium, an exercise room, and an indoor pool. Breakfast is available for an extra $10 per night.... *Tel 617/783–0090, 800/222–8733, fax 617/783–0897. 400 Soldiers Field Rd., 02134, Harvard Square or Central Square T stops. 310 suites. $$$*

82 Chandler St. Spacious guest rooms at this friendly B&B, close to Copley Square, Amtrak, downtown. A super penthouse suite.... *Tel 617/482–0408. 82 Chandler St., 02115, Back Bay T stop. 5 rms. No credit cards. $$–$$$*

Eliot Hotel. A 1990s renovation transformed the dowdy old Eliot into a chic all-suite hotel with a sophisticated clientele. Its suites—living room, bedroom, kitchenette—are furnished with mahogany antique reproductions and handsome couches, and they have Italian marble bathrooms.... *Tel 617/267–1607, 800/44-ELIOT, fax 617/536–9114. 370 Commonwealth Ave., 02215, Hynes/ICA T stop. 91 suites. $$$$*

Eliot and Pickett Houses. Owned by the Unitarian Universalists, these Beacon Hill homes make an excellent self-catering option. Breakfast is provided (you make it yourself), and you can use the kitchen to cook other meals as well.... *Tel 617/ 742–2100, ext. 679, 617/248–8707, fax 617/742–1364. 25 Beacon St. (mailing address); 6 Mt. Vernon Place, 02108, Park Street T stop. 20 rms. AE, DC not accepted.* $$

57 Park Plaza. This Howard Johnson branch is bang in the middle of the Theater District, with an on-site cinema. Free parking.... *Tel 617/482–1800, 800/654–2000, fax 617/ 451–2750. 200 Stuart St., 02116, Boylston T stop. 350 rms.* $$$

Four Seasons Hotel. A mighty modern palace overlooking the Boston Common that every luxury, including an on-site health club.... *Tel 617/338–4400, 800/332–3442, fax 617/423–0154. 200 Boylston St., 02116, Boylston T stop. 288 rms, 80 suites.* $$$$$

Harborside Hyatt Conference Center and Hotel. This brand-new, lighthouse-shaped hotel has great views over both the inner harbor and the airport, where it's located. You'll find good-size rooms and a modern health club.... *Tel 617/568–1234, 800/233–1234, fax 617/567–8856. 101 Harborside Dr., 02128, Airport T stop. 270 rms, 11 suites.* $$$$

Howard Johnson's Fenway. This HoJo branch has an outdoor pool and backs onto Fenway Park. Free parking.... *Tel 617/ 267–8300, 800/654–2000, fax 617/267–8300. 1271 Boylston St., 02215, Kenmore Square T stop. 94 rms.* $$

Hyatt Regency. Another fancy Hyatt, this one sits beside the river rather than the harbor. Excellent weekend packages; health club, restaurants.... *Tel 617/492–1234, 800/233– 1234, fax 617/491–6906. 575 Memorial Dr., Cambridge 02139, BU/Central Square T stop. 500 rms.* $$$$

The Inn at Harvard. The atrium lobby steals the show here, but guest rooms are impressive too, with courtyard balconies, original artwork from Harvard's Fogg Art Museum, and chocolates at bedtime.... *Tel 617/491–2222, 800/222– 8733, fax 617/491–6520. 1201 Massachusetts Ave., Cambridge 02138, Harvard Square T stop. 113 rms.* $$$$

Le Meridien. Smart, glass-roofed hotel occupies a landmark building surrounded by skyscrapers in the Financial District. The inside is loaded with marble, and large guest rooms have recently been redecorated.... *Tel 617/451–1900, 800/543–4300, fax 617/423–2844. 250 Franklin St., 02110, State Street T stop. 326 rms, 22 suites. $$$$*

Lenox Hotel. At this friendly, centrally located hotel, recent renovations have raised the atmosphere from bland to elegant.... *Tel 617/536–5300, 800/225–7676, fax 617/266–7905. 710 Boylston St., 02116, Copley T stop. 222 rms, 3 suites. $$$$*

Logan Airport Hilton. The only obvious reason to stay here is to ease an awkward flight time. The hotel has an outdoor pool and offers free transportation to all airport terminals 24 hours a day.... *Tel 617/569–9300, 800/722–5004, fax 617/567–3725. Logan Airport, East Boston, 02128, Airport T stop. 540 rms, 27 suites. $$$$*

Midtown Hotel. Inexpensive, if not charming, this is one step up from a motel, with reasonably large rooms and an outdoor pool; about five minutes' walk from Copley Square.... *Tel 617/262–1000, 800/343–1177, fax 617/262–8739. 220 Huntington Ave., 02116, Prudential T stop. 159 rms. $$*

Milner Hotel. This is not a glamorous place to stay, but it's inexpensive, clean, air-conditioned, and centrally located.... *Tel 617/426–6220, 800/453–1731, fax 617/350–0360. 78 Charles St., 02116, Boylston T stop. 68 rms. $$*

Newbury Guest House. A sure winner from the day it opened in 1991, this handsomely furnished B&B expanded into the house next door in 1994 and doubled the room count— and it's still always full. Reserve your parking spot ($10 for 24 hours—a bargain for a Boston hotel) in advance.... *Tel 617/437–7666, fax 617/262–4243. 261 Newbury St., 02116, Copley T stop. 32 rms. $$$*

Omni Parker House. This 19th-century classic has updated its fixtures but not its atmosphere. The rooms—small by newer hotel standards—come with suit hangers and formal striped fabrics, and will appeal most to conservative businessmen who need to hang up their suits.... *Tel 617/227–8600,*

800/843–6664, fax 617/742–5729. 60 School St., 02108, Government Center, Downtown Crossing, or Park Street Ts. 535 rms, 12 suites. $$$$

The Ritz-Carlton Boston. The traditional place to stay in Boston, if you have the cash. Private Club suites upstairs have their own lounge with free food, drink, and entertainment, for a mere $840 per night.... *Tel 617/536–5700, 800/241–3333, fax 617/536–1335. 15 Arlington St., 02116, Arlington T stop. 278 rms, 48 suites. $$$$$*

Royal Sonesta. This fun hotel on the Charles River is close to shops and museums and has excellent family packages. Guest rooms have museum-quality artwork from the hotel's own collection.... *Tel 617/491–3600, 800/SONESTA, fax 617/661–5956. 5 Cambridge Pkwy., Cambridge 02142, Lechmere T stop. 400 rms, 28 suites. $$$$*

Sheraton Boston Hotel and Towers. This vast, twin-tower high-rise has 29 stories and a health club. If you need a personal butler you can find one in the Towers, the executive section that takes up the top three floors of the hotel.... *Tel 617/236–2000, 800/325–3535, fax 617/236–1702. 39 Dalton St., 02199, Prudential T stop. 1,208 rms, 100 suites. $$$$*

Tremont House. Built in 1925, this old-fashioned grand hotel in the Theater District has smaller rooms than the modern high-rises do, but they're pleasant. Ask about packages, some of which include parking.... *Tel 617/426–1400, 800/331–9998, fax 617/338–7881. 275 Tremont St., Boston, 02116, Boylston T stop. 281 rms, 34 suites. $$$*

Westin Hotel. Rooms at this 36-story hotel are top-class Business Generic, with smart oak and mahogany Colonial-style furniture. Thick towels, thick carpets, thick bedcovers, and huge windows with awesome city views.... *Tel 617/262–9600, 800/228–3000, fax 617/424–7483. 10 Huntington Ave., Copley Place, 02116, Copley T stop. 800 rms, 45 suites. $$$$*

YMCA of Greater Boston—Central Branch. Small rooms with shared bathrooms; on the plus side, you get TVs, maid service, free breakfast, and use of the excellent recreational facilities (including track, pool, and sauna).... *Tel 617/536–7800. 316 Huntington Ave., 02116, Northeastern T stop. 40 rms, most share baths. $*

BOSTON | ACCOMMODATIONS

38

Boston Accommodations

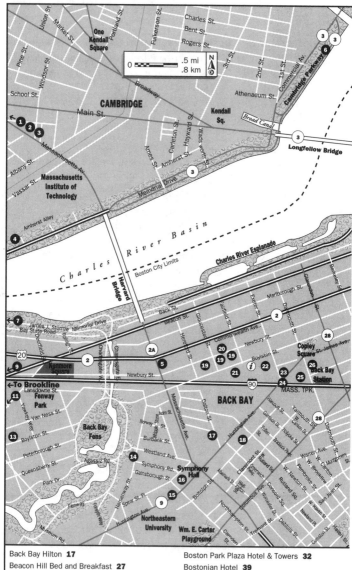

Back Bay Hilton **17**

Beacon Hill Bed and Breakfast **27**

Beacon Inn Guest Houses **19**

Beacon Inns **9**

Berkeley Residence **30**

Boston Harbor Hotel **43**

Boston International Youth Hostel **14**

Boston Marriott Copley Place **24**

Boston Marriott Long Wharf **45**

Boston Park Plaza Hotel & Towers **32**

Bostonian Hotel **39**

A Cambridge House Bed and Breakfast **1**

Chandler Inn **37**

Charles Hotel **2**

Colonnade Hotel **18**

Copley Plaza Hotel **26**

Copley Square Hotel **23**

Doubletree Guest Suites **7**

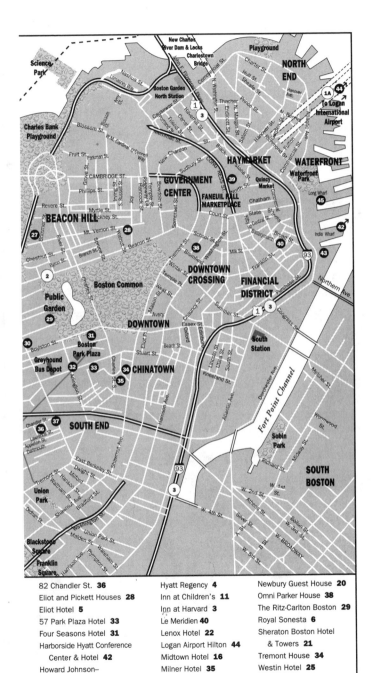

82 Chandler St. **36**	Hyatt Regency **4**	Newbury Guest House **20**
Eliot and Pickett Houses **28**	Inn at Children's **11**	Omni Parker House **38**
Eliot Hotel **5**	Inn at Harvard **3**	The Ritz-Carlton Boston **29**
57 Park Plaza Hotel **33**	Le Meridien **40**	Royal Sonesta **6**
Four Seasons Hotel **31**	Lenox Hotel **22**	Sheraton Boston Hotel
Harborside Hyatt Conference	Logan Airport Hilton **44**	& Towers **21**
Center & Hotel **42**	Midtown Hotel **16**	Tremont House **34**
Howard Johnson–	Milner Hotel **35**	Westin Hotel **25**
Fenway **13**		YMCA Central Branch **15**

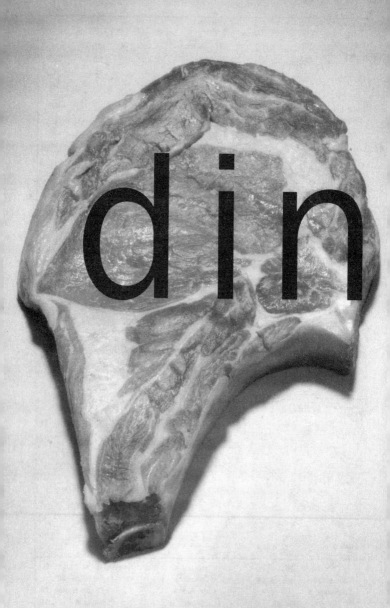

ing

How far wrong
can you go when
dropping a lobster
into a pot of boil-
ing water? New
England's first
settlers screwed

up the next step, feeding lobster to farm animals instead of to the family. But the hapless Pilgrims were saved from making the standard British fare of boiled beef America's staple by savvier Native Americans, who taught them about corn and corn bread, cranberries, and roast wild turkey.

Although traditional Yankee boiled dinners can be sampled in some spots, the modern New England specialty is seafood. And in Boston, you can find it raw, boiled, deep-fried, or cooked by Italian, Chinese, French, Indian, or South American chefs. For every highfalutin city chef presiding over a pedigree kitchen, there are scores of ethnic cooks at hot stoves dishing up childhood recipes from Bologna, Beijing, Bombay, or Ballyshannon.

Jumping on the cuisine-as-cultural-statement bandwagon, trendy restaurants are mixing and matching as many spices and vegetables as they dare. You'll find "Pacific Rim" cuisine, "Southern Mediterranean" specialties, and wide-ranging "European" menus. Less trendy kitchens turn out the same basic Italian, Irish, or Chinese fare year after year. Boston dining can be formal, hip, simple, or spicy, but thanks to the ethnic melting pot, it is never boring.

Only in Boston

Lobster, shellfish, and Boston scrod (it's not a breed—it's the best whitefish of the day) are the local seafood specialties; New England clam chowder, made with potatoes and onions and *no* tomatoes (New Yorkers put red stuff in theirs) is also available everywhere. Yankee cuisine (an oxymoron?) consists of thick pork chops, boiled cabbage, chicken potpies, and heavy puddings. If you really want to, you can find it at traditional restaurants like **Durgin-Park** and **Parker's** at the Omni Parker House hotel (see Accommodations). The local brew that just went public, Samuel Adams, comes in many colors, most of them dark and tasty. Those who prefer British beers to pallid Bud and Miller will like Sam Adams' concoctions.

How to Dress

Several top Boston restaurants require jacket and tie; others don't want to offend anyone, so they state "jacket preferred." Most ethnic restaurants don't care what you wear.

When to Eat

To avoid crowds and get the "early bird specials," join the families and seniors and eat between 4 and 6. Any time after

7 you might have to wait for a table, and most tables are wiped and polished by 11, when good God-fearing Yankees are headed for bed.

Getting the Right Table

The only way to do this, especially between July and November, is to book ahead. Ask for a table by the window, ask for nonsmoking, ask for a booth, ask for a seat by the fire—and arrive on time. Boston restaurants are usually crowded, and parking can take a while. Ask about parking (and the cost of it) when you call to make reservations. If there's no car park (and there probably isn't), there may be expensive valet parking or inexpensive validated parking at a local garage.

Where the Chefs Are

At four-star **Aujourd'hui**, Jamie Mammano serves traditional New England fare and healthy, spa-inspired variations. **Biba Food Hall**'s Lydia Shire outdoes Wolfgang Puck with her delicious, newfangled inventions. On the haute French front, Raymond Ost runs with the haughty best at **Julien**, as does **Maison Robert**'s Lucien Robert. Frank McClelland serves fresh, organic produce at **L'Espalier**. The high end of hotel dining includes **Seasons** at The Bostonian Hotel, with chef Peter McCarthy, and the **Rialto** at Cambridge's Charles Hotel, where new-kid-on-the-block Jody Adams has a memorable repertoire of Southern European dishes. For fine Northern Italian dishes, Deborah Hughes excels at **Upstairs at the Pudding**, where they hand roll and cut the pasta, serve white truffles from Italy, and make a mean black pepper polenta.

The Lowdown

Something fishy (in town)... Near City Hall, the **Union Oyster House**, established in 1826, was popular with Daniel Webster, and so beloved by John F. Kennedy that his favorite booth upstairs (#18) is marked by a plaque. But Kennedy probably didn't have to wait hours for a table, and you probably will. Last time we ate here, the predicted wait was off by 45 minutes, so be sure to make reservations. If you really want to taste the place for its history, snack at the raw bar and drink a beer downstairs—you can find equally good seafood elsewhere.

BOSTON | DINING

Once a little Cambridge seafood store, **Legal Sea Foods**
is now a burgeoning Boston restaurant chain famous for
a vast variety of super-fresh fish ("if it isn't fresh, it isn't
Legal") cooked any way you want it, but usually without
fancy dressings. Most of the branches sport white ceramic tile walls and big mirrors—a simple, shiny look that
echoes the purist's menu. Though most branches don't
take reservations, they offer "preferred seating." Call early
in the day, and when you arrive they'll offer you the next
available table; otherwise you might grow old while waiting. **Skipjack's** offers slightly fancier (but not better)
seafood than Legal, with many exotic varieties and Cajun
cooking in a jazzy, multicolored setting downtown. Their
Brookline outlet is less eye-catching, and it attracts an
incompatible mix of families and aged patrons. For a different take on seafood, **Grand Chau Chow** and its sib-
ling **Chau Chow** across the street serve up Chinatown's
best fish and shellfish dishes.

Something fishy (by the sea)... Smack on the end of a
pier, **Anthony's Pier 4** is surrounded on three sides by
water, with glorious views through its glass walls. You can
take in the harbor, the airport, and downtown all at once,
making dining here downright exciting. Although the
place seats 1,000, the large dining rooms have got plenty
of character. The "Run Room" looks over the water
towards the city; sea breezes waft through open windows,
and the white wrought-iron chairs and tables make it
seem like a huge wedding marquee (there's limited outdoor seating in summer as well). The main dining room
feels like the prow of a ship about to cross the harbor. On
top of this, the seafood is great and the service superb:
Anthony's has got it just right. Still, many Bostonians
drive past Anthony's regularly on their way to **The No
Name**. Out on the restored but workaday Boston Fish
Pier, The No Name is squeezed between dozens of
seafood companies (and is just beyond the "Super Snooty
Seafood Company"); it's hard to spot until the lines build
up by 8pm. The No Name offers generous, well-cooked
portions at low prices, sea views if you manage to sit in the
small, glassed-in addition out back, and authenticity. Step
outside and you're among boats, nets, and gulls. Modern
Boston could be a million miles away. Also at the Fish
Pier, **Jimmy's Harborside Restaurant**, established in

1924, has big harbor-view windows in a vast, rectangular, three-tier dining room where everyone can see the sea. Specialties include baked or smoked finnan haddock, arctic char, and tuna kebab. Across the street, **Jimbo's** is a smaller, darker (no sea view), less expensive offshoot of Jimmy's, with miles of electric train tracks hanging from the ceiling. The food is good and inexpensive, but I find the dim lighting, exposed pipes, and dark wood a bit depressing. *All* the above restaurants are Greek-owned ("We have 150 Greek on staff and 50 foreigners," quipped the waiter at Jimmy's). For Italian seafood on the Fish Pier, try **The Daily Catch**. Incidentally, it's a dusty, uninspiring, 30-minute to walk to the Fish Pier from the T at South Station. Take a taxi or drive: All these restaurants have parking.

Something fishy (in a shack)... For a big choice of out-doorsy, inexpensive restaurants you should head for the North Shore, particularly Essex. **Woodman's of Essex**, where they claim to have invented the fried clam in 1916, is the classic seafood-in-the-rough wood shack. Back in Boston, there's the **Barking Crab**. Order seafood at the window, then sit on wooden picnic tables beside the harbor and watch fishing boats prepare for the next morning's outing until your number is called. Compared with indoor spots, large seafood platters with fries, coleslaw, and corn are a bargain here.

For chowder lovers... City restaurants compete every year in the Boston Harbor Chowderfest. The chowder at **Turner Fisheries Bar and Restaurant** won the title of "Best Chowder in Boston" for three straight years and was retired to the Boston Chowderfest Hall of Fame. If you like people-watching you'll enjoy this open part of the Westin lobby.

For oyster lovers... The best bit of the **Union Oyster House** is the raw bar. On a busy Saturday, the shuckers serve over 3,000 oysters. You'll also find an excellent raw bar at **Turner Fisheries**.

For lovers who just ate oysters... You can linger over a romantic dessert at the Custom House Lounge in **Bay Tower**, which overlooks the harbor and Faneuil Hall from the 33rd floor. There's live music and dancing nightly, a bar, and special nightcaps. If you prefer to stroll through the Back Bay holding hands and sharing ice cream, pick something up from **J.P. Licks**—preferably white-coffee or chocolate-chip-cookie-dough ice cream with hot fudge sauce (but it's all delicious).

Isn't it romantic... The Copley Square Hotel is quaint and quirky, so it's somehow fitting that their showpiece restaurant, the **Cafe Budapest**, serves Hungarian food. Billed as "one of the country's leading Hungarian restaurants" (it's good, but how much competition can they have?), this place has three theme dining rooms; even those of us who've never been near Hungary can relate to the trio of design schemes. The dark red hunting lodge has leather chairs and gloomy paneling. Next comes the glassy, glittery, pink palace room, and finally the peasant's blue room, with its long leather couch and patterned china on the walls. Equally otherworldly is the menu, which includes such specialties as *szekley gulyas* (sauerkraut stuff), *nokkedli* (noodles), Russian caviar, *tournedo à la Rossini* (goose liver and truffles), and, for the plebeians, steak *à l'Americaine*. Right next door on Copley Square, the glamorous Copley Plaza Hotel has a romantic, candlelit dining room serving classic American cuisine. As you hold hands beneath the gas lamps on Charles Street, you could drop into the cozy (that is, little) basement restaurant at **The Hungry i** and stare into each other's eyes over more candles, or whisper sweet stuff in the cute courtyard. The menu offers contemporary American cuisine with rich sauces and delicious European desserts. If you can't afford that European honeymoon but want to pretend you're in Italy anyway, go to the North End and try **Mamma Maria**, a stunning little restaurant on flowery North Square with several intimate, dimly lit dining rooms (one seats just two people) in a converted town house and an unusually imaginative Italian menu. In Cambridge there's **Rialto** at the Charles Hotel, and the floral splendor of **Upstairs at the Pudding**, where chef Deborah Hughes, who's also a passionate gardener, tends to a balcony full of herbs and edible flowers for outdoor dining in summer. On the green walls hang 18th-century posters advertising productions by Harvard's Hasty Pudding Theatrical Group (still alive downstairs; see

Entertainment). The menu features locally farmed meats and vegetables, and might include Vermont pheasant with smoked barbecue sauce, lobster with garlic and ginger fettucine, or littleneck clams from Cape Cod.

For aspiring lovers... If you're lonely and don't want to be, try **Durgin-Park**. They'll sit you at a long table with an amazingly varied crowd of lone diners, and since no one ever comes here looking for a mate, chances are you'll meet one. On top of that, it's like taking the singles line at the ski lift. Unlike those cumbersome families of four, you won't have to wait for hours. Gay or straight, you'll feel comfortable at the South End's **Club Cafe**, an "all-inclusive" establishment, where singles are always welcome, and the men at the bar are glorious to look at, even those who (from the female viewpoint) are batting for the other team.

For same-sex romance... The **Club Cafe** restaurant is attached to a gay bar, with a health club in the basement, and is a popular spot for gay couples, though not exclusively so. **Jae's** in the South End attracts a sizeable gay crowd, as does the **Black Crow Caffe** in Jamaica Plain.

Kid pleasers... At any **Ground Round** restaurant the kids will love the free popcorn, big-screen videos, crayons, and balloons; in fact, they'll be so distracted they might even let you eat in peace. Unfortunately, the food is unremarkable. Though the burgers, potato skins, and pseudo-Mexican entrees are edible, you'd hardly go back without the kids. The local chain **Bertucci's**, on the other hand, has great (Italian) food and caters to kids—it's our favorite family restaurant. Children get (genuine) Play-Doh and unspillable cardboard drink cartons, while some branches have giant chalkboards and others have outdoor boccie courts. What's more, the plates are unbreakable, and the staffers are speedy and long-suffering. Faneuil Hall's **Durgin-Park**, with its noisy, lively atmosphere and long tables, is another good bet. In the North End, **The European** is loud and kid-friendly. If you want to eat seafood, try the informal **No Name** or the outdoor **Barking Crab**, where the kids can wander about and make as much noise as they like. In Chinatown, **Grand Chau Chow** has high chairs, super-speedy service, and so much activity the tots will be mesmerized.

BOSTON | DINING

For loud families... We take ours to **Doyle's** and **Nick's Beef and Beer**, where the hustle bustle is certain to entertain your kids.

Dining rooms with views... Sometimes you have to sacrifice seasoning for scenery. Not so at the **Rowe's Wharf Restaurant**, where you can dine on top-quality American entrees while watching the exciting waterfront activity through enormous picture windows. On the other hand, you visit pricey **Bay Tower** restaurant for the spectacular view of Faneuil Hall and the harbor, rather than the prettily prepared nouveau American dishes, from lobster to veal, pasta to lamb.

Most abrasive wait staff... Looking for Yankee-style verbal abuse? Last time I was at **Durgin-Park** a waitress apologized to a diner, and he complained, "You're not supposed to do that!" Durgin-Park wait staff are renowned for their rudeness, but more often they're humorous and good-natured, with a bit of bossiness thrown in. At **Nick's Beef and Beer** in Cambridge, however, the red-clad waitresses, who look like Oprah interviewees, either call you "darlin" and complain about their job, or swipe your plates in terrible silence. Eating at Nick's always was a masochistic experience, thanks to the big bar scene and loud crowds, so the wait staff fit right in.

Landmarks... For seaside, try **Anthony's** on Atlantic Avenue, on the way to the Fish Pier. A classic Boston bar is **Doyle's**. Don't be fazed by its location in an unfashionable section of Jamaica Plain—Bostonians flock here from all over the city. Dining is mainly at high wooden booths beneath carved plaster moldings and ceiling fans. The walls sport old newspaper clippings and a mural showing Doyle's famed political patrons, like Ted Kennedy. Choose British or Irish beer, or ask for a separate drinks menu listing "the largest collection of single malt scotches in America." Stick to traditional pub fare (potato skins, spaghetti, fish and chips, onion rings, steaks); pass on the disastrous—and dated—attempts at sophistication (quiche or sauerkraut). **Jacob Wirth** dates from 1868; having survived two world wars and Prohibition, it must be doing something right. A long mahogany bar dominates the room; German beers,

Rhenish wine, and hearty German dishes abound at what's basically a German beer hall. If your pocket runs deep, try **Biba Food Hall**, twice awarded the annual "Best Restaurant in Boston" by *Boston* magazine. The biggest "institution" of them all, **Durgin-Park** in Faneuil Hall has been here forever and, simply by maintaining its informal, ordinary, Yankee, inexpensive style in an area that has become increasingly formal, refined, touristy, and expensive, this restaurant has become a popular legend. Diners eat "family style" at long tables with red-and-white-check tablecloths—you may sit next to seniors wearing trolley tour stickers, bureaucrats from city hall, or some famous Boston sports star. Overheard on a recent visit: a middle-aged tourist from San Francisco discussing the cannibalistic habits of lobsters with a suited Bostonian gent who said he "comes here every week to sit and yak and watch the world go by." Generous portions of seafood, ribs, and onion rings are served with hunks of corn bread and pitchers of ice water. Be prepared to wait ages with fellow tourists vying for seats.

Overrated... **The European**, established in 1917, is the oldest and most famous place to eat, yet the menu is stuck in another decade and the (lack of) decor is depressing. Nonsmoking patrons sit in a faded gray (oops, that's cream) room with a false ceiling and faded Italian piazza scenes on the walls. Smokers sit at wood-grain Formica booths and red tables in a darker room with Tiffany-style lights. When we ate here, we just couldn't work out what all the fame and fuss was about—especially with so many other excellent Italian restaurants around. There's nothing wrong with the food at the **No Name** seafood restaurant out on the Fish Pier, but again, having heard it praised to the heavens, we couldn't figure out anything extra-special about this admittedly inexpensive but otherwise unremarkable spot—except perhaps the trendy lack of a name.

Neighborhood bars ("Cheers" redux)... Check out the Jamaica Plain landmark **Doyle's**, or if you like bratwurst, **Jacob Wirth**. For haute beer fanatics, **Samuel Adams Brewhouse** in the Lenox Hotel is a sort of Lourdes, where they serve six types of Sam Adams beer (it's not brewed on the premises, in spite of the name). The "Cheers"-like atmosphere includes dark wood panel-

BOSTON | DINING

ing, TV screens, and photographs of old Boston. In Brighton, **The Sunset Grill and Tap** proclaims, "So many beers, so little time," and offers an eight-page beer list as well as taste-tester glasses and good pub food. Somerville, a working-class version of neighboring Cambridge, is famed for **Redbones**, and Redbones is famed for barbecued ribs. While you're there check out a few of the great bar's 24 handcrafted beers on tap. And then, of course, there's "Cheers" itself, really the **Bull and Finch**, which attracted the TV producers and inspired, as a location at least, the TV series. The exterior of the Bull and Finch (iron railings and all) appears on TV, but of course the TV interior was somewhere on a Los Angeles studio lot. Though it's trendy to trash such an obvious tourist attraction, the place isn't too bad (it even has a regular crowd)—if you can stomach the hordes of eager sitcom fans.

Beer brewed here... Microbreweries are a growing fad in Boston, and nowhere is more faddish than **brew moon** in the Theater District. Cozy old "Cheers" it ain't. Aspiring to sophistication, it achieves in-your-face po-mo trendiness. A squeaky-clean steel microbrewery bubbles away behind glass panels in the bar, and the food—contemporary American (what did you expect, a terrine of foie gras?)—is delicately arranged. In the workshop-like **Cambridge Brewing Company** you can swill homemade ale and try an eclectic American menu. The setting: exposed brick and beer-making equipment. The **Boston Beer Works** is a good place to stop in before (maybe even better after) a Red Sox game across the street. Sacks of hops are piled above the bar, shelves of beer bottles teeter over your head; the place shines with steel and copper brewing equipment, and it offers about 15 home-brewed flavors on tap each night. Blueberry ale, complete with floating berries, is rich and fruity; raspberry ale is sweet and dreamy; watermelon ale is lighter and a touch tarter. Incidentally, the **The European** in the North End recently started microbrewing, but the waitress advised us against drinking the home brew.

Sports bars... The Original Sports Saloon at the Copley Square Hotel is famous for its award-winning ribs and barbecue dishes, as well as for the noise of 10 regular TVs and two big-screen versions. Dishes have corny names (try a "hat trick," a "green monster," or "Clemens heater" chili) but taste great. Big-name players as well as fans frequent the place. **Jacob Wirth** is also popular with local sports heroes, notably Larry Bird of the Boston Celtics.

For politicos and back-room dealers... Irish bars and Boston politics go hand in glove. **Doyle's** (established 1882) is the unlikely capital of social politics in Boston. We've seen more politicians masquerading as men or women of the people here than on TV. Ted Kennedy opened the bar's newest room, and erstwhile Boston mayor Ray Flynn, who virtually lived here, brought Bill Clinton in for a beer during his '92 presidential campaign (Clinton subsequently made Flynn ambassador to the Vatican). During national elections, news cameras wheel in to test post-poll waters in a merry Doyle's throng of Irish immigrants, off-duty cops, TV anchors, Harvard professors, and families. Boston politicians also favor the Boat Bar at **Jimmy's Harborside Restaurant**, another local institution. More upscale is **Seasons** at the Bostonian Hotel, where city politicians from city hall, one block away, bring people for power lunches. When they don't need to look like men (or women, but usually in this case, men) of the people, politicians pull up the pink velvet wing chairs at the old **Parker's** at the old Omni Parker Hotel. The place serves traditional New England food in a grandiose setting of high ceilings, walnut paneling, ornately carved pillars, brass statues, and large mirrors festooned with grapes.

For Edwardian gentlemen... Women have been allowed to eat here for over 20 years (wow!), but **Locke-Ober** in Downtown Crossing, with its crested menus, stained glass, dark wood paneling, red leather, and long, intricately carved bar has been a Brahmin stronghold since it opened in 1879. It still exudes a haughty men's club attitude.

Haute hotel... The **Ritz-Carlton** has a formal, stuffy dining room with an overpriced wine list, and the **Plaza Dining Room** at the Copley Plaza seems to trade as much on its Waterford crystal chandeliers as on its seasonal French offerings, though both restaurants serve impeccable if unimaginative dishes. At the Four Seasons

BOSTON | DINING

Hotel, award-winning **Aujourd'hui** is rated by some as the best hotel dining in New England. Panelled in dark oak, the restaurant overlooks the Public Garden's duck pond; and fine white linens and antique china grace its tables. Chef Jamie Mammano specializes in New England dishes and "Alternative Cuisine," a Four Seasons–trademarked style of low-calorie, low-sodium, low-cholesterol food. Start with Oregon white truffles, dine on rack of Colorado lamb, and end with chilled Grand Marnier soufflé. Or whatever. It's always good. **Seasons**, at the Bostonian Hotel (not at the Four Seasons!) offers a tasty menu that changes, you guessed it, with the seasons. A summertime menu might include grilled rabbit, yellowfin tuna, lobster, and three different preparations of Long Island duck. Finish it off with white-chocolate or peach cheesecake. The four-course dinner comes at a prix fixe of $39. In Cambridge, the most exciting hotel dining is **Rialto** at the Charles Hotel. At the former Rarities restaurant, green velour banquettes with triangular backs, striped lamp shades, dark wooden floors, and dim lighting have replaced the de rigueur black and chrome decor. Chef Jody Adams, an already-risen young star who's been associated with several excellent local restaurants, surpasses herself here with a southern European menu focusing on French, Italian, and Spanish cuisine. Try the grilled mussels, *soupe de poisson*, roast pork loin, or lobster-and-shellfish stew, and end with hot chocolate cream and ginger Anglaise.

Bangs for your (big) bucks... Biba Food Hall will cost you an arm and a leg, but your taste buds will thank you. Where else does pizza crust melt in your mouth? (The flaky, pastry-like pizza crust comes in the bread basket.) The dishes are as imaginative as they are well-prepared: Try the salmon club sandwich, lobster pizza, or foie gras with garlic and mashed potatoes for lunch. For dinner, there's chicken with lilac smoke and potatoes roasted in coals, with pheasant pâté and grappa; or pan-roasted hake with cockles and chilies. Diners sit beneath colorful ceiling panels with bright geometric patterns based on Albanian rug motifs, and one side of the room has floor-to-ceiling windows overlooking the Boston Public Garden. The black-clad wait staff are low-key and suitably reverent as they transport your triangular butter pat to your plate with special tongs. Some rate the service as slow, but "leisurely" is a better term—you're supposed to relish the experience. Back Bay's **L'Espalier** has been run by a husband-and-wife team of top chefs, Frank and Catherine McClelland, since 1988. Whenever possible, they purchase seasonal organic products from local farmers—this partly explains the high prices. The menu changes every week or so, but there's always caviar, a vegetarian selection, and a taster menu.

For yuppies... Davio's offers good, modish, Italian food—sun-dried tomatoes, squid-ink sauce, goat cheese—(you get the idea)—in an intimate candlelit basement, with red tile floor, redbrick walls, and arched windows. In warm weather, you can eat outside on the obligatory Newbury Street iron tables and chairs. Lunchtimes, you'll overhear yuppie businessmen and women doing deals; evenings, you'll overhear them discussing the movie scripts they're writing in their spare time. With branches in Cambridge and the South End, the cuisine at **Jae's** is nouveau Pacific Rim—beat that for trendiness. Korean, Japanese, and Thai dishes are cooked with flair, and restaurant favorites include Korean-style spicy squid, Ok Dol Doo Boo Bi Bim Bab (rice, tofu, and veggies in a hot stone pot), cellophane noodles, and a big sushi bar. Yuppies will also like **Biba Food Hall** (get mommy to pay). Beer-loving yuppies will enjoy the septic atmosphere of **brew moon**, a Theater District microbrewery.

For earthy, crunchy yuppies... Like arty, popular, gay Jamaica Plain where it's located, the **Black Crow Caffe** attracts a funky mix of all sexual orientations and races. The wait staff is as delectable as the menu. Goat cheese, lentils, herbs, and curries get put to imaginative use—it's all theoretically healthy but well-dressed and calorie-stuffed, rather like the clientele. We sneak in and buy the triple chocolate cheesecake to go. You can also try **Small Planet** in Copley, worth a visit just to see the stunning artwork. Superb photographs of remote corners of the world grace the walls. Pelicans hang from the cloud-painted ceiling, and there's a sculpted mini rain forest, complete with giraffes and a brewing tropical storm. The one-world-is-enough menu includes Asian noodles, Cuban sandwiches, conch fritters, and Aztec pizza.

Cheap eats... One of those rare finds, **Soleil**, near Harvard Square in Cambridge, serves "peasant foods from sunny lands" at prices American "peasants" can afford. Main courses for as little as $6 include bean dishes, burritos, risottos, and vegetarian entrees. Also in Cambridge, but in a totally different universe, **Nick's Beef and Beer** is greasy, loud, cheap, and meaty. Go for the Greek salads, baked half chickens, and plastic pitchers of beer. On the edge of the Theater District, the mystifyingly popular **Blue Diner** serves similarly unhealthy food. The homemade corned beef hash is famous, but we're put off by slow service and too much grease. Much better is **Boston Market**, where home-style cooking meets fast food. The result? Soft and succulent spit-roasted chicken. It's a national chain.

For committed carnivores... **Redbones** in Somerville is famous everywhere for its barbecue dishes, ribs, and 10 types of sausage. The Barbecue Belt Platter lets diners try out the varied styles of Arkansas and Tennessee ribs. **Jacob Wirth** is famous for its prime rib, while **The Last Hurrah**, downstairs at the Omni Parker, has a good reputation for meats, offering strip steak, grilled beef tenderloin, Yankee pot roast, and mixed grill in a traditional New England–style bar/restaurant. Along Newbury Street, the **Capital Grille** offers dry-aged porterhouse steaks, double-cut lamb chop, filet mignon, and a few seafood entrees; the meat is dry-aged in the open kitchen in a glass-cased meat locker. The area's most famous meat restaurant is a 20-minute drive north of Boston on Route 1, in the unlikely town of Saugus. An even unliklier herd of life-size plastic cows graze outside the enormous **Hilltop Steakhouse**, which seats 1,500, cooks great steak, and always has a (long) line.

Vegging out... Perhaps it's the Yankee heritage, but Boston doesn't have a really outstanding vegetarian restaurant. Having said that, you can get good vegetarian dishes in many places, including the Pacific Rim specialist **Jae's**, most Italian restaurants (try **Bertucci's**), **Chau Chow** in Chinatown, Brookline's **Indian Cafe**, and Mexican eateries including **The Border Cafe**. The **Milk Street Cafe** *is* vegetarian, but it's more of a lunch bar than a dinner spot.

Global harmony... Ethnic eating is in, and some restaurateurs figure what the hell, all types of cuisines go together as long as they're kind of exotic. **Soleil** cooks up anything from "sunny lands," while **Jae's** casts a net from California to Korea. Not to be outdone, **The Blue Room** in Cambridge covers half the world—its "Latin trio" includes shrimp with chilies, chicken chorizo, coleslaw, corn bread, salad, and black beans. You can also order spicy Hong Kong shrimp and Asian entrees. Another interesting combination is the mixture of French and Cambodian food at the exquisite **Elephant Walk** restaurants in Brookline and Somerville, where specialties include sweet-and-sour lemongrass fondue, chicken with basil and kaffir lime leaves, and marinade of lamb tenderloin with mushrooms.

Mama and papa Italian... Let's face it, there are too many Italian family restaurants in the North End, and some families cook better than others. Try **Pagliuca's**, where three brothers cook generous portions of rural Italian dishes and the warm, European atmosphere soothes. Another pleasant spot is **La Piccola Venezia**, where you dine beneath oil paintings of Venetian gondolas. Ectomorphs will want to look into "the Godfather platter"—a feast fit for Marlon Brando on a beef bender, with veal and chicken cutlets, eggplant parmigiana, meatballs, sausage, peppers, and pasta. The famous **Felicia's** serves above-average Southern Italian home cooking in a formidable upstairs chamber. A dark red ceiling and red velvet drapes go with the frightening maitre d', scarlet cummerbund and all. Photos on the staircase show Felicia with Bob Hope, Felicia with Frank Sinatra, and the Pope blessing Felicia. Bob and Frank are still patrons; one can only guess about the Pope.

Nouvelle Italian... When you're sick of red sauce, try **Mamma Maria's Ristorante**, a neat little town house restaurant that serves delicious new Italian cuisine in striking two-tone surroundings. Window boxes of white impatiens trail between black shutters, and a long black staircase leads to a series of small dining rooms with heavy white drapes and dark gray walls. Off the main Hanover Street drag, **Sage** is an undiscovered refuge from spaghetti and meatballs (try rabbit, roast salmon, or grilled octopus), while North End old-timer **Bernardo's** recently dropped some of the red-sauce dishes and replaced them with Sicilian cuisine. Outside the North End, the **Bertucci's** chain is always a good bet, with pizzas made in giant brick ovens leaping with flames. The sauce on their new mushroom-and-chicken ravioli dish is divine!

Designer pizza... If you're no longer satisfied by just pepperoni and mushrooms on your pizza, go to the **Bella Luna** in Jamaica Plain, where you can top it with pretty well anything, from bamboo shoots to baby corn. The **Bluestone Bistro** is a similar establishment, where you can experiment with ham and pineapple. Why this South End restaurant moved into boring Brighton, an unremarkable suburb populated by students, third-generation Irish, and first-generation Asian immigrants (none of whom talk to each other) is a mystery. For less complex but still good pizza, you can go to the North End's **Pizzeria Regina**, which is packed on weekends, or escape to the reassuring anonymity of Chicago's **Pizzeria Uno** chain.

The tastiest Tex-Mex... Is **The Border Cafe** the best Mexican restaurant outside Mexico? I'm an enchilada aficionado, and I've yet to top this glorious Harvard Square extravaganza. Is Tex-Mex better than Mexican? The Tex-Mex food is fabulous, portions are big, prices are little, and it's served with flair—waiters make a point of leaping the stairs two at a time, loaded trays aloft (do they practice in off hours?). Order the mountainous, sizzling Cadillac fajitas and stuff 'em in. The fruity margaritas are legendary (but bring your ID—my husband was once refused a drink and he's really old.) Beer is served from an ice-filled, claw-footed bathtub. The problem? The wait. The answer? Leave your name at 6:30, collect your free beeper, then shop at nearby bookstores until it buzzes (it could take two hours on a Saturday). The restaurant is expanding into a space next-door, which may or may not ease the situation. If the line at the Border Cafe is just too long, try the **Cottonwood Restaurant and Cafe**, one stop up the Red Line at Porter Square (there's another downtown off Boylston Street). It's more peaceful; you can make reservations. But the food's fancier, and it costs twice as much.

More Mex than Tex... For a Mexican fix in the Back Bay, try the quiet **Casa Romero**. The tiny, flower-filled courtyard with its terra-cotta fountain is perfect on summery evenings; unusually rich sauces (for Mexican cuisine) give the dishes a unique flavor, and who could resist cactus salad? A caveat: The basic (cheapo) margaritas are too harsh, even for veteran tequila lovers. Another downtown option, **Fajitas and 'Ritas** is pleasantly quirky. You're handed a menu-cum-order sheet and a crayon, and you fill in what you want. All they serve is fajitas (chicken, beef, shrimp, turkey, and a whole lot more) and excellent margaritas.

Bombay on the Charles... If **The Border Cafe** is the tastiest place north of Mexico, **Bombay Club** serves some of the best Indian food west of London. We dragged ourselves away from our favorite hole-in-the wall Indian hideouts to this fashionable Harvard Square restaurant, and we weren't disappointed. Located upstairs in a trendy shopping mall, it has a big airy dining room and two walls of windows overlooking busy JFK Street. The sauces are exquisite, the tandoori is crisp but tender, and the breads are delicious. We rather missed the wailing music and Indian-goddess-seduction prints that characterize every other Indian restaurant we've ever known, but the flavors more than compensated. Cambridge generally is a good place for Indian food. In North Cambridge, the **Maharaja** stands out. Try their dinner for two, and save space for the excellent, warm, *gulab jamen* and the spiced Indian tea. Otherwise, take your pick from the glut of Indian restaurants around Central Square: Our top two are the **Indian Globe**, which attracts many Indian diners (always a good sign), and **Shalimar of India**. In Brookline, go for the **Indian Cafe**, which has above-average food and decor and some excellent vegetarian entrees, including *shahi paneer korma* and *malai kofta*.

High-end French... **Julien** at the Hotel Meridien in the Financial District has to be the poshest restaurant in town. Don't come here in casual clothes, even at lunchtime—the maître d' is a master of the disdainful stare. Opulence is the name of the game. The former reception room for the governors of the Federal Reserve Bank, with its ceiling resplendent in gold leaf and two original murals by N.C. Wyeth, houses the bar; the airy dining room, with elaborately carved stone walls, used to be the "Members' Court". The chef consults on a regular basis with visiting kitchen gurus from France; the result is a sumptuous menu including chateaubriand; terrine of smoked salmon and sturgeon, with *blinis* and horseradish caviar cream; and roasted monkfish with garlic and bacon for two. *Le vin* might cost $200 a bottle. **Maison Robert** is another fine French restaurant, in the Old City Hall building along the Freedom Trail. In summer, incongruous yellow-striped umbrellas surround the solemn stone statue of Benjamin Franklin in the forecourt (Ben was an alumnus of the original Boston Public Latin School, founded in 1635 on this site, as commemorated by a sidewalk mosaic). Specialties include dover sole, rack of lamb, dessert soufflés, crêpes suzette, in the cafe you'll find French provencial cuisine.

Kosher corner... **Aujourd'hui** at the Four Seasons Hotel in the Theater District has a separate, strictly supervised kosher kitchen preparing kosher meals for the main dining room. More casual, the **Milk Street Cafe** is also kosher, though most of the customers aren't, and you'd hardly notice unless someone told you. For a wide choice of kosher foods, from Chinese to bagel shops, go to Brookline, the heart of Boston's Jewish community.

It's all Greek... Dozens of Boston restaurants are owned by Greeks, but they're cooking seafood, pizza, steaks and chicken. **Omonia** actually produces Greek dishes: moussaka, lamb, spinach pies, flaky pastry, and baklava. The cuisine is authentic, the service is more polite than in most Greek tavernas, and if you close your eyes to the Theater District outside, you might imagine you're in Greece.

Thai one on... One of the city's best Thai restaurants is in fashionable Brookline village. **Sawasdee** has a discreet wait staff and a colorful menu: yellow curry (potatoes, onions, and pineapple in coconut milk), red curry (eggplant and bamboo shoots), and emerald curry (fish balls, green peas, asparagus, string beans, and green bell peppers). The *pad thai* and vegetarian dishes are also delicious.

When in Chinatown... Eat Chinese where the Chinese eat—in Chinatown. Most Chinatown restaurants are enormous, unpretentious institutions. At **Chau Chow**, fish comes fresh from the tanks to the table, and the Chinese customers order tons of food off the menu. Across the street, **Grand Chau Chow**, under the same ownership, has the same menu with slightly higher prices; it's bigger, with typical Chinatown linoleum floors, rowdy atmosphere, and large round tables. **East Ocean City** is slightly smarter than the competition, with marble floors and tablecloths, but the food is much the same as elsewhere.

Pass the dumplings, darling... Dim sum, the Chinese version of brunch, served every day of the week, comes to your table on little carts in silver dishes and wicker baskets, and you order whatever takes your fancy. On noisy, frenetic weekends, you point and yell, and non-English-speaking waiters guess. You'll often end up with mystery dishes. Come in a good, adventurous mood, and don't panic about the price as the dishes pile up. Unless you accidentally order some wildly exotic import from China, dim sum is always affordable. **Dynasty**, with enormous upstairs and downstairs dining rooms and a big Chinese crowd, serves some of the best dim sum in Chinatown. Also known for their dim sum are **Grand Chau Chow** and the **Imperial Seafood Restaurant**, which specializes in Cantonese cuisine.

Brunch secrets... When we want to eat Sunday brunch, we break down and head for a big hotel. After feasting on those sinful mountains of endless delicacies at the Marriott (any Marriott), the Sheraton, or the Westin, brunch anywhere else seems like a letdown. Personally, I'd pick the nearest, biggest hotel and dive in. Most charge a flat rate for an all-you-can eat extravaganza that will fill you up until Tuesday evening. Alternatively, the **Café Promenade** offers an à la carte brunch, with cream-and-mint smoked salmon, filet mignon, and duck salad. The **Milk Street Cafe** makes a fixed-price kosher vegetarian brunch. Harvard Square's **Bombay Club** has Indian food, and Jamaica Plain's **Doyle's** does American egg dishes to a T.

Lunch munchies... Slip off the Freedom Trail and catch lunch with half the population of the Financial District at the bright and cheerful **Milk Street Cafe**, which serves homemade vegetarian soup, sandwiches, salads, and the like over the counter. If you really want to join the workers, take your food out and eat with the throng in Post Office Square. If you're antiquing along Charles Street at lunchtime, try the gourmet sandwiches at

Rebecca's, where you can eat in-or outside amid plants in terra-cotta pots under yellow umbrellas. The **Caffe Bella Vita** on the same street offers Italianate sandwiches, salads, and pastries amid pale orange stucco walls and original artwork. You can browse a catalog of for-sale artwork over lunch.

After hours... Boston is not known for late-night frivolity. However, you can live it up in a few places, most of them around the Theater District, and notably the **Blue Diner**, which doesn't close between 7am Thursday and 11pm Sunday (Monday through Wednesday, it's open from 7 am until 11 pm). The mixed-use **Club Cafe** is open nightly until 1:30. **Jae's** in Cambridge serves sushi until 1, Thursday through Saturday nights. In Chinatown, many restaurants stay open until 2 weekdays and until 4 Friday and Saturday; **Dynasty** goes until 4 every day of the week.

When the play's the thing... **Rocco's** borders the Theater District and is suitably dramatic. With its great high ceilings, false stone arches, stuffed peacock, and abstract modern artwork, it looks like a modern opera set. Before a play, you can also get some Christmas shopping done, as the wild and wonderful table artwork (pretty painted pitchers, ceramic frogs, candle holders shaped like cows, carrots, or chilies) is for sale. A price list sits right beside the menu, which features Italian American cuisine. In the Theater District, **David's** is styled like a Medieval puppet theater with castellated moldings, pennants hanging from the ceiling, and shields on the walls. It's Mr. Rogers' Land of Make Believe in navy, red, and orange. The delicious cuisine is billed as European, but it's heavily influenced by the good ole USA (when did cranberries last grow in Europe, and which European country does Cajun cooking make you think of?). Next door, the microbrewery-cum-restaurant brew moon is painfully à la mode. It's more accurate to say that the Theater District came to **Jacob Wirth** than vice versa, since the restaurant was here first.

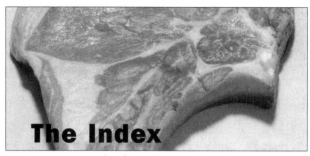

The Index

$$$$$	over $30
$$$$	$20–$30
$$$	$15–$20
$$	$10–$15
$	under $10

Prices reflect per-person cost of a main course, appetizer or dessert, and one alcoholic drink.

Anthony's Pier 4. Anthony's is big, bustling, and exciting. You'll see lots of fellow tourists. Photos of the more famous visitors, from Liza Minelli to Richard Nixon, are plastered up in the reception area. Make reservations to avoid hours of waiting.... *Tel 617/482–6262. 140 Northern Ave., South Station T stop. Jackets recommended.* $$$$

Aujourd'hui. One of the best (and most expensive) restaurants in town, Aujourd'hui, at the Four Seasons Hotel has four stars and two executive chefs, one of whom specializes in pastries. Don't come in athletic wear or jeans; they won't let you in.... *Tel 617/451–1392. 200 Boylston St., Arlington St. T stop. Jackets preferred.* $$$$$

Barking Crab. This restaurant keeps changing its name, and each change seems to bring a price increase; still, it's cheaper to eat lobster outdoors on the harbor with plastic forks and paper plates than at most other seafood restaurants.... *Tel 617/426–2722. 88 Sleeper St., South Station T stop. No reservations. DC not accepted.* $$

Bay Tower. Thirty-three stories above Faneuil Hall, the high price reflects the high-rise setting rather than the quality of the nouveau American food.... *Tel 617/723–1666. 60 State St., State St. T stop.* $$$$$

Bella Luna. Lunar themes dominate this funky gourmet pizza restaurant with an open kitchen in Jamaica Plain. Exotic toppings include clams and spinach; the Pizza Menino (Italian sausage and pepperoni) is named for Boston's mayor. They also make "extraterrestrial insaladas," "stellar sandwiches," "pasta constellations," and desserts.... *Tel 617/524–6060. 405 Centre St., Jamaica Plain, Heath St. T stop. $*

Bernardo's. Simple Sicilian dishes star at this old-fashioned North End eatery. Try olive and celery salad, diced fresh tomatoes over spaghetti, or grilled mackerel.... *Tel 617/723–4554. 24 Fleet St., Haymarket T stop. $$*

Bertucci's. A successful local chain that is constantly expanding, Bertucci's has branches in Boston, Cambridge, Brookline, Somerville, Newton, and West Roxbury. Brick-oven-pizza and good pasta dishes with upscale yet kid-friendly decor appeal to almost everyone except my uncle from Denver, who wanted spaghetti with tomato sauce (they don't have it). He did, however, enjoy his linguine. *Tel 617/227–7889, Faneuil Hall, Haymarket T stop. Tel 617/247–6161, 43 Stanhope St., Copley T stop. Tel 617/661–8356, 799 Main St., Cambridge, Central Sq. T stop. Additional locations. Reservations not accepted. $$*

Biba Food Hall. Twice awarded "Best Restaurant in Boston" by *Boston* magazine's annual awards, the Biba Food Hall caters to society matrons, wealthy businessmen, and everyone in between with good money and good taste. Unusually, lunch here costs almost the same as dinner.... *Tel 617/426–7878. 272 Boylston St., Arlington St. T stop. AE not accepted. $$$$–$$$$$.*

Black Crow Caffe. It's in an unsalubrious section of Jamaica Plain, but this restaurant sparkles from within. Marble-topped and wooden tables are crammed in dangerously close to enormous cacti, and royal blue walls support striking floodlit artwork. The flashy cars outside bring diners from nearby, snooty Brookline. If you're not driving, take a cab; you won't enjoy walking this bit of Boston.... *Tel 617/983–9231. 2 Perkins St., Jamaica Plain, Heath St. T stop. Reservations not accepted. D not accepted. $$$*

Blue Diner. Surprisingly, you can make reservations to eat in this
genuine 1940s, shining-steel diner, and you should, or you'll
have to wait hours.... *Tel 617/338–4639. 150 Kneeland
St., South Station T stop. Open 7am–11pm Mon–Wed, Thur
7 am–Sun 11 pm. $$*

The Blue Room. Wildly eclectic ethnic food in a restored mill
building. Cooking classes are held some summer nights on
the patio.... *Tel 617/494–9034. 1 Kendall Sq., Kendall Sq.
T stop. $$$$*

Bluestone Bistro. Lively and serves excellent pizza as well as
pasta and delicious appetizers, like mussels and hot bean
dip. Often packed, there's little space to wait, but you can
take the pizza out.... *Tel 617/254–8309. 1799 Common-
wealth Ave., Brighton, Chiswick Rd. T stop. $*

Bombay Club. Famous because all Indian restaurants are simi-
lar but this one isn't. A low-cost lunch buffet is served from
gleaming copper pots; dinner items are full-flavored, and the
mango margaritas are otherwordly.... *Tel 617/661–8100.
57 JFK St., (the Galleria Mall), Cambridge, Harvard Sq. T
stop. D, DC not accepted. $$*

The Border Cafe. Half the population of Cambridge crams into
this wildly and justifiably popular Tex-Mex restaurant on
weekends. Hefty, scrubbed wooden tables and chairs scrape
on unpolished wooden floors; Harvard students jam-pack
the bar, and everyone tramps up and down the wide wood-
en staircase to the basement-level dining room with its loud,
messy murals of donkeys and cacti. Be prepared to wait, but
don't miss it! *Tel 617/864–6100. 32 Church St., Harvard
Sq., Cambridge. Harvard Sq. T stop. No lunch. Reservations
not accepted. D not accepted. $$*

Boston Beer Works. A mixture of smart students, young
couples, beer lovers, and Red Sox fans (the bar's across the
street from Fenway Park) drink and eat at this long, airy,
two-level restaurant that focuses on beer but does not for-
get food. The burgers are great and so are the ribs and steak
tips, but you can also order hummus and tahini, jambalaya,
mako shark sticks, or Thai salad.... *Tel 617/536–BEER. 61
Brookline Ave., Kenmore Sq. T stop. $$*

Boston Market. At locations all over town, these fast-food restaurants offer healthy (unfried) chicken dinners to eat in or to go. New locations are springing up all over town—all over the world, in fact: We even found one in Athens, Greece! A good alternative to the burger joint.... *Tel 617/ 542–2449. 232 Tremont St., Boylston T Stop (and other locations). Reservations not accepted. AE, D, DC not accepted. $*

brew moon. "welcome to the moon," says the menu. "our fresh in time philosophy ensures that your meal and your beer will always be freshly made, never compromised. brew moon is the fulfillment of a dream." Boogie on down, sample the ale, the artichokes, the lack of capital letters, and the we're-so-cool atmosphere.... *Tel 617/742–5225, 617/523–6467. 115 Stuart St., Boylston T stop. D not accepted. $$$–$$$$.*

Bull and Finch. Blame the pub for its name (a tacky pun on Boston's famous architect, Charles Bulfinch), but don't blame it for the fact that this innocent neighborhood bar beside the Public Garden inspired the TV sitcom "Cheers." After all, the bar was here first.... *Tel 617/227–9605. 84 Beacon St., Arlington St. T stop. $$$*

Cafe Budapest. A romantic, surreal place with super soups (try the iced cherry), veal, schnitzel, and delicious pastry desserts.... *Tel 617/734–3388. 90 Exeter St., Copley T stop. $$$$$*

Café Promenade. This American, bistro-style restaurant at the Colonnade Hotel serves a good à la carte brunch. Best dinner bets include lobster lasagne with tomato-tarragon cream, signature pizzas, and steaks.... *Tel 617/424–7000. 120 Huntington Ave., ICA/Hynes T stop. $$$*

Caffe Bella Vita. Kids' high chairs are imaginatively painted in primary colors; you can purchase the artwork, and the salad and sandwich menu is complemented by dinner specialties like spinach lasagna. End it all with genuine gelato.... *Tel 617/720–4505. 30 Charles St., Charles St. T stop. Reservations not accepted. No credit cards. $*

Cambridge Brewing Company. The beer is brewed on the premises, and the food's good too. Try the mussels

steamed in beer, or the paella, with its generous portions of
seafood and chicken.... *Tel 617/494–1994. 1 Kendall Sq.,
Cambridge, Kendall Sq. T stop. $$*

Capital Grille. A paradise for meat lovers. This steak house has
a clubby feel, with wooden and leather furniture.... *Tel 617/
262–8900. 359 Newbury St., Hynes/ICA T stop. $$$$*

Casa Romero. Unusually rich Mexican entrees are served in two
dining rooms with low, ceilings, hardwood floors, ceramic
tables, and Aztec murals. Or you can dine outside in the
courtyard.... *Tel 617/536–4341. 30 Gloucester St. ICA/
Hynes T stop. $$*

Chau Chow and Grand Chau Chow. Your dinner swims before
your eyes in these award-winning Chinatown Chinese
restaurants. Efficient service whizzes the food to the table
almost as you order, and main courses can easily precede
the appetizer. The vast menu specializes in seafood, and you
can eat for a few bucks or spend a fortune, depending on
whether you dine on lobster and eel, or duck's feet and
bean soup.... *Chau Chow tel 617/426–6266, 52 Beach St.
Grand Chau Chow tel 617/292–5166, 45 Beach St.,
Chinatown T stop. Reservations not accepted. No credit
cards. $–$$$$*

Club Cafe. South End types (young, open-minded, professional,
gay) will enjoy the lively gay and singles scene at this cafe
that's part of a health club and jazz bar.... *Tel 617/536–
0966. 209 Columbus Ave., Prudential T stop. $$*

Cottonwood Restaurant and Cafe. Art deco meets the Wild
West. The waiters wear purple shirts and turquoise Western
ties; neon strip lights shine on Native American artifacts in
a series of small dining alcoves. Try the peach maragaritas
and "snakebites"—fried, spicy jalapeños stuffed with jack
cheese and shrimp, and served with cilantro mayonnaise....
*Tel 617/247–2225, 222 Berkeley St., Copley T stop. Tel
617/661–7440, 1815 Massachusetts Ave., Cambridge,
Porter Sq. T stop. $$$$*

The Daily Catch. The Boston Fish Pier restaurant with no sea
view. A lone Italian seafood restaurant in a throng of Greeks.
The Daily Catch has tubular steel stools, an open kitchen,

and suitably Italian tile floors.... *Tel 617/523–8567. 261 Northern Ave. (Boston Fish Pier), South Station T stop. No credit cards.* $$$$

David's. Opened in 1993, this Theater District restaurant is one of Boston's best new eateries. Try steamed salmon with basil dumplings or Cajun-rubbed tuna steak.... *Tel 617/367–8405. 123 Stuart St., Arlington St. T stop. D, DC not accepted.* $$$$

Davio's. Come here for good food and cute waiters who say "Let me make you a nice drink with cranberry juice and seltzer" when it's hot.... *Tel. 617/262–4810. 269 Newbury St., Copley T stop.* $$

Doyle's. A Boston classic, where politicians swap war stories, and the high wood booths are always packed. A special list boasts America's largest collection of single-malt Scotches.... *Tel 617/524–2345. 3484 Washington St., Jamaica Plain, Green St. T stop. No credit cards.* $

Durgin-Park. "There's no place like this place anywhere near this place, so this must be the place," says the notice at the entrance, and it's right. Hearty plates of seafood (fried or broiled, but usually fried), prime ribs, and Boston baked beans are dished up in a big exposed kitchen beneath lots of exposed plumbing. This popular, busy restaurant takes no reservations. Guess what happens? Get here early and be prepared to wait.... *Tel 617/227–2038, 617/227–2877. 340 N. Market St., Government Center T stop. Reservations not accepted.* $–$$$

Dynasty. This barn of a restaurant serves good dim sum in bare-bones surroundings until 4 every morning.... *Tel 617/350–7777. 33 Edinboro St., Chinatown T stop.* $–$$$$

East Ocean City. It looks fancier, but the food's par for China-town. Best bets are crab or other seafood entrees.... *Tel 617/542–2504. 25–29 Beach St., Chinatown T stop. AE, D, DC not accepted.* $$

The Elephant Walk. A mother-and-daughter team run this excel-lent new restaurant with two branches serving French and "aristocratic Cambodian" cuisine in a gracious, airy dining room with elephant motifs and objets d'art. The Beacon Street branch is bigger, airier, and louder; Union Square more intimate.... *Tel 617/247–1500, 900 Beacon St., St. Mary's T stop. Tel 617/623–9939, 70 Union Sq., Somerville, Central Sq. T stop (one mile away). No reservations Fri or Sat. $$*

The European. The best thing about this restaurant is the validated parking: only $1 for two hours (at the lot beneath the expressway). The menu lists 15 veal dishes and over 100 other options—play it safe and order pizza or pasta, and avoid anything fancy-sounding because it won't be.... *Tel 617/523–5694, 218 Hanover St., Haymarket T stop. $$*

Fajitas and 'Ritas. A small, bright, new restaurant with butcher paper on each table, and do-it-yourself ordering. Fajitas proved highly successful downtown, and it recently opened a brand new branch in Brookline. It's cheerful, friendly, informal, relaxing, and still somehow hip. The Brookline branch gets busy after 7:30, and service suffers (they need more wait staff). Portions are inexpensive but a tad small. Two hungry diners will need three orders of fajitas. Order an extra margarita while you're at it.... *Tel 617/426–1222, 25 West St., Downtown Crossing T stop. Tel 617/566–1222, 48 Boylston St., Brookline, Brookline Village T stop. Reservations not accepted. $*

Felicia's. Above-average Southern Italian home cooking. A tower of Italian wines is the dining room's centerpiece.... *Tel 617/523–9885. 145 Richmond St.. Haymarket T stop. $$$*

Grand Chau Chow. See Chau Chow.

The Ground Round. This friendly chain offers so-so American food in cheerful, kid-oriented surroundings. Adult diners can usually take refuge in the bar.... *Tel 617/247–0500. 800 Boylston St. (Prudential Center), Prudential T stop (and other locations). Reservations not accepted. $$*

Hilltop Steakhouse. The region's best known steak house, 15 minutes north of town by car. It's kitschy, enormous, and serves marvelous steak.... *Tel 617/233–7700. 855 Broadway St. (Rte. 1), Saugus, No T stop. Reservations not accepted. No credit cards. $*

BOSTON | DINING

The Hungry i. In a tiny Charles Street basement, this intimate restaurant with redbrick walls and patterned china serves quail, duckling, and contemporary American fare.... *Tel 617/227–3524. 71½ Charles St. Charles St. T stop. D not accepted. $$$$$*

Imperial Seafood Restaurant. Cantonese cooking, excellent dim sum. Newly renovated.... *Tel 617/426–8439. 70–72 Beach St., Chinatown T stop. D not accepted. $*

Indian Cafe. If you're south of the river and crave Indian food, this is the place. We love the food here, especially the rich sauces on the *korma* and chicken *tikka masala* dishes. Romantic and understated atmosphere.... *Tel 617/277–1752. 1665 Beacon St., Brookline, Washington St. T stop. DC not accepted. $$*

Indian Globe. Come here for good, traditional Indian food at low prices. Overhead are shiny goddess-seduction prints.... *Tel 617/868–1866. 474 Massachusetts Ave., Cambridge, Central Sq. T stop. AE, D, DC not accepted. $*

J.P. Licks. The roof ornament, a larger-than-life plastic cow, was recently rescued from cow thieves on the Charles River. "J.P." stands for Jamaica Plain, the Boston neighborhood where this business originated; "Licks" is for the delicious ice cream, frozen yogurt, and hot fudge sauce (pass on the low-fat hot fudge sauce). (See You Probably Didn't Know).... *Tel 617/236–1666. 352 Newbury St., Hynes/ICA T stop. No credit cards. $*

Jacob Wirth Company. Who can argue with a tradition? Dates to 1868, and serves good German and American bar grub, from burgers to knockwurst to taco salad.... *Tel 617/338–8586. 31 Stuart St., Boylston St. T stop. $*

Jae's Cafe. Large and preppy, the Cambridge branch has a glorious, room-size, saltwater tropical fish tank (the inhabitants are *not* on the sushi menu). The South End restaurant is cozy and dimly lit. The menu proclaims, "Eat at Jae's and live forever"; perhaps that's why both places are permanently packed. Be prepared for a wait: They take reservations only for parties bigger than six. Sushi novices can try the "designer tidbits" menu. Jae's also serves many vegetarian and Chinese entrees.... *Tel 617/421–9405, 520 Columbus Ave., Prudential T stop. Tel 617/497–8380, 1281 Cambridge St., Cambridge, Central Sq. T stop. D not accepted.* $$$

Jimbo's Fish Shanty. This down-market version of Jimmy's (below) serves good, inexpensive seafood in a rather gloomy atmosphere.... *Tel 617/542-5600. 245 Northern Ave. (on the Fish Pier), South Station T stop.* $$

Jimmy's Harborside Restaurant. Great sea views make Jimmy's better than the downtown fish restaurants. Otherwise, it's the kind of place you'd take your parents. Median prices, formal service, bright lights.... *Tel 617/423–1000. 242 Northern Ave. (on the Fish Pier), South Station T stop (1-mile walk). Reservations recommended.* $$$

Julien. Presumably they write the menu prices in longhand because they're less shocking that way. Expect to pay through *le nez*. Enjoy the grandiose setting. The food is *très bien*, and by the time you get the bill, it's *trop tard*.... *Tel 617/451–1900. Le Meridien Hotel, 250 Franklin St., State St. T stop. Reservations recommended. Jacket and tie required for men.* $$$$$

La Piccola Venezia. A picturesque, inexpensive little trattoria. Carved mahogany bar, brick oven, and a healthy row of tomato plants and fresh herbs in the window.... *Tel 617/ 523–3888, 263 Hanover St., Haymarket T stop.* $$

The Last Hurrah. Leather booths, carved wainscot, Tiffany lamp shades, and a long bar claim allegiance to a bygone era. In a concession to contemporary dining habits, there's a token salad bar and three "healthy choice" entrees. Otherwise, expect lots of meat, mashed potatoes, and flaky pastry. The menu features a black-and-white photograph of "the magnificent Miss Lillian Russell." *Tel 617/725–2181. 60 School St., Park St. T stop.* $$

Legal Sea Foods. The people want fresh fish well cooked, and that's what they get here. Probably the best all-around fish fleet in New England, the Legal chain just keeps on growing. Homemade ice cream makes a great dessert.... *Tel 617/426–4444, Park Plaza Hotel, 35 Columbus Ave., Arlington St. T stop. Tel 617/266–7775, 100 Huntington*

Ave., Copley T stop. Tel 617/864–3400, 5 Cambridge Center (Kendall Sq.), Cambridge, Kendall Sq. T stop (and other locations). $$$

L'Espalier. High-end French and New England cuisine on a fixed-price menu. Three intricately carved dining rooms open off a wide spiral staircase. Current specialties include rack of lamb in portabello shallot crust, glazed lobster with peas and radish salad, and chocolate soufflé with pistachio ice cream, but the menu changes frequently.... *Tel 617/262–3023. 30 Gloucester St., Auditorium T stop. DC not accepted. Closed Sun. $$$$$*

Locke-Ober. A formal, Brahmin institution between the statehouse and city hall. Filet mignon, Wiener schnitzel, chicken, a famous lobster Savannah...you get the idea. City men headed for cardiac arrest have the surprising option of low-fat selections including shrimp, swordfish, and even vegetables with tofu.... *Tel 617/542–1340. 3 Winter Place, Downtown Crossing T stop. Jacket and tie required for men. No lunch weekends. $$$$$*

Maharaja. A favorite Indian restaurant. It sits unobtrusively on a street corner in North Cambridge. The food's great, there are plenty of choices; you can have your vindaloo (relatively) mild, or ask for a "hot" version of *korma*. The stern proprietress softens up if you smile at her.... *Tel 617/876–8664. 2088 Massachusetts Ave., Cambridge, Porter Sq. T stop. $*

Maison Robert. In summer you can eat al fresco, or indoors at the informal cafe with its brick walls and arches, floral oil paintings, and silver champagne buckets. The cafe serves "peasant fare" at nonpeasant prices (or else you're a peasant after paying them), though the two prix fixe menus ($17 and $23) are good values for three-course French meals in the middle of Boston. The formal Bonhomme Richard dining room offers French haute cuisine (*saumon fumé*, rabbit, veal, or *"le steak grille maître d'hôtel"*), and claims to have the "best French wine list" in town.... *Tel 617/227–3370. 45 School St., Government Center or Park St. T stop. $$$$$*

Mamma Maria's Ristorante. An unusually intimate North End restaurant. Dim lighting, private tables, and imaginative dishes like Atlantic salmon over red-beet salad, and beef tenderloin with truffle oil, asparagus, and semolina mushroom dumplings. The maître d' hails not from Rome but from London.... *Tel 617/523–0077. 3 North Sq., Haymarket T stop. $$$$*

Milk Street Cafe. A favorite with city workers, this counter-service cafe has daily specials like veggie melts and vegetarian burritos. It's all kosher, though nonkosher customers would never know.... *Tel 617/542–2433. 50 Milk St., State St. T stop. $–$$*

Nick's Beef and Beer. Much like hell (I assume), Nick's is dark and cavernous, with flames leaping about the open kitchen, red plastic booths, and scary waitresses howling above the din from the bar. Plates are piled diabolically high with meat, and it's dirt cheap.... *Tel 617/492–4284. 1688 Massachusetts Ave., Cambridge, Porter Sq. T stop. $*

No Name. You'll find excellent boiled lobster, broiled shrimp, fried clams, and all the rest, right beside the sea and $10 per plate cheaper than your average Boston seafood restaurant. On the other hand, the interior decor is basic (hanging plants, Formica tables); beverages are served in paper or plastic; and the atmosphere is hardly *sophistique*. Diners come in big, cheerful groups, prepared to wait for tables.... *Tel 617/423–2705, 617/338–7539. 15 ½ Fish Pier (off Northern Ave.), South Station T stop (1-mile walk). Reservations not accepted. No credit cards. $$*

Omonia. The Greek Omonia is a noisy, polluted main square in Athens. This, by contrast, is a neat, quiet little restaurant in the Theater District where you *won't* see the staff breaking plates or dancing on the tables. The food is authentic enough—it just seems a bit *subdued* for the Greeks (and our family should know).... *Tel 617/426–4310. 75 South Charles St., Boylston T stop. D, DC not accepted. $$*

The Original Sports Saloon. A "Cheers-like", neighborhood atmosphere and good BBQ and ribs.... *Tel 617/536–1904. 47 Huntington Ave., Copley T stop. Reservations not accepted. $*

Pagliuca's. Veal *braciolettini*, chicken *campagna*, and Italian vegetable soup are served in a cheerful little dining room

BOSTON | DINING

with brick walls and a wine rack around the ceiling.... *Tel 617/367–1504. 14 Parmenter St., Haymarket T stop. D not accepted. $$*

Parker's. China, sterling silver flatware, and pink wingback chairs set the tone at this stodgy restaurant in the Omni Parker Hotel. The summer lobster-bake menu includes a pound of lobster, a dozen steamers, corn, chowder, and Boston cream pie, which was created in this very restaurant more than 130 years ago.... *Tel 617/227–8600. 60 School St., Government Center or Park St. T stop. Jacket and tie required for men. $$$$*

Pizzeria Regina. Seek out the original version of this restaurant in the North End, where an old brick pizza oven creates a delicious, crispy-yet-flaky pizza crust. Like most North End eateries, it's crowded on weekends.... *Tel 617/227–0765. 11½ Thatcher St., Haymarket T stop. Reservations not accepted. No credit cards. $*

Pizzeria Uno. It's a Chicago import and it's a chain, but this place still serves up the best deep-dish pizza in town.... *Tel 617/523–5722, Faneuil Hall, Haymarket T stop. Tel 617/ 497–1530, Harvard Sq., Cambridge, Harvard Sq. T stop. Tel 617/262–4911, Kenmore Sq., Kenmore Sq. T stop (and other locations). $*

Plaza Dining Room. The ornate restaurant at the Copley Plaza Hotel brings you duck *à l'orange*, lobster-tail medallions, and sautéed gulf shrimp beneath the chandeliers.... *Tel 617/267–5300, 138 St. James Ave., Copley T stop. $$$$*

Rebecca's. Squeezed onto Charles Street between dozens of antique stores and real estate agents, Rebecca's is a pleasant stop for lunch or a light dinner.... *Tel 617/742–9747. 21 Charles St., Charles St. T stop. Reservations not accepted. $*

Redbones. Come here for meat and beer in a genuine, low-maintenance neighborhood bar.... *Tel 617/628–2200, 617/661–3254. 55 Chester St. (Davis Sq.), Somerville, Davis Sq. T stop. No credit cards. $$$$*

Rialto. Dining here is an exciting experience, with a young team of hosts and chefs, and a marvelous southern Mediterranean menu.... *Tel 617/661–5050. 1 Bennett St., Cambridge, Harvard Sq. T stop. D not accepted. $$$$$*

Ritz-Carlton Dining Room. Chateaubriand, rack of lamb, and Dover sole are the staples in this formal, stuffy dining room with an expensive wine list. As of July 1995, the Ritz dropped its mandatory jacket-and-tie policy in the bar and public areas, but of course, it's unthinkable to drop either in the dining room.... *Tel 617/536–5700. 15 Arlington St., Arlington St. T stop. Jacket and tie required for men. $$$$$*

Rocco's. There's never a dull moment at Rocco's. High ceilings boast grand bacchanalian murals with grapes and bottle-clutching angels. The ever-changing artwork is wildly abstract, and, at last check, the place was piled high with bronze birdhouses. The food is imaginative Italian American—try the *raviolini* with brown butter-walnut sauce, or leg of lamb with feta-stuffed zucchini.... *Tel 617/723–6800. 5 Charles St. S., Arlington St. T stop. $$$$*

Rowe's Wharf Restaurant. The Boston Harbor Hotel is the most exciting place to stay in town, and you can sample the excitement by dining at this restaurant. If nothing else, you'll remember the view of the busy inner harbor and the wharf, with its commuter crafts and luxury yachts.... *Tel 617/439–3995. Boston Harbor Hotel (Rowe's Wharf), Aquarium T stop. $$$$$*

Sage. A small dining room, a tiny kitchen, and an ambitious menu come together at this little-known North End restaurant. The cuisine is, of course, Italian, but of a newer vintage, with plenty of goat cheese, artichokes, beets, and fine Italian spices.... *Tel 617/248–8814. 69 Prince St., Haymarket T stop. AE, DC not accepted. $$$$*

Samuel Adams Brewhouse. A friendly sports pub at the Lenox Hotel, where you can nosh on inexpensive bar food like chili, sandwiches, burgers, and nachos.... *Tel 617/536–5300. 710 Boylston St., Copley T stop. Reservations not accepted. $*

Sawasdee. Boston's best modest-but-tasty Thai house. Quiet and subdued, and mercifully free of beaded curtains and other kitsch. Try the satay chicken, or anything in peanut sauce.... *Tel 617/566–0720. 320 Washington St., Brookline, Brookline Village T stop. $$*

Seasons. Take the glass elevator four floors up from the atrium lobby of the Bostonian Hotel, and you arrive at this glass-enclosed rooftop restaurant overlooking the Boston skyline and Faneuil Hall. Strips of lightbulbs and full-size trees add to the airy atmosphere.... *Tel 617/523–3600. The Bostonian Hotel, North and Blackstone Sts., Government Center T stop. $$$$$*

Shalimar of India. This is another good Central Square Indian restaurant offering all the basics and plenty of wailing music.... *Tel 617/547–9280. 546 Massachusetts Ave., Cambridge, Central Square T stop. $*

Skipjack's. Some people rave about this seafood restaurant. I've tried both branches and have never been inspired to return to either. Your parents might like it.... *Tel 617/536–3500, 199 Clarendon St., Copley T stop. Tel 617/232–8887, 2 Brookline Place, Brookline, Brookline Village T stop. $$$*

Small Planet Bar and Grill. If you like your dining experiences to express your eco-conscience, check out this funky watering hole. The menu is global; the decor is *National Geographic*.... *Tel 617/536–4477. 565 Boylston St., Copley T stop. Reservations not accepted. $$*

Soleil. A bargain! Incredibly inexpensive dishes from Mexico, the Mediterranean, Africa, and the Caribbean—Soleil specializes in (you guessed it) food from sunny places. Crammed with multiculti arts and crafts; small booths. The wait staff practice their Spanish as they go, in an attempt, they say, to communicate with the kitchen.... *Tel 617/876–7018. 18 Eliot St., Cambridge, Harvard Sq. T stop. D not accepted. $*

The Sunset Grill and Tap. The beer's good in this downscale Brighton bar, and so are the ribs. Meet the local college crowd as they try to outdrink each other....*Tel 617/254–1331. 130 Brighton Ave., Brighton, Harvard St. T stop. $*

Turner Fisheries Bar and Restaurant. Famed for its chowder, this seafood restaurant in the Westin's hyperactive

lobby also claims to have "New England's largest selection
of single-malt Scotches." See Doyle's, above: chance's are
someone's not telling the truth.... *Tel 617/424–7425.
Westin Hotel, at Dartmouth St., Copley T stop. $$$*

Ye Olde Union Oyster House. The oldest restaurant in Boston
and, they claim, the oldest continuously serving restaurant
in the country, the Oyster House is famed for its extensive
raw bar and its olde New England, pub-like atmosphere....
Tel 617/227-2750. 41 Union St. Haymarket T stop. $$$$

Upstairs at the Pudding. Above Harvard's famous theater
group, the "Hasty Pudding Club," this romantic restaurant
specializes in Northern Italian and Continental cuisine.... *Tel
617/864–1933, 10 Holyoke St., Cambridge, Harvard Sq. T
stop. D not accepted. $$$$*

Woodman's of Essex. Come here for the unique experience of
eating fried seafood at picnic tables at a small New England
town in the middle of a salt marsh.... *Tel 508/768–6451.
Rte. 133, Essex, No T stop. Reservations not accepted. No
credit cards. $*

Boston Dining

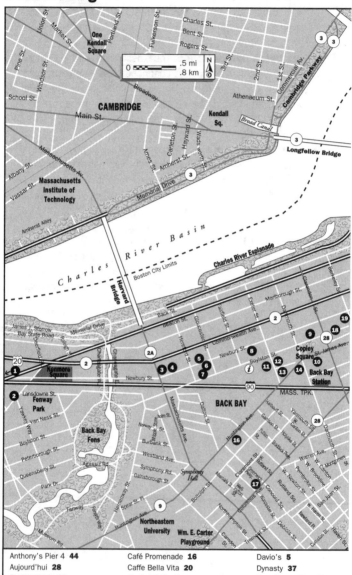

Anthony's Pier 4 **44**
Aujourd'hui **28**
Barking Crab **49**
Bertucci's **43**
Biba Food Hall **27**
Blue Diner **39**
Boston Beer Works **2**
Boston Market **33**
brew moon **31**
Bull and Finch **23**
Cafe Budapest **12**

Café Promenade **16**
Caffe Bella Vita **20**
Capital Grille **3**
Casa Romero **6**
Chau Chow **36**
Club Cafe **25**
Cottonwood Restaurant
  and Cafe **19**
The Daily Catch **45**
David's **30**

Davio's **5**
Dynasty **37**
East Ocean City **35**
The Elephant Walk **1**
Fajitas and 'Ritas **40**
The Ground Round **8**
The Hungry i **21**
Imperial Seafood
  Restaurant **37**
J.P. Licks **4**

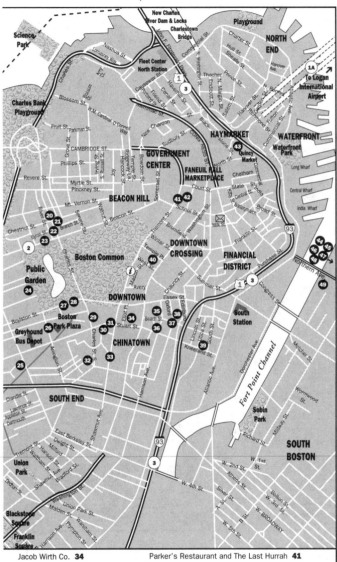

Jacob Wirth Co. **34**
Jae's Cafe **17**
Jimbo's Fish Shanty **48**
Jimmy's Harborside Restaurant **46**
L'Espalier **7**
Legal Sea Foods **26**
Maison Robert **42**
No Name Restaurant **47**
Omonia **32**
The Original Sports Saloon **13**

Parker's Restaurant and The Last Hurrah **41**
Plaza Dining Room **10**
Rebeccas's **22**
Ritz-Carlton Dining Room **24**
Rocco's **29**
Sam Adams Brewhouse **11**
Skipjack's **18**
Small Planet **9**
Turner Fisheries **14**

Downtown and North End Dining

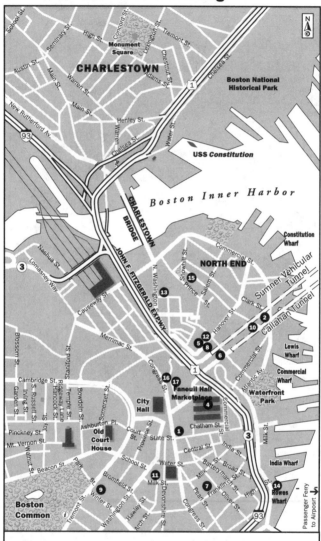

Bay Tower **1**
Bernardo's **2**
Durgin-Park Inc. **4**
The European **5**
Felicia's **6**
Julien **7**
La Piccola Venezia **8**
Locke-Ober **9**
Mamma Maria's **10**

Milk Street Cafe **11**
Pagliuca's **12**
Pizzeria Regina **13**
Rowe's Wharf Restaurant **14**
Sage **15**
Seasons **16**
Union Oyster House **17**

Cambridge Dining

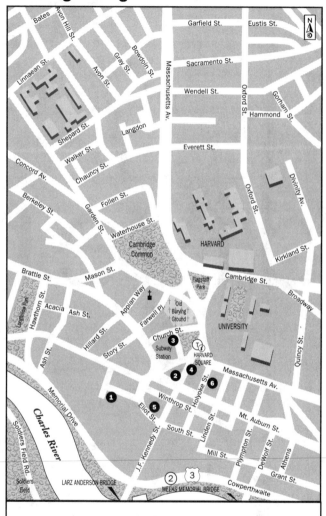

Bombay Club **2**
The Border Cafe **3**
Pizzeria Uno **4**
Rialto **1**
Soleil **5**
Upstairs at the Pudding **6**

LEGEND
✝ Church
ⓘ Information
✉ Post Office

3 sions

Got your walking
shoes, change for
subway tokens,
money for cab
fare? Good,
because it's total
madness to take

your car sightseeing in Boston. You're bound to get lost or have an accident on your way there, and you won't be able to find a parking space when you do get there. Boston is a city of neighborhoods built long before the automobile, and in these hoods, people walk, take the T or bus, or spring for cabs. All those cars you'll see lining city streets are just stereo thefts waiting to happen. Trust us.

Boston's a small city of about 43 square miles—and even that figure represents a lot of annexed "streetcar suburbs," which tourists rarely pass through. The tiny, original Shawmut Peninsula colonized by John Winthrop's settlers in 1630 has been augmented by landfill, but the whole deal still takes up very little of the planet's surface. **Beacon Hill**, **Back Bay**, **downtown** (including the **Theater District** and **Chinatown**), the **North End**, and the **Fenway** contain most of the city's attractions. Restaurants and cafes may lure you to the **South End. Cambridge** is a separate town, as old as Boston and with its own left-of-liberal, multicultural gestalt, but geographically it's only a quick hop on the T across the Charles River—and it's a vital part of the whole Boston experience.

These days, the "Cheers" bar and the Hard Rock Cafe have more drawing power than the American Revolution, but you really shouldn't visit Boston without attempting to follow at least part of the **Freedom Trail**, the nifty historical walking route marked out with a red line on the sidewalk (sometimes made of contrasting bricks). Like most visitors, you'll probably lose the trail at one baffling intersection or another; on the other hand, if you decide not to follow the trail, you'll find yourself continually running into it by accident. The entire 2.5-mile trail officially includes 16 historic sites of early American history, from the Boston Common to the Bunker Hill Monument and the USS *Constitution* in Charlestown. To get started, pick up a map at the **Boston Common Visitor Information Center**, on the Tremont Street side of Boston Common, where the trail begins. (You can also grab flyers here for nearly every other tourist destination in the area.) A lot of people cop out at the point where the trail leaves the North End and wanders over the nonscenic Charlestown Bridge to Bunker Hill—instead they take the water shuttle from Long Wharf to the Charlestown Navy Yard or a bus from Haymarket to Charlestown's City Square. Or, what the hell, they skip the Charlestown side altogether, which is the smart thing to do unless you're a fan of military history, or one of those obsessive types who has to finish everything they start. Even the National Park

Service's free guided walking tours of the trail, which start at the visitors center by the Old State House, skip Charlestown, on the theory that there are rangers on the other side who can fill you in.

Getting Your Bearings

In Boston's earliest years, everyone lived in the **North End**, cut off from the rest of the Shawmut Peninsula by the now vanished Mill Pond and Mill Creek; today it's cut off from the rest of Boston by the Central Artery, the stretch of I-93 that slices right through town. After Beacon Hill siphoned off the North End's wealthy white population and its working-class, free, black residents in the early 1800s, the North End became an immigrants' welcome center, first for Irish and Eastern European Jews, and, more recently, for Italians. Across the Central Artery to the southwest sprawls the bland, modern **Government Center**, which segues southward into **downtown**, where high-rises tower over 17th- and 18th-century streets with noteworthy Colonial-era sites hidden like Easter eggs among them. Duck back under the highway to the east and you'll hit the harbor, where the Aquarium presides over a handful of busy,

Freedom Trail

The number of official stops on the Freedom Trail and even its length depend on whose mouthpiece is talking and how good you are at not getting lost. A generous list of notable sites in early American history along the 2.5- (or maybe 3-) mile trail:
1. *Boston Common*
2. *Massachusetts State House*
3. *Park Street Church/Old Granary Burying Ground*
4. *King's Chapel and Burying Ground*
5. *First Public School marker*
6. *Old Corner Bookstore*
7. *Old South Meeting House*
8. *Benjamin Franklin Birthplace*
9. *Boston Massacre Site*
10. *Old State House*
11. *Faneuil Hall*
12. *Paul Revere House*
13. *Old North Church*
14. *Copp's Hill Burying Ground*
15. *USS Constitution*
16. *Bunker Hill Monument*

BOSTON | DIVERSIONS

tourist-thronged wharves. In downtown's southern reaches, the somewhat dilapidated **Theater District** surrounds the juncture of Tremont and Stuart streets, while **Chinatown** snuggles beside the Central Artery to the east, joining the Theater District at a very seamy seam known as the **Combat Zone.** Its adult-entertainment businesses are disappearing, but the atmosphere on Washington Street and around the New England Medical Center at night is still far from welcoming.

The side-by-side **Boston Common** and **Public Garden** cut off downtown on its western edge. North of them lies **Beacon Hill**, with its cozy streets and grand but not gaudy homes. Beacon Hill impresses many as the epitome of Boston Brahminism, but the truth is that the neighborhood has always been ethnically and economically diverse, particularly on the north slope, which borders busy, gritty Cambridge Street. There are multimillionaires on famous Louisburg Square, and there are people living off their Social Security checks in boardinghouses several blocks above. Many Brahmins left their charming but cramped quarters in the late 19th century for the new, higher and wider homes of **Back Bay**, built on landfill with large, straight streets running westward from the Public Garden and parallel to the Charles. Today most of the elegant Back Bay row houses have been subdivided into condos, where an ever increasing student population takes on extra roommates to afford the extravagant rents. Every other block in the Back Bay has a fabulous church, and Newbury Street is a must for shoppers, a great street scene as it gradually gets down and dirty at Massachusetts Avenue. Copley Square and the Prudential Center abut the Back Bay on its southern edge; south of that, I-90— the Massachusetts Turnpike, a k a the Mass. Pike—divides the Back Bay from the **South End**, a Victorian megalopolis with narrow brownstone-lined streets. Gays played a big role in gentrifying the South End; parts are still in serious disrepair, but other parts are as manicured and charming as the best of Beacon Hill and Back Bay.

Westward, cultural diversions abound in the **Fenway**, which has Frederick Law Olmsted, New York's Central Park designer, to thank for its green space. Here you'll find Symphony Hall, the New England Conservatory of Music, the Museum of Fine Arts, the Isabella Stewart Gardner Museum; for fans of pop culture, baseball's Fenway Park backs into nightclub-laden Lansdowne Street, land of 1,000 dances. The flashing Citgo sign above **Kenmore Square** signals that you're moving into Boston University territory, with little of interest until the trolley stops at Coolidge Corner in **Brookline**, the first of the streetcar suburbs. Or, if you're feeling adventurous, take the No. 39 bus west from the Boston Public Library in Copley Square to **Jamaica Plain**, also served by the Forest Hills stop on the Orange Line. Better known as "J.P.," this is a well-integrated, mixed-income community with a few funky restaurants and cozy pubs on or around Centre

Street, plus an urban oasis known as Jamaica Pond. This is probably where the Boston catchphrase "You can't get there from here" originated; Bostonians who aren't from J.P. are usually helpless to give exact directions to the area.

Charlestown lies across the Charles from the North End; **Cambridge** stretches along the north bank of the Charles westward from there, connected to Boston by a number of bridges. The Harvard Bridge, which carries Massachusetts Avenue (locally called just Mass. Ave.) across the river, leads not to Harvard but to MIT—to get to Harvard you'll take the Larz Anderson Bridge, which empties onto JFK Street (not to be mistaken for the JFK Expressway). Just to confuse you.

The best way to get around is by subway, the famous **Boston "T."** The T has four lines, distinguished by color (see You Probably Didn't Know) and runs from 5am to 12:45am. While you're at it, buy a **tourist pass** for the T at the Airport subway station or the Boston Common Visitor Information Center, which will also get you discounts at a lot of attractions (see Hotlines & Other Basics). Buses are convenient for a few far-flung sights, but the routes are not as easy to figure out, and for most visitors, won't be a required mode of transportation.

The tunnels

Heading out of Boston to Logan Airport, you take the **Callahan Tunnel**, *which feeds out of the North End. A snarl of highways—I-93, Route 1, the JFK Expressway—all suck into this long tiled chute under Boston Harbor. Coming into Boston from Logan and the North Shore, you'll take the* **Sumner Tunnel**, *which is really just the other tube of the Callahan Tunnel, but hey, why not commemorate two obscure local heroes instead of one? Bostonians were perplexed when the* **Ted Williams Tunnel** *opened in January 1996, named after a truly famous Red Sox batter. But only taxis can use the Williams tunnel, and it goes nowhere (someday it will link the Mass. Pike and Route 1). If you're nuts enough to fly into Boston on a Friday evening between 5 and 7, you'll have to drive north on Route 1, away from Boston, then make a U-turn after a couple exits and join the honking melee heading south. Traffic backs up for hours, waiting to funnel from eight tollbooth lanes into the Sumner's two lanes. Be smart and take a taxi instead—cabs are the only vehicles allowed to turn south from Logan on Route 1 during Friday rush hour, which means they can barge into the goddamn mess closer to the tollbooths. Or be really smart and book a flight that arrives Saturday morning.*

BOSTON | DIVERSIONS

Tour Time

If you don't mind looking like a tourist, sling a camera around your neck and hop onto one of the ubiquitous narrated "trolley" tours that trundle around the city's main sights; they're actually pretty convenient, and they're an especially good deal in bad weather—either snow, rain, or muggy heat. The **Blue Trolley** (tel 617/876–5539); the **Red Beantown Trolley** (tel 617/236–2148); and **Old Town Trolley** (tel 617/269–7010), which has orange and green cars, offer essentially the same tours of Boston, with unlimited reboarding during the day. You can buy tickets on board at any stop along their routes; the official first stop for all three is at Long Wharf. Here are the only differences: only the Blue Trolley goes across the Longfellow Bridge to Cambridge (mostly to pick up passengers at the Cambridge Center Marriott) and crosses Fort Point Channel to Fish Pier (weekends only); only the Red Trolley goes all the way down Huntington Avenue to the Museum of Fine Arts and the Fenway (it also has the only Filene's Basement stop); only Old Town stops at the Museum of Science, Hard Rock Cafe, and Boston Tea Party Ship. Old Town also runs a separate Cambridge tour from April through October, which starts at Harvard Square and heads to the Science Museum. Late May through Labor Day, the Red Trolley's special "Twilight Mystery Tours" (tel 617/542–2525) leave from Park Square at Boylston and Charles Streets. **Boston Duck Tours** (tel 617/723–DUCK, mid-April through fall) which use renovated World War II amphibious vehicles, are also great for an overview, since passengers ride high up. Unlike the trolley tours, you can't get on and off the "ducks," but these 80-minute tours do go out onto the Charles River, as well as on city streets. Pick up tickets at the Prudential Center (800 Boylston St.). Despite what your conductor may tell you, please don't yell "Quack, quack" at passers-by. True Bostonians yell four-letter words at people in traffic, or they don't yell anything at all.

The Lowdown

The fast-track Freedom Trail... Okay, you've only got an hour to spend on matters historical. If you're with a significant other, head straight to the North End and **Copp's Hill Burying Ground**, which will give you a view of the Charlestown sites on the Freedom Trail. From there it's a brief walk to the **Old North Church** and the **Paul Revere**

House, and you'll still have time left for a cappucino on Hanover Street. If you're by yourself, start at the Park Street T entrance, where you can wave at the gold-domed **State House** to your left and then read the **Boston Common** tablet in front. Crossing the street takes you to the **Park Street Church** and its **Old Granary Burying Ground**, final resting place of patriots Samuel Adams and Paul Revere. Follow the trail *past* sites four through 11 (see sidebar), snapping away with your camera; theres not much reason to go inside anywhere until you reach **Faneuil Hall**, and even that should only take a few minutes. You'll end up at **Faneuil Hall Marketplace**, where you can buy postcards of whatever you missed.

Don't believe the brochures... Faneuil Hall Marketplace, a much-copied re-creation of a Colonial-era market (including the long, parallel Quincy Market, North Market, and South Market), revived the economically sagging Boston waterfront when it opened in 1976. Sure, the original buildings set among cobblestones have great historic weight: Patriots such as Samuel Adams fanned the fires of liberty here, as abolitionists like Charles Sumner did later. Faneuil Hall itself—a gift to the people of Boston in 1742

Blackstone vs. city living
Anglican minister William Blackstone (sometimes written Blaxton) had no problems with pedestrians or drivers of any kind when he moved to the Shawmut peninsula, as the native Americans called it, in 1625. He lived by himself there until 1630, when he took pity on the disease-plagued shlubs in John Winthrop's recently established Massachusetts Bay Colony across the harbor and invited them over. For Winthrop, who had told colonists they should consider themself as a "city on a hill," the grass did prove greener on the other side, and in 1634 the settlers designated Blackstone's former stomping ground as the Boston Common, for "the grazing of cattell" and other public needs. Sociable only to a point, and a fan of religious tolerance, Blackstone soon took off for his own greener pastures, in Rhode Island. The dark warren of 17th-century passageways known as the Blackstone Block (near Faneuil Hall) give you an idea of the crowded city living he passed up. At the State House, the statues of Mary Dyer, hanged as a Quaker in 1660, and Anne Hutchinson, banished in 1637 for heretical views, give you an idea of the narrow-mindedness he left behind.

BOSTON | DIVERSIONS

and a tongue twister for tourists ever since ("fannel" or "fanyull" are acceptable)—was remodeled and enlarged in 1806 by Charles Bulfinch, the Boston architect you can't avoid; you can still climb up to the handsome, white-walled second-floor assembly room, where the tradition of patriotic oratory and civic functions continues. The statue of Samuel Adams on cobblestones outside, facing City Hall, makes a good meeting point, and you can check out the golden grasshopper weather vane, recalling one atop the Royal Exchange in London. But very few come today for the history. They come for the shopping, and as the restoration enters its third decade, that shopping has sunk to the level of suburban malls. Cutesy outplays Colonial, with "theme" stores focusing on inanities: every conceivable item that can be carved into the shape of an animal, or more flavors of jelly beans than you ever thought you'd need. Looking for real Boston memorabilia? Sure, you'll find that here, too, but at a get-rich-off-the-*turistas* price. The food stands that flank the long building still offer some of the best noshing around, from *gelati* and cookies to baked beans and lobster rolls; if you buy something in the claustrophobic food court, take it outside near the Bostix kiosk, where steps lead up to an out-of-the-way plaza for picnicking. But why not follow the red line of the Freedom Trail (often indistinct under the feet of so many visitors) to Union Street, where you'll find another batch of reasonably priced, if touristy, taverns? Try the corn chowder at the friendly bar of **Marshall House** (15 Union St.), which looks (but isn't) just as antique as the famous **Union Oyster House** down the street (see Dining). Serious shoppers will prefer to make the short walk or take the T at State Street (for one stop) to grubby **Downtown Crossing**, the area where Macy's, Filene's, and the famous Filene's Basement offer serious department store shopping, and dozens of boutiques and specialty stores flank the giants like so many pilot fish.

Where to feel like a student... Harvard Yard's the obvious place to pretend you're a student at **Harvard University**, an institution so overbearingly excellent that *Boston Globe* columnist Alex Beam refers to it simply as "WGU," for "world's greatest university." The college's oldest buildings are clustered behind redbrick walls in the Yard, which adjoins manic Harvard Square; in the cloistered quiet of the Yard, look for Bulfinch's Stoughton and University Halls, as well as the 1742 Holden Chapel and its Georgian Revival counterpart, the 1931 Memorial Church. Sever Hall and Widener Library are impressively massive. Don't miss the whimsical Harvard Lampoon Castle (at Mount Auburn and Plympton Streets), with its facelike front and stork weather vane. Plenty of students—whether Harvard enrollees or not—seem to be taking Outdoor Terrace 101 at the Au Bon Pain cafe on the Mass. Ave. end of Harvard Square—playing chess, suffering existential crises, and sipping endless cups of Peet's coffee. It's conveniently near the Harvard University Information Office in Holyoke Center, which can arrange a free, official tour of the campus for you. **MIT** (Massachusetts Institute of Technology) students scarf down Chinese food at Mary Chung's restaurant in Central Square (464 Massachusetts Ave.) or drink microbrews at the Cambridge Brewing Company (One Kendall Square); otherwise, they're squir- reled away studying on the decidedly modern campus between the Longfellow and Boston University Bridges. You'll know you've found the campus when you spot its main building, Rogers, which is topped by a shallow dome that looks like a roll-on deodorant. Take a tour starting at the MIT Information Center in the Rogers Building. **Boston University** students patronize restaurants and fast-food places on Commonwealth Avenue west of Mass. Ave., and the pubs and clubs on Brighton Avenue in Brighton. They come together with the **Berklee School of Music**'s guitar players and jazz singers in Kenmore Square, where they can mill around the mammoth six-story BU Bookstore (660 Beacon St.) or scout for used CDs in tiny neighborhood stores. The artsy **Emerson College** crowd is spreading from the northwest corner of the Public Garden into the Theater District along the eastern edge of the Boston Common, an area that can stand some rejuvena- tion. **Tufts University** students gravitate to newly hip Davis Square, on the Red Line in Somerville, where they can hang at the Someday Cafe (51 Davis Sq.), catch a cheap movie or concert at the Somerville Theater (see Entertainment), or nosh at the Rosebud Diner (381 Summer St.).

Where to act like a Brahmin... Even though their numbers are dwindling, you can still sample a bit of

Brahmin culture. Their private clubs are still notoriously private; on Beacon Hill, the disdainful lion's-head knockers on the castlelike front of the **Somerset Club** (42 Beacon St.) practically dare you to knock. (A popular story says that even firemen were once required to use the servants' entrance during an emergency.) The **Boston Athenaeum** at the top of the Hill also has private membership, but several floors of its library and eclectic art gallery are open to visitors (for free!), while guided tours reveal even more of the inner (and upper) sanctum. Balconies where gentlemen (and gentlewomen) scholars bury their heads in a wide variety of tomes look down on the **Old Granary Burying Ground**. When the thinkers get peckish, they can walk across the top of the Common to **Locke-Ober** (see Dining), a handsome, dark-paneled restaurant that didn't admit women until the 1970s. Jacket and tie are required, of course.

The Brahmins that still live on Beacon Hill are most likely on Chestnut and Mount Vernon Streets, and on the "flat of the hill" below Charles Street; in Back Bay, they're likely to be on relatively quiet Marlborough Street. The only way you'll gain entrance to one of their houses is to take a tour of an unoccupied one. The **Gibson House** in Back Bay captures upper-middle-class Victorian clutter—photos, curios, plush furniture and carpets, and gloomily tasteful woodwork. On Beacon Hill, the **Nichols House**, an 1804 Bulfinch town house, is a cozy showcase for art and antiques, including pieces by 19th-century sculptor Augustus St. Gaudens. Landscape architect and de facto feminist Rose Standish Nichols turned her family home into this museum at her death in 1961; if the museum director leads your tour, you're in for a gossipy treat. The **Harrison Gray Otis House** is another Bulfinch town house, this one on the "wrong" side of Cambridge Street, but not to worry—old man Otis, a Boston mayor and congressman, later moved into another Bulfinch house on the Hill proper (at 85 Mount Vernon St.), and then another (45 Beacon St.). The footloose Otises didn't leave much of the original furniture and decor, but content yourself with admiring the restored bright Federalist colors and noble proportions, and possibly hooking into a two-hour neighborhood walking tour, on summer Saturdays. Both of these Beacon Hill houses are administered by the Society for the Preservation of New England Antiquities, which could also be the nickname of the stereotypical Brahmin closet. The **Brooks Brothers** store, at the corner of Newbury and Berkeley Streets, is where they shop—but only when their clothes have completely worn out.

Common ground... Note the division between the scruffy, practical **Boston Common** and the polished, decorative **Public Garden** where the Swan Boats glide and the world's shortest suspension bridge crosses a cunning little lagoon. The Common has more places for homeless people to sleep; you might see Chinese women serenely doing tai chi exercises early in the morning in the Public Garden. The Common was founded in 1634, partly for "the grazing of cattell." Today it's mostly drab open space, with a playground, two tennis courts, some ugly statuary, and a shallow concrete wading pool known as the frog pond. The Public Garden, founded in 1839, is a carefully manicured horticultural garden with maddeningly indirect walkways and the "Make Way for Ducklings" sculpture. Please don't confuse the two open spaces in conversation—Charles Street is the border between them, if that helps.

Matters of state... There are two statehouses on the Freedom Trail, both fascinating, but only one free. The **Massachusetts State House** looms above Beacon and Park Streets, where a third of the people are snapping photos of its gleaming golden dome, a third are turned in the other direction snapping photos of the Shaw Memorial (where the Black Heritage Trail begins), and the other third are waiting to get on one of the tourist trolleys. You can wait an eternity for a "walk" signal at the intersection, but it's worth crossing the street to explore the grounds and interior of the Charles Bulfinch–designed State House, a neoclassical redbrick structure built on John Hancock's former pasture in 1798. To the far right and left of the grand main entrance, where statues of Daniel Webster and Horace Mann stand triumphantly in the sun, somber bronze statues of Mary Dyer and Anne Hutchinson are tucked into shady corners. (Of course, you'd be somber too if you'd been hanged on the Boston Common, as Dyer was, or been banished, as Hutchinson was, for nonconformist religious views.) Also on the right, facing the Common, is a bronze statue of John F. Kennedy walking purposefully through autumn leaves; a wreath of real fall leaves usually lies on the pedestal. In the second floor's elegant Doric Hall (designed by Bulfinch), you can pick up a map for a self-guided tour or join a free guided tour on weekdays. Highlights include mosaics, stained glass, ornate carvings, replicas of historic American flags (the originals are too fragile for viewing anymore), large-scale paintings of Colonial history, and best of all, the Sacred Cod. State legislators refuse to conduct their business unless this fish, carved out of pine in 1784, hangs over the gallery in the House of Representatives. (Yes, the Senate now has in its own gallery a Holy Mackerel.) Note that you can't leave the State House via the main entrance; that's reserved for outgoing U.S. presidents and Massachusetts governors departing their offices. So go out the side, and stop by the **Daily Grind** (168 Cambridge St.) nearby, to revive with a cup of joe or roll-up sandwich—the oatmeal-maple scones sell out early.

For Revolutionary history, you'll need to visit **The Old State House**, rebuilt and restored several times since 1713, which stands surrounded by modern high-rises at the corner of Washington and State Streets. The Congress Street balcony, where the Declaration of Independence was first read to Bostonians on July 18, 1776, overlooks a cobblestone ring marking the site of the Boston Massacre; on the building's exterior are mounted replicas of the gold lion and gold-topped unicorn—symbols of the British crown—that jubilant Americans tore down in 1776. In the spirit of forgive-and-forget, Queen Elizabeth II went inside during the U.S. bicentennial celebrations, but don't feel that you have to—for one thing, you have to pay a fee (it's run by a private society), and for another, there's nothing too thrilling inside, just historical curios such as a vial of tea leaves from the Boston Tea Party.

Secrets of the North End... From Faneuil Hall, a sunken pedestrian way (which construction workers are trying to place underground) takes you under the Central Artery and over to the North End, which is chockablock with food markets, restaurants, and cafes. Soak up the atmosphere by strolling down Hanover or Salem Streets in the evening, when elderly residents chat in Italian as they sit in lawn chairs watching the tourists. Stop in a *caffe* for an espresso, like the newer wave of immigrants, who are probably discussing soccer and the difficulty of parking. (That empty lawn chair in the street? That means the residents expect to find "their" parking space ready for them when they get back—or else.) Try Hanover Street's multilevel **Caffe Vittoria** (296 Hanover St.) for a *latte* when it's cold out, or nearby **Caffe dello Sport** (308 Hanover St.) for a lemon sorbet when it's warm; you may have to wait there for a seat at the **Daily Catch** (see Dining) or the intimate, hip **Pomodoro** (319 Hanover St.), a rustic-style trattoria across the way. You may hear exaggerated accounts of the presence of the Mafia here—something which really pisses off North End residents—but petty turf wars are not uncommon, and there are a few storefronts that don't seem particularly interested in their advertised line of business. This gives the North End its hint of the Casbah, a place where tourists are generally welcome but secrets are rarely revealed.

Small wonders on the Freedom Trail... Between Faneuil Hall and the North End, the trail darts through the **Blackstone Block**, a 17th-century neighborhood riddled with tiny lanes and 18th-century architecture, including the house of John Hancock's brother Ebenezer at **10 Marshall Street** (now private offices). Walk through the amazingly narrow, dark **Scott Alley**, between North Street and Marshall Street, which was called Marshall's Lane back in 1652. A kiosk in tiny **Creek Square** records some finds from architectural digs in the area, including remains of smuggled goods from times of British embargoes. Once in the North End, the trail veers off busy Hanover Street to North Square, where the small Tudor-style **Paul Revere House**, built after the Great Fire of 1676, still stands. Revere bought it in 1770, when he already had five children, and lived here nearly 30 years, by which time his wife had given birth to 16 (not all lived). Contrast his compact house, the oldest surviving frame house in Boston, with the more gracious interior of the adjacent **Pierce-Hichborn House**, built in 1710 and home to Revere's cousin. Or, since both houses charge admission fees, just glance from the outside and continue on to an even smaller treasure, the narrowest house in Boston: a three-and-a-half-story clapboard home less than 10 feet wide at **44 Hull St.**, across from Copp's Hill Burying

Ground. A window on each floor faces the street; the entrance is on the side, facing the wall of the next building. It's not open to the public, but then there wouldn't be room for anyone, anyway. Not quite as small, but still charmingly intimate, is the **Old Corner Bookstore** at the corner of School and Washington Streets, also known as the Globe Corner Bookstore. The unfortunate Anne Hutchinson used to live on this site, before she was banished for religious dissidence (and later killed by Indians—life was *not* easy in Colonial days). A new house was built here around 1718, with a quaint gambrel roof. Used first as an apothecary, it later became a bookstore and publishing house. **Atlantic Monthly** became a national presence from this spot, while publishers Ticknor & Fields spread the words of Longfellow, Hawthorne, Thoreau, Emerson, and Harriet Beecher Stowe from their presses. Today it's a bookstore with a thoughtful selection of Americana and travel literature. The *Boston Globe* intervened financially to help preserve the site, which accounts for the dual name; the other Globe Corner Bookstores in Back Bay and Harvard Square are larger but a wee bit less historic.

Small wonders on Beacon Hill... Beacon Hill's tiny alleys and mews, once home to tradesmen, servants, and horses, now harbor fashionable residences; all over the Hill you'll see smaller-than-average entranceways, along with diminutive balconies and window boxes. Narrow, cobblestoned **Acorn Street**, off West Cedar between Mount Vernon and Chestnut Streets, is to Boston what Lombard Street is to San Francisco: a photo opportunity that countless postcard manufacturers have already seized. Create your own Kodak moments by exploring other equally picturesque hideaways, like **Cedar Lane Way** (behind busy Charles Street between Chestnut and Pinckney Streets), which looks especially Dickensian when the gaslights glow at night. Peer through tunnels at 9 and 74 Pinckney, which lead to homes hidden from view. On the less-vaunted north slope, just above West Cedar Street off of Phillips, is **Primus Avenue**, a grand name for a terraced brick walkway; the gate is usually unlocked, so walk on through, so long as you're duly quiet. Across the way is an even narrower passage nicknamed **Flower Lane**, with a gaslight beckoning at the end. Around the corner, off of Revere Street, are four cul-de-sacs lined by two- and three-story brick houses, with a few surprises thrown in. The elegant, plantation-style white house at the end of **Rollins Place**, for example, is actually just a facade, while the windows at the end of **Sentry Hill Place** are not. There's a lovely oasis at the end of **Bellingham Place**; up the hill you can slip through the iron gate and meander around the attractive courtyard at **Joy Place**, as long as you don't act like a thief or a tour guide. No one minds if you walk through **Holmes Alley**, either, which is not at all pretty but historically more significant: Walk to the end of Smith Court (home of the African Meeting House, off of Joy Street), and turn left, where a two-foot-wide path goes behind several residences; makes a sharp right through a brick tunnel, which leads to South Russell Street. You've just walked on the tracks of the Underground Railroad, which had several depots in this part of Beacon Hill, a bastion of white abolitionists and free blacks.

Church and state on the Freedom Trail... Okay, so you can't always separate them. The **Old South Meeting House**, at the corner of Milk and Washington Streets, across from Benjamin Franklin's birthplace, is where colonials came to debate pressing matters and plot acts like the Boston Tea Party, when the crowds at Faneuil Hall grew too large. The second oldest church in Boston (founded in 1670, rebuilt in 1729), this graceful building is now a museum, but it closed in 1995 for 18 months of renovation and restructuring of its thoughtful but text-heavy exhibits (the revamped versions are expected to be more interactive). We hope Old South will still document the life of Phyllis Wheatley, the first published African American poet, who worshipped here. Gloomy-looking granite-hewn **King's Chapel**, at the corner of Tremont and School Streets, was the first Anglican church in Boston, founded in 1686 and rebuilt in 1749. First the church ran out of money for a steeple; then, after the evacuation of the British, it ran out of Anglicans, eventually becoming the world's first Unitarian church in 1789. A bell cast by Paul Revere's foundry still signals Sunday worship. The handsome brick **Park Street Church**, built in 1809, lists its historic claims on a plaque out front: the founding of the Handel & Haydn Society in 1815, William Lloyd

Garrison's abolitionist sermons beginning in 1829, the debut of the anthem "America" in 1831, and so on. The clock on the steeple still works, greeting passengers from the facing Park Street T station with the time of day and tolling bells to match. You can take guided tours in July and August, but with so much history and so little time, it's best to save your energy for Christ Church, better known as **Old North Church**, on Salem Street in the North End. Here, most historians believe, signal lanterns were hung on April 18, 1775, to warn those across the shore that the British were coming. (Just to confuse the historians, there was another "Old North" church in North Square, conveniently near Paul Revere's house; the British burned it in 1776.) Built in 1723 and replaced twice since, the tall steeple of Old North beckons from many vistas in Boston, while the original bells still peal. The gleaming white interior houses an antique clock and organ, plus touching tributes to slain British soldiers; for more history, stop in the funky museum and gift shop next door. Abandoning the trail, cut back to the cafes on Hanover Street through brick-lined **Paul Revere Mall**, known as "the Prado" to Italian residents. With its statue of Paul Revere, the mall would be a nicer place to hang out if wind didn't blow street trash through it so often. Here on Hanover Street you'll find the only Charles Bulfinch church left in Boston: **St. Stephen's Church** (formerly New North), an 1804 gem that seriously rivals Old North for charm. Thanks to the North End's flood of immigrants, it's Catholic today; Rose Kennedy was christened here.

Back Bay churches even atheists might enjoy...

You can't escape organized religion in Boston, so you may as well enjoy its outstanding architecture, most of it in the Back Bay. **Trinity Church** in Copley Square may not look like it's floating, but approximately 2,000 submerged wooden piles help hold up its massive square tower, designed by Henry Hobson Richardson. A small colonnaded courtyard lets you escape from the bustle of Back Bay. On the side plaza is Augustus St. Gaudens' outdoor statue of Jesus blessing the church's first rector, Phillips Brooks (who wrote "O Little Town of Bethlehem")—it's over the top in Boston's typically self-congratulatory way. Nearby, another of Richardson's Romanesque churches, **First Baptist** (Commonwealth Ave. and Clarendon St.), has the best nickname: "Church of the Holy Bean

Blowers," a waggish reference to the trumpeter angels perched on its belfry over sacramental scenes by Auguste Bartholdi, sculptor of the Statue of Liberty. Another fun name, **New Old South Church**, was given to the impressive Italian Gothic church across from Copley Square where the congregation of the Old South Meeting House moved in the 1870s. At any rate, it's near a good place to buy a magazine—there's a newsstand just outside next to the Copley Square T entrance.

Fans of Tiffany glass should head for Newbury Street to check out the Tiffany lamp and windows in the Gothic Revival **Church of the Covenant** and the 16 Tiffany windows in the stately brown **Arlington Street Church**, with its steeple inspired by London's St. Martin's in the Fields. In Boston, a church is rarely just a church: the Church of the Covenant also houses Gallery NAGA, showing contemporary art, while Arlington Street has flocks of vendors outside selling African tchotchkes and its congregation is young, urban, integrated Unitarian Universalist (gays who don't like bars should try meeting people here). The Gothic Revival **Emmanuel Church** (15 Newbury St.), draws Bach fans, with a different, professionally performed cantata every Sunday except in summer (see Entertainment); its richly decorated Leslie Lindsey Memorial Chapel, named after a victim of the sunken *Lusitania,* is poignant. Looking more like it belongs in Dresden or Hiroshima than Boston, the **First and Second Church**, at Marlborough and Berkeley Streets, kept its fragmented 1867 facade after a fire in 1968. Paul Rudolph, the architect responsible for the hideous rippled-concrete state-services building on Cambridge Street, put a similarly modern building behind the ruins, like a ghastly phoenix rising from the ashes.

Grave concerns on the Freedom Trail... You've heard of living history, right? Boston has its share of costumed performers (a whole colony thrives 40 minutes south at the 17th-century-styled **Plimoth Plantation** in Plymouth), but the city's *dead* history is even more rewarding. The Freedom Trail alone takes you by three 17th-century cemeteries where you can scout for interred Colonial celebrities and gravestones with intriguingly dour inscriptions and macabre engravings such as skulls with angel wings (sorry, no rubbings allowed). The oldest is **King's Chapel Burying Ground**, which serves as the final resting

BOSTON | DIVERSIONS

place for, among others, Elizabeth Pain (died 1704), whom Nathaniel Hawthorne apparently immortalized as Hester Prynne in *The Scarlet Letter*, and William Dawes, Paul Revere's riding mate, whom Longfellow doomed to obscurity by leaving him out of his famous poem "The Midnight Ride of Paul Revere." The **Old Granary Burying Ground**, a few blocks away by the Park Street Church, contains the graves of Revere, Samuel Adams, three signers of the Declaration of Independence, Crispus Attucks, the four others slain in the Boston Massacre, and Benjamin Franklin's parents. Most people with children try to find the tombstone of "Mother Goose," believed to be in a family plot. In the North End, the **Copp's Hill Burying Ground** rises high above Charter Street for a pleasant view across the water to Charlestown. Unable to enjoy the view, however, are the cemetery residents, who include the Puritan dynasty of the Mathers (Increase, Cotton, and Samuel); African-American abolitionist and Revolutionary soldier Prince Hall; and the remains of thousands more ordinary folk, including the dead of Boston's first black settlement (an area of Copp's Hill known as New Guinea). The British used to shell Bunker Hill from here, while riflemen used the gravestones for target practice; you can still see the bullet holes.

Other grave concerns... The **Central Burying Ground** isn't on the Freedom Trail, but it's close enough for a detour. Tucked in a corner of the Common by the Boylston T station, this lonely, fenced-off 18th-century resting place holds the remains of British casualties of the Battle of Bunker Hill, and portrait artist Gilbert Stuart, among others. Across the river, Cambridge's **Old Burying Ground**—near Harvard Square and adjacent to the First Parish Church (3 Church St.; more recently known for its free coffeehouse where Tracy Chapman got her start)—is dense with Harvard presidents and Revolutionary War soldiers, including the memorably named Neptune Frost and Cato Stedman, two African-Americans. Follow the path between the graveyard and the church to a quiet oasis of quaint old houses; after a block you're back on busy Church Street, not far from the Harvard T stop. A short bus (or cab) ride from Harvard Square, **Mount Auburn Cemetery**, which opened in 1831, was the country's first garden cemetery, and is still one of its finest. Although picnicking isn't allowed on the rolling grounds, many area residents hang out here on sunny afternoons, bird-watching and taking scenic strolls between the monuments and crypts. (In a lot of ways, this is a more comprehensible place for budding botanists than the enormous **Arnold Arboretum** across town, a 3-mile walk from Kenmore Square along Frederick Law Olmsted's "Emerald Necklace"). You'll pass by the graves of many 19th-century New England luminaries, including Henry Wadsworth Longfellow, Oliver Wendell Holmes, and "Battle Hymn of the Republic" author Julia Ward Howe (maps are available at the guardhouse). And on a clear day the small Norman tower at its center offers a grand view of Boston, Cambridge, and environs, all the way to the Blue Hills.

End of the Trail... Hearty souls who complete the entire Freedom Trail wind up at the **Charlestown Navy Yard**, where you might find a fife and drum corps or high school bands performing in summer, distracting weary tourists standing in line for a tour of "Old Ironsides," as the **USS Constitution** is nicknamed. The *Constitution* was commissioned in 1797 and is still active and undefeated today—though an annual spin around the Harbor on July 4 is the extent of its sailing today. Young, eager-to-please sailors in vintage uniforms (kind of like the Cracker Jack kid's) lead free tours of the ship, whose sturdy wooden hull deflected cannonballs during the War of 1812. The tour focuses not only on the ship, but on the life of those who served on it; you learn that the medical quarters, for example, were deliberately located far from the crew, so the screams of patients undergoing amputation wouldn't demoralize other sailors. You do have to pay to visit the **USS Constitution Museum**, which is best left to Navy buffs and hyperactive children (kids can jump in a hammock or play captain at the helm, which they can't do on the real thing). Instead, soak up the museum's scrimshaw-and-salt-air ambience for free in the museum store, one of the better souvenir stops on the trail. The Navy Yard's other attractions include the **USS *Cassin Young***, a World War II destroyer, and visiting ships from other country's navies and merchant marines; the **Commandant's House**, an 1809 brick mansion on a little hill overlooking the Harbor, which you can tour; and the country's last ropewalk building, which you can't. One good reason for taking the trail all the way to Charlestown is so you can rest your bones at the historic **Warren Tavern** (2 Pleasant St.), built in 1780 near Bunker Hill. Then the truly obsessive will press on to the gray granite **Bunker Hill Monument**, at the top of a pretty steep hill—those who get winded easily should take a cab. (Even the tourist trolleys only go as far as the Navy Yard.) It may look like a smokestack in the distance, but it turns out to be an obelisk of Quincy granite atop Breed's Hill, where the Battle of Bunker Hill was fought on June 17, 1775. You can sift through the functional but low-tech dioramas inside the base, or climb up the monument's 294 steps (strictly optional, especially for the claustrophobic). An easier way to grasp the situation is to visit the **Bunker Hill Pavilion** near the entrance to the Charlestown Navy Yard, where you can see a multimedia presentation about the source of "Don't fire until you see the whites of their eyes." But, shoot, if you came this far, you're probably nuts enough to climb all the way to the top.

Art museums (the biggies)... Designed in the style of a 15th-century Venetian palazzo to satisfy the whims of one of the grandest 19th-century Boston grande dames, the **Isabella Stewart Gardner Museum**—call it the Gardner, as locals do—shows off the irreverence of its socialite founder, who scoured all of Europe for her booty. In galleries set around an ever blooming interior courtyard, you'll find some real treasures—paintings by Rembrandt and Titian, Whistler and John Singer Sargent. The casual way it's organized makes meeting each gem feel like a personal discovery: Etruscan pottery and Papal robes both get classified as "Early Italian," for example. To Isabella, whose Sargent portrait is hung in a prominent central spot, this would have made sense, as would having lunch in the Gardner's arty little cafe, which opens in good weather on to a charming outdoor courtyard. Don't bother trying to strike up a conversation with the security guards about the 1990 burglary that cost the museum its Vermeer and a dozen other artworks; they prefer to let the empty spaces on the walls tell the story. The **Museum of Fine Arts** (MFA), Boston's greatest cultural gem, is only a short walk around the corner from the Gardner; depending on your tolerance for staring at art, you can actually do both in one day, if you plan efficiently. Much more of a traditional museum than the Gardner, the MFA—found-

ed in 1870 as part of the Boston Athenaeum—contains a
great collection of American and European art. While
most adults check out the Renoirs, Rembrandts, and 43
Monets, and kids flock to the Egyptian wing with its
newly renovated Nubian section, those of us in the know
find inner peace in the quiet, rice-paper-shaded rooms of
one of the finest Asian art collections in the country. Along
with art and artifacts from Cambodia, Thailand, and
India, as well as China and Japan (seek out the intricately
decorated tiny glass snuff bottles, actually painted from the
inside), this collection houses a serene Buddhist temple
room and an attached Japanese garden. If you get hungry,
you can dine in a classy sit-down restaurant or gaze at the
equally tranquil courtyard from the downstairs cafeteria.
With a collection as expansive as the Museum of Fine
Arts', it's easy to miss some of its more unusual items.
Check your coat in the older section, off Huntington
Avenue, and you'll see one of the few pieces of art you're
actually encouraged to touch: a bronze model of Daniel
Chester French's statue of Abraham Lincoln, which is
housed in the Lincoln Memorial. Visitors' fingers have
kept his knees gleaming; on this small scale, Abe seems
downright cuddly. Upstairs in the Greek and Roman galleries, look for an ancient Cretan ivory statuette less than
eight inches tall, who holds up gold snakes with a deter-
mined look on her remarkably unblemished face (whether
a goddess or a priestess, she's certainly formidable, despite
being a wee thing encased in glass). Any notions you may
have about Boston prudishness will be laid to rest here by
two pieces of ancient Greek porn: an Athenian water jar
decorated with copulating couples, whose contortions
have led curators to nickname the unknown artist "Elbows
Out"; and another Athenian vessel with red figures, on
which a man in a satyr costume sports a phallus with a cap-
tion translated as "Handsome!" One last naughty bit: A
bacchante statue of a blithely naked nymph once on display at the museum's Huntington Avenue entrance caused
such a stir a century ago when it was donated to the
Boston Public Library that it had to be removed. Compared to the "Elbows Out" jar of course, the nymph is practically Puritan, and it has found a more enlightened public
at New York's Metropolitan Museum of Art, where it currently resides. A bronze casting of the statue quietly
returned to the library at last during its recent renovations,

and can currently be viewed in front of the book delivery room (by the turn of the century it will make its way to its originally intended perch in the courtyard fountain). Architect Philip Johnson built an addition in 1971 to the library's grand 1895 Renaissance Revival building, decorated outside with the names of the Western World's geniuses, replete with marble, mosaics, and murals inside. But skip the plain-Jane modern part, and head to the original's contemplative courtyard or its third-floor Sargent gallery.

Most underrated museums... The trio of **Harvard Art Museums**—the Fogg Art Museum, the Busch-Reisinger Collection in Werner Otto Hall, and the Sackler Museum—are often overlooked by visitors to Boston, which is too bad: they're an easy walk from Harvard Square, cheaper than either the Museum of Fine Arts or the Gardner Museum (one admission gets you into all three; free on Saturday mornings), and open on Mondays, when the MFA and Gardner are locked tight. And did we mention the art? This trio is considered the finest university collection outside of Oxford's. The **Fogg Art Museum** has works by big-name Impressionists and modernists in its Italian loggia-style galleries, plus pieces by less-famous artists from the Middle Ages to the current day, with curators who like to keep viewers on their toes. The decorative arts collection is an antiquer's dream; look for the President's Chair, an unpromising-looking seat in which every Harvard president since the 18th century has rested his buns. Behind the Fogg, in the new Otto Hall, is the extensive **Busch-Reisinger Collection**, home of art the Nazis considered "degenerate" and lots of other Teutonic treasures; some of the collection remains in its former home, Adolphus Busch Hall, an ornate building with Wagnerian motifs, just a block away. The **Sackler Museum**, like its namesake in Washington, D.C, features Asian and Middle Eastern art treasures that rival the MFA's in quality, if not quantity. Harvard also boasts four museums of natural history, with a four-in-one admission deal, but only one—the **Peabody Museum of Archaeology and Ethnology**—is really worth its salt. The oldest ethnographic museum in the hemisphere, it holds an abundance of information on native peoples and early European settlers, much of it excavated by Harvard's own archaeologists. From Iron

Age relics to beautifully carved Northwest totems, this is one museum that successfully mingles science and beauty.

Most overrated museums... These would be the rest of Harvard's natural history museums, which a lot of folks praise just to prove they're intellectuals. The glass flowers at the **Botanical Museum** are marvels of design and detail, most guide books tell you, but these delicate botanical models, crafted in the 1880s, are also dusty and—unless you're seriously into herbaria—a bore. This famous collection of meticulously reproduced stamens, petals, and pistils still draws the crowds each weekend; skip it and go to the archaeology museum (see above) instead. It's not essential to visit the tedious rock collections at the **Mineralogical and Geological Museum**, either, and only bone and fossil fans will love the **Museum of Comparative Zoology**.

On the waterfront... Sometimes you can forget Boston has a waterfront, with the Central Artery (and now the Big Dig) blocking access to the harbor. When all the construction is done early next century, though, the Harborwalk along the waterfront should be a terrific stroll. Besides taking a cruise or whale-watching tour from Long Wharf or Rowes Wharf (see "Boston by boat," below), you can connect with the city's maritime heritage by simply hanging out in **Christopher Columbus Park**, across from Cross Street where Commercial Street becomes Atlantic Avenue. You can watch the bustling harbor while picnicking here (Quincy Market is directly on the other side of the highway, and the North End delis are only a few blocks away), or eat at one of the seafood establishments near by, such as the **Chart House** restaurant (60 Long Wharf), housed in a late-18th-century warehouse on Long Wharf. Go into the **Long Wharf Marriott** (296 State St.) to see displays on how long the wharf really was in Colonial times. Nathaniel Hawthorne worked in a customhouse at the very end of Long Wharf. Even if you're not taking the water shuttle to the airport, or staying at the extremely upscale **Boston Harbor Hotel** (see Accommodations) at Rowes Wharf, it's worth walking through the monumental brick arch off of Atlantic Avenue to see where the really big yachts stay when they're in town. For the price of a drink, you can enjoy the view at leisure in the hotel's Harborview Lounge or outdoor cafe (in season); if you're a sailor yourself, you can even take a boat out on the water by stopping by the **Boston Harbor Sailing Club** (see Getting Outside). In summer, some of those Onassis-style luxury craft will sail over to Fan Pier, across the Fort Point Channel, to eavesdrop on a pop concert at **Harborlights** (see Entertainment), where pop concerts are held in a cool white tent that resembles the Sydney (Australia) Opera House. Landlubbers will have to walk or drive over the unscenic Northern Avenue Bridge to the seasonal venue, but once inside you can all enjoy the same dynamite views of the skyline and waterfront.

How to feel like you're in a foreign country...
Local color doesn't necessarily mean red, white, and blue in Boston. In late summer, head to the **North End**'s *festes*, weekend celebrations of patron saints from the Southern Italian and Sicilian towns that sent their populace to Boston earlier in this century. Flyers posted in storefronts and cafes tell which streets will be blocked off for all the food stalls, carnival games, entertainment, parades, and often elaborate religious processions. For the Madonna del Soccorso *festa*, for instance, which celebrates the Feast of the Assumption on August 15, a young girl dressed as an angel "flies" several stories high in the air, releasing a basket of white doves before gently descending to the statue of the Holy Virgin which was paraded through the streets earlier that day.) It's traditional to pin money to these religious icons (the proceeds go to charities), and to pig out on fried calamari, pasta, *arancini* (fried rice balls filled with meat), and Italian ice. Boston's **Chinatown** is pretty rinky-dink compared to the larger West Coast versions, but like the North End, it offers a sense of otherness within the city, numerous restaurants and markets, and something to do in August—namely, the **August Moon Festival** in mid- to late August, which, like **Chinese New Year** in early February, features dragon parades, firecrackers, martial arts demonstrations, and dances (call 617/542-2574 for info on both). Chinatown is really Pan-Asiatown these days, with more recent Vietnamese and Cambodian immigrants thrown into the mix. The shopping isn't exceptional, but the sticky sidewalks always seem crowded. Many restaurants down here stay open till 4am, the better to serve club hoppers after clubs shut down at 2.

Black Boston... The history of African-Americans in
Boston goes well beyond Crispus Attucks, who made the

history books in 1770 as the first victim of the Boston Massacre. Not far from his resting place in the **Old Granary Burying Ground** lies the starting point of the **Black Heritage Trail**, at the **Robert Gould Shaw Memorial** facing the State House. The memorial's bas-relief, by Augustus St. Gaudens, honors the leader of the 54th Massachusetts Regiment in the Civil War, immortalized in the 1989 movie *Glory*. Two young Gould groupies leave a weekly bouquet of fresh flowers in the hands of Gould, who sits on horseback above members of America's first black regiment. Head from there to the **Museum of Afro American History**, in the former Abiel Smith School (the city's first school for black children) on Joy Street, where well-versed National Park Service rangers leading guided tours will point out overlooked details on St. Gaudens' statue (such as the almost worn-out inscription on the Boston Common side). They'll also take you into the austere upper-level church of the **African Meeting House** on Smith Court, off Joy Street; the lower level has changing exhibits on African-Americans in New England. Many illustrious blacks lived on Beacon Hill from its earliest days: the **Middleton-Glapion House** (5 Pinckney St.) was built in the 1790s by a black veteran of the American Revolution, George Middleton, and a barber, Louis Glapion. Underground Railroad sites are all over the Hill, including **Holmes Alley** at the end of Smith Court, and the **Lewis Hayden House** (66 Phillips St.), named for its abolitionist owner who was himself a former fugitive slave; Hayden threatened to blow the house up if anyone came looking for runaways there, and he had two kegs of gunpowder in his basement to back him up. Abolitionists such as William Lloyd Garrison and Sojourner Truth spoke at the **Charles Street Meeting House** (corner of Mount Vernon and Charles Streets), which later became an African Methodist Episcopal church (it's now offices and shops). The Freedom Trail's **Park Street Church** is also identified with Garrison's antislavery sermons. The irony of all this is that very few blacks could afford to live on Beacon Hill these days: Bostonians of color tend to live in the depressed areas of the South End, Roxbury, and Dorchester, where no tourist ever treads.

Where everybody knows your name... Sure, they're always glad you came at the **Bull and Finch**, the original model for the pub in the TV show "Cheers." But if you think all the folks waiting in line to get into this small basement-level pub on Beacon Hill are regulars who come for the atmosphere, think again. Beacon Hill residents are permitted to jump ahead of the line if they want to, but the truth is the regulars stopped coming here long ago. These days, the Bull and Finch is more theme park than local watering hole, with overpriced drinks, T-shirts, and other paraphernalia. And did we mention the wait to get in? Skip the line: walk into the upstairs gift shop and take a peek down into the bar, then ditch the joint. If you want that chummy feel of a neighborhood bar, try a lower-profile establishment like the straightforward **Brendan Behan Pub** in Jamaica Plain (see Nightlife), which gathers to its smoky bosom this outlying community's poets, musicians, and quite a few savvy pols. Music and poetry readings keep this very Irish watering hole full, and the diversity of the neighborhood nearly guarantees that anyone will feel at home here, except maybe a right-wing preacher. (For other authentic Boston pubs, see Nightlife.) Instead of heading to the overrated **Hard Rock Cafe**, a tourists-only destination that has eclipsed even the Freedom Trail in popularity, join the hybrid mix of patrons at **Johnny D's Uptown**, a lounge in Somerville's Davis Square. A family-owned joint (the current boss, Carla, inherited the bar from her dad, Johnny DeLillis), Johnny D's attracts both working-class Somerville regulars and artsier Cambridge bohemians, many of whom have crossed the city line for more affordable housing. Johnny D's presents a steady lineup of blues and, of all things, zydeco; although the club has won a W.C. Handy "Keeping the Blues Alive" award, cover (on music nights) rarely exceeds $10. Neighborhood folks come also for Johnny D's big weekend brunches and Monday night swing or Cajun dance lessons. (See Entertainment.)

The view from above... If you're into panoramic views stretching to New Hampshire, you've got two choices in the Back Bay: the **John Hancock Tower**'s sixtieth-floor observatory and the **Prudential Center**'s fiftieth-floor Skywalk. The Hancock observatory, besides being higher up (it's the tallest building in New England), has more exhibits: You can hear Boston historian Walter Muir Whitehill's recorded comments on the architecture—and aroma—of the city, listen to air-traffic controllers at

Logan Airport, or see a display on Boston as it appeared in 1775, with spoken and sung voice-overs about Revolutionary events (a song about gunshots "peppering the bums" of soldiers might get kids' attention). On the other hand, go to the Pru and you can have a drink at its newly remodeled Top of the Hub lounge. Outdoors, head for the **Copp's Hill Burying Ground** in the North End for a sweeping view of Charlestown, or go to Charlestown itself and climb the 294 steps of the **Bunker Hill Monument.** The view's not all that spectacular; most of the way up, the narrow windows are on the same side, looking at the Charlestown projects in increasing increments of altitude, while at the top there are windows on the other sides but not much room to enjoy them. But, hey, you'll feel so virtuous (and so out of breath), you won't care.

The view from a bridge... One of the best views of Boston and Cambridge isn't especially elevated; it's at the **Harvard Bridge**, which carries Massachusetts Avenue from Boston to Cambridge (and to the MIT campus, not Harvard). Looking east you can see the golden dome of the State House nestled among downtown high-rises, atop the rising brick-red smudge of Beacon Hill, as well as the Longfellow Bridge with its sleek Red Line T trains bustling across to Kendall Square in Cambridge. South and west are the backside of Back Bay's grand Beacon Street row houses, with the John Hancock Building and the Prudential Center piercing the sky at either end; the comforting kitsch of Kenmore Square's lit-up Citgo sign; the hills of Brookline and Newton; the dwindling curve of the river as it heads toward Harvard. To the north are the many architectural flavors of the MIT campus and the smokestack remnants of industrial Cambridge.

Boston by boat... If you just want to get out on the water for a quick view, take one of these inexpensive minicruises: the one-dollar, East Boston-to-North End water shuttle that also goes to the Charlestown Navy Yard (tel 617/222–3200, Navy Yard weekends and midday only, leaves from Long Wharf); the **MuSEAm Ferry** from the Children's Museum to the Museum of Science; or, for a rock-bottom buck, **Bay State Cruise Company**'s 45-minute summer lunchtime harbor cruises from Long Wharf. Several companies offer narrated trips through the Boston

BOSTON | DIVERSIONS

Harbor, leaving from either Long Wharf (**Boston Harbor Cruises** or Bay State Cruise Company) or Rowes Wharf (**Massachusetts Bay Lines**). You can also dive right in, so to speak, from the airport, by taking the seven-minute water shuttle to Rowes Wharf (see Hotlines & Other Basics), but it's a bit expensive for such a short trip. The Long Wharf companies also cruise around the intriguing Harbor Islands (see Getting Outside), which may become a national park if Massachusetts politicians have their way. You can stay in the calmer waters of the Charles River, and compare the skylines of Cambridge and Boston, by taking the popular **Boston Duck Tours** in refurbished World War II amphibious craft; on the water portion of these 80-minute tours, you'll putter around from the locks around the Museum of Science, under the Longfellow Bridge, and back again. The **Charles Riverboat Cruise** picks up and drops off passengers in a more conventional craft at the CambridgeSide Galleria and the Esplanade and heads down the river to near Harvard Square before looping back, for a round-trip that lasts nearly an hour. The highlights-only narration isn't the reason to go; getting nautical for under $10 is. You can take your time heading back, too: Disembark for a stroll along the Esplanade not far from the Hatch Shell, where the Esplanade Cafe is open spring through early fall; or take time out for noshing at CambridgeSide Galleria, where the same company also rents paddleboats for use in the small lagoon. And then, of course, there are the **Swan Boats**, those bulky paddleboats that churn slowly around the lagoon at the Public Garden. Tame as hell, but kinda pleasant on a hot Boston summer day.

A whale of a time... You're unlikely to see Moby Dick, but several cruise companies (including **Boston Harbor**) and the **New England Aquarium** offer whale-watching tours leaving from Boston Harbor; the Aquarium's generally are the best. Such tours can run up to six hours; naturalists are on hand to point out interesting marine life and to ensure the captains don't steer too close to these massive mammals. Although the ships all have amenities to help pass the time, make sure no one in your group is prone to seasickness before committing such a large chunk of time to tail animals who occasionally act like Greta Garbo. Bring something to keep the kids entertained, and definitely bring jackets, no matter how warm the day on shore seems.

Excursions to Plymouth and Cape Cod... Three miles south of Plymouth on Route 3A is **Plimoth Plantation**, a meticulously researched living re-creation of the Colonial village in 1627, weird accents and all. Also on hand: the Mayflower II replica, a Native American homesite, and a visitors' center examining the "irreconcilable differences" between Pilgrim and Native American life. It only takes about 40 minutes to get here by car—one of the few justifications for having wheels during a Boston vacation. Kids love to ask the Pilgrims about Colonial hygiene and other mysteries, while history buffs will be hard-pressed to trip up the well-trained docents. It's a great way to get outside; anyone heading to the Cape should also plan on stopping here, the least kitschy "living history" park you're likely to find. Every summer, Cape Cod lures thousands of Bostonians away from the stifling city... and into traffic along Route 3. Even travelers to the islands of Martha's Vineyard and Nantucket are bound to hit traffic heading to the ferries from Woods Hole and Hyannis, unless they fly over (don't expect the cast of "Wings" if you do). But if your itinerary can handle a round-trip of six hours at sea (shorter than the bus), **Bay State Cruises** will take you to Provincetown, at the tip of Cape Cod. Leave the city in the morning, have lunch at a sidewalk cafe where you can observe the vibrant gay and lesbian street scene (it's changed a bit since the Pilgrims first landed here) or head out to the incredible sand dunes, and return three hours later—if you have to. Just make sure to bring a good book and munchies for the long trip back. Beware of onboard karaoke and ho-hum refreshments.

Best places for gallery hopping... Most visitors to Boston end up on **Newbury Street**, where art lovers can quickly pick the better galleries from the lesser, the originals from the touristic. But those in search of real value, contemporary originals, or a taste of the *vie bohèmien* should check newspaper listings in fall or spring for open-studio weekends. The concept is simple: Twice a year, usually for one long weekend, each artist-dense neighborhood opens its doors to the public. Usually some central gallery or cooperative space serves as an information depot, with

BOSTON | DIVERSIONS

maps and sometimes refreshments. From there, you're on
your own. Wear comfortable shoes, as you may be climb-
ing stairs or hiking over old paving stones. Bring your
curiosity and your checkbook. These days, open studios
seem to be everywhere. Along the waterfront across the
Congress Street or Summer Street bridges, the old warehouses of Fort Point Channel have been adopted by
artists for their light and space. Within an area of six
blocks, you'll see over 100 studios. Start with the **Fort
Point Artists' Community Gallery.** Painting, photogra-
phy, ceramics, bookbinding, jewelry making, and more
thrive here, and collectors can pick up pieces without the
hefty gallery markups. Or check out the tonier, and somewhat older, **South End Artists Association.** Artists
across the river have been carving smaller but more
affordable spaces out of three-family houses in
Cambridgeport, the loop of Cambridge held by the
Charles; contact the **Cambridge Art Association** for
details (tel 617/876–0246).

Weirdest bunch of public statuary... In Back Bay's
Commonwealth Avenue Mall, puzzle over a series of
unrelated statues, from Leif Eriksson to William Lloyd
Garrison, with the obscure Domingo Sarmiento and others in between. Off Charles Street on the **Boston
Common** is the much-maligned contemporary sculpture
The Partisans, dejected-looking soldiers on weary horses.
No one really knows what it's doing there; the artist claims
it's a gift to the city. In **Liberty Square**, between Kilby,
Batterymarch, and Milk Streets downtown—originally
intended to honor the Stamp Act protests of 1765—
there's now a monument to the Hungarian uprising of
1956 ("to those who never surrendered"). Even though it's
a dramatic testament to liberty in its own right (the bronze
Hungarian flag has a hole where the Communist symbols
were torn out), the modern sculpture intrudes on the
quaintness of the square; look up instead at the curving
Appleton Building, with its delightful friezes showing
different artisans at work. Even stranger is the contrast
between two nearby statues—one seated on a park bench,
one standing—of the unorthodox mayor famous for the
slogan "Vote often and early for James Michael Curley"
and the recently installed **New England Holocaust
Memorial** (between City Hall and Union Street). Visitors
wander, dazed, through the somber new memorial of six

glass towers, reading plaques bearing the testimonies of Holocaust survivors and witnesses, along with a grim chronology of the horrors that Jews and other groups suffered during World War II. Another plaque ties the whole memorial into the Freedom Trail by hectoring passersby to remember what happens in a world without freedom. Then you practically bump into Curley, that merry old pol, who kept his job as mayor even while serving time for fraud. Hmmm…. The empty brick plaza on the other side of brutally modern City Hall might have been a better place for the Holocaust Memorial.

Bigger isn't always better… The **Christian Science World Headquarters** is kind of like the Vatican meets the National Mall: a chilly modern complex contains the "Mother Church," a giant basilica built around a small Romanesque chapel; a 700-foot-long reflecting pool; and an I.M. Pei office tower. In the Christian Science Publishing Society building, there's the Mapparium, an odd walk-through stained-glass globe, and headsets are available to hear answers to commonly asked (and some unintentionally funny) questions about the religion. The hourly tours of the Mother Church, founded by Mary Baker Eddy in 1879, are worth it to see the massive organ and the unusual inscriptions, but on the whole, the megaplex creates a desolate, windswept sprawl on the Huntington Avenue border between Back Bay and the South End. Having the unattractive 52-story **Prudential Center** office and retail complex nearby doesn't help either. The 62-story **John Hancock Tower** looms over the Copley Square area, its sheer glass walls reflecting Trinity Church, the nearby old John Hancock tower (200 Claridence St.), and clouds. Sure, the reflection is breathtaking, but the old Hancock building has a useful beacon on top that predicts the weather: clear blue, clear view; flashing blue, clouds due; steady red, rain ahead; flashing red; snow ahead. Flashing red in summertime doesn't mean a blizzard in July: It means the Red Sox game has been canceled due to rain.

Best patriotic festivals… On **Patriot's Day**, the Monday nearest April 19, "Paul Revere" rides on horseback all the way from Boston's North End to the Minuteman-filled Middlesex village of Lexington, and does shout "The British are coming." On or around June 17, **Bunker Hill Weekend** restages the Battle of Bunker

Hill in Charlestown (which actually took place on Breed's Hill, as nitpickers can't wait to tell you); every year, it's still a Pyrrhic victory for the redcoats. Both Bunker Hill Day and Patriots' Day are city holidays, which means free metered parking—if you can find it. Nobody does the Fourth of July quite like Boston, as those who've seen the annual Boston Pops concert and fireworks on public television may guess. Sure, Washington, D.C., has an equally famous pyrotechnical and musical to-do, but the District of Columbia is just a Yankee Doodle-come-lately in Bostonians' minds. In Beantown the celebration lasts a whole week, beginning in late June with **Harborfest** (tel 617/227–1528), a waterfront festival that includes a concert and fireworks over the harbor, and wrapping up with **Chowderfest** (or Chowdafest, as locals call it) at City Hall, a massive cook-off of the regional specialty. On **Independence Day** itself, events include a costumed "John Hancock" and other Revolutionary look-alikes reading the Declaration of Independence from the balcony at the Old State House. But the real draw is the Pops' celebrity-studded shebang at the Hatch Shell on the Esplanade, which starts drawing picnicking crowds early that morning; by midday, it's not a good place for the claustrophobic, with the Cambridge side of the river only marginally less packed. Is it worth waiting all day to watch the John Phillip Sousa-laden concert in cramped quarters, or jockeying for a spot on the Esplanade just to listen to it on tinny speakers, all to have prime seats for the fireworks over the river at its conclusion? Well, several hundred thousand people seem to think so—and there is a charming kind of hush for the 15 minutes or so of the stunning display. When everyone attempts to leave the dimly lit Esplanade at once, though, Cambridge Street, Embankment Road, Storrow Drive, and other arteries, not to mention the narrow footbridges, turn into evacuation scenes from Japanese horror movies. If you don't like crowds, and you really are interested in middle-of-the-road orchestral pablum, catch the rehearsal concert (sans stars and explosions) the night before, instead.

Tea time... Tea looms large in Boston lore, even if today's Bostonians are more likely to be caught drinking coffee from the ubiquitous Dunkin' Donuts and Starbucks (which bought out the homegrown Coffee Connection a few years ago). The staff at the **Boston Tea Party Ship and Museum** will be happy to tell you about the events of December 16, 1773, when colonials disguised as Indians dumped an entire cargo of highly taxed tea leaves into the harbor (actually at Griffin's Wharf, in an area that's now dry land). But this replica ship is a pretty lame attraction, packaged strictly for tourists; you get a cup of tea with your admission, but it's better to imbibe tea in high style, overlooking the Public Garden, at the Bristol Lounge of the **Four Seasons Hotel**, or at the **Ritz-Carlton**'s elegant upstairs tearoom (see Accommodations for both). Although the conversations are louder at the Four Seasons, its finger sandwiches, scones, and pastries are better than those at the Ritz-Carlton; both charge a pretty penny for what is essentially an afternoon snack. Although it doesn't appear to be issuing steam anymore, the 227-gallon gilded teakettle hanging from the exterior of the **Sears Crescent** building next to Government Center has fascinated Bostonians since it was made in 1873 for the Oriental Tea Company. So have the elephants on the circa 1929 **Salada Tea Building** (Stuart and Berkeley Streets, in Back Bay), which lumber across its bronze doors, columns, and frieze, in scenes of the tea trade.

Beer here... Of course, you can always skip the tea and head straight for the strong stuff, as long as you're of legal drinking age (21 in Massachusetts). The microbrew revolution has come to Boston, and once again Sam Adams is a patriot leading the way, although Jim Koch's Samuel Adams Brewing Company is definitely a macro among micros. You can browse through the **Boston Beer Museum**— really just the archives of the Koch brewing family—as you tour the Sam Adams brewery in Jamaica Plain, or sample the wares on tap at the **Samuel Adams Brewhouse** (see Dining) in the Lenox Hotel near Copley Square; fresh pretzels (with gourmet mustards) and sausages are draws even for nondrinkers. The **Back Bay Brewing Company** is a real brew pub—that is, its beers are made and served on site—on Boylston Street one block away, with a larger menu than the small Sam Adams bar. The gleaming vats and brewery apparatus is plainly visible at **Boston Beer Works** (see Dining), which has the widest variety of ales and lagers and a sprawling menu. Before- and after-baseball crowds pour in here from Fenway Park, its neighbor across the street. Serving a flight of tasty malt beverages, the **Commonwealth Brewing Company** needs two floors to handle the crowds of Celtics fans streaming in from nearby FleetCenter, the soulless modern successor to the Boston Garden. On weekends, beer hounds can take a free tour of the brewery here, while live music echoes off the copper vats at night. No need to drink and drive, or even ride the T: **Old Town Trolley** offers special Boston and Cambridge brewpub tours. (See Hotlines & Other Basics.)

Pure fun for little kids... For little ones, schedule a *Make Way for Ducklings* **Tour** (spring and summer only), which will let them follow in the footsteps of Robert McCloskey's classic children's tale, or at least show them the Mallard family statues, waddling dutifully single-file in the Public Garden. You want statues? We got statues—the giant bronze teddy bear outside of **F.A.O. Schwarz**, the bronze Bugs Bunny outside of the Warner Brothers store in Faneuil Hall Marketplace, and the less commercial *Tortoise and the Hare* near the Boston Marathon's finish line in Copley Square. Chugging along at a snail's pace around one small lagoon, the **Swan Boats** in the Public Garden may not wow kiddies who've cut their teeth on Great Adventure and Six Flags, but parents enjoy catching their breath in the well-manicured surroundings. The **Franklin Park Zoo**, although recently renovated, is more of a draw for in-towners than for families coming from towns with major-league zoos; even Providence, an hour away, has a better zoo. If your kids are under 10, they may like the Children's Zoo exhibit.

Secretly educational stuff for older kids... The much-touted Mapparium, a stained-glass walk-through globe at the **Christian Science World Headquarters** that hasn't changed since completion in 1935, won't hold the video generation's attention for very long. The map's geography is outdated, but kids may dig the acoustics: Whisper in one corner and you'll be heard plainly in the opposite corner. The sharks and jellyfish at the **New England Aquarium**, however, may appeal to their bloodthirsty side, even if they've grown too old to get a kick out of fondling starfish in the touch tanks. The kitsch factor is high and the history factor is low, but some kids enjoy dumping tea off the side of the **Boston Tea Party Ship and Museum** in Fort Point Channel; the museum's neighborhood is also good for gazing at ships and bridges. The real draws here, however, are a few steps away: the **Computer Museum**, with enough interactive stuff to engage kids up to age 12 (don't miss the giant walk-through computer and robot exhibits), and the totally hands-on **Children's Museum**, best for ages 3 to 10. Multicultural activities such as a Latino market and a Tokyo subway ride are part of the changing exhibits here; recent installations include a state-of-the-art performance space known as KidStage, a tool-toting hard-hat area called "Build It," a 14-foot lobster you can climb in "Under the Dock", and a playroom for children under five. The giant Milk Bottle in front of the Children's Museum is an outdoor snack bar that's a fun place to get lunch. An even better interactive experience is at the **Museum of Science** over in Cambridge, which fairly crackles with kinetic energy; it's got a planetarium, loads of hands-on exhibits, and a 20-foot T. Rex. Take sports nuts to the so-so **New England Sports Museum** at the CambridgeSide Galleria, where they can feel what it was like to be on the receiving end of a Roger Clemens pitch. And if you must feed the kids "culchah," go to the **Museum of Fine Arts** on Sundays, when special activities are organized for youngsters. On any day at the MFA, follow the signs that say "To the mummies" to find children's all-time favorite exhibit.

Author, author... Edgar Allan Poe was born in Bay Village, in a house that no longer exists. Henry Wadsworth Longfellow, however, put down roots almost as deep as those of the spreading chestnut tree under which his village smithy stands. He lived at 105 Brattle Street in Cambridge for the latter half of the 19th century; nearly a hundred years before, George Washington had slept and strategized here, during the siege of Boston, when the stately mansions of Brattle Street were still known as "Tory Row." The **Longfellow House** is now a national historic site, and even if you can't quote a single Longfellow poem, it's worth a visit to get a fair glimpse of 19th-century Boston life. You can see a memorial to Longfellow's chestnut tree ("Under the spreading chestnut tree/The village smithy stands"), forged by the actual anvil shown under the tree, next to the house where the real smithy lived. That's the **Dexter Pratt House** (56 Brattle St.), where the Blacksmith House Bakery Cafe now has a pleasant terrace in season. *Little Women* fans will want to make the half-hour drive out to Concord to Louisa May Alcott's **Orchard House**, where she and her family enjoyed relative prosperity after years of sporadic income (as a teacher, Bronson Alcott was considered a free thinker—perhaps too literally). After her literary ship finally came in, Louisa also lived on Beacon Hill at **10 Louisburg Square** (between Mount Vernon and Pinckney Streets, two blocks up from Charles Street), an overpraised, oft-photographed spot that can be a little dreary, with tall, unornamented row houses staring across a dark, fenced-in park and cobblestoned streets. *Jurassic Park* author Michael Crichton and Senator John Kerry and his wife, Teresa Heinz, have two of the more famous households on today's square.

Kennedy country... The Kennedys may not be universally revered in Boston, but they have been repeatedly elected, with their dynasty spreading to Rhode Island and Maryland. Rose Kennedy's funeral in 1994 brought out thousands of mourners, and her admirers still like to view (from the outside only) her birthplace at **4 Garden Court** in the North End. Her father, Boston mayor John "Honey Fitz" Fitzgerald, was also born in the North End, on Ferry Street. JFK devotees will want to tour the **John F. Kennedy National Historic Site** in Brookline, though he only lived here until he was three (get a life, folks!). Since he has to spend time there, Senator Ted Kennedy might have wished a better homage to his brother than Government Center's sterile **John F. Kennedy Federal Office Building,** by the firm of Walter "Mr. Bauhaus" Gropius. Much more appealing is the I.M. Pei–designed **John F. Kennedy Library and Museum**, on Columbia Point by the University of Massachusetts (UMass) Boston campus. The angular white building juts into the bay, while inside, newly revamped exhibits look at the life and times of Oliver Stone's favorite conspiracy victim, with lots of videos to explore his personal and political life. The dramatic waterfront site allows you to check out his yacht, too. It's a good thing there's a cafe on site, because there's absolutely nothing else within walking distance. **Old Town Trolley**

has a three-hour tour visiting his birthplace, Harvard University, his statue at the State House, and the library/museum. Fans of John F. Kennedy Jr., alas, will have to travel all the way to Martha's Vineyard, where his annual summer appearances cause a stir.

Ethereal Bulfinch... Just before he set off to build the U.S. Capitol, Mr. Bulfinch was tapped to design a hospital for Boston. He complied with the **Bulfinch Pavilion and Ether Dome**, now obscured by the Massachusetts General Hospital Complex in the old West End, across from Beacon Hill. The first public use of ether as an anesthetic (others may have tried it at home) was in the medical amphitheater under Bulfinch's skylit dome in 1846 (there's a monument to the occasion in the Public Garden). When the amphitheater is not in use, you can go inside; exhibits of medical memorabilia are ad hoc. Since it can be hard to find, only medical students, architecture buffs, and fans of the TV series "St. Elsewhere" should make the trek.

High-tech hangouts... The entire MIT campus could be included here, but hackers will also feel at home in the **Cybersmith** in Harvard Square—pick up a drink from the coffee bar and a computer card from the front desk, and you're ready to go at this on-line cafe. You can test-drive CD-ROMS, cruise the Internet, play computer and virtual reality games, and create screensavers and mousepads with your image on them. At the **Computer Museum**, daily Internet lessons can help anyone get up to speed on the information superhighway. If you want to go on-line before you actually go to Boston, the *Boston Globe* and other local organizations contribute to the city's World Wide Web page (http://www.boston.com).

Free spirit... Not everything is free along the Freedom Trail, and certainly not elsewhere in Boston and Cambridge. In addition to the commons, churches, college campuses, and cemeteries which charge no admission fees, these attractions are free: the **Massachusetts State House**; **Faneuil Hall**; the USS *Constitution* at the **Charlestown Navy Yard**; the **Bunker Hill Monument**; all historic cemeteries and burial grounds (see "Grave concerns," above); and the **Frederick Law Olmsted**

National Historic Site—the landscape designer's house, archives, and appropriately verdant grounds in Brookline. Others sites have discount admission at certain times: the **Museum of Fine Arts** on Wednesday afternoons; the **Harvard University art museums** and **Harvard University museums of natural history** on Saturday mornings; and Thursday evenings at the **Institute of Contemporary Art**, a provocative gallery in an old Back Bay firehouse (though its recent "Elvis and Marilyn" exhibit provoked more titters than anything else).

The Index

Arlington Street Church. This Unitarian Universalist church has an ultraliberal congregation behind its ultraconservative brownstone exterior.... *Tel 617/536–7050. 351 Boylston St., Arlington T stop. Open weekdays 10–5. Admission free.*

Arnold Arboretum. This horticultural collection managed by Harvard University for the Boston parks department is at its blooming best April through September. Green thumbers will definitely want to check out the gift shop.... *Tel 617/ 524–1718. The Arborway and Centre St., Jamaica Plain, Forest Hills T stop. Open daily sunrise–sunset; visitors center open 10–4. Guided tours Sun at 2, May–Nov. Admission free.*

Back Bay Brewing Company. The latest entrant into Boston's brewpub wars. Food is available, although not the point here.... *Tel 617/424–8300. 755 Boylston St., Copley T stop. Upstairs 11:30–12 Mon–Sat, 12–12 Sun. Downstairs 5:30–10 Mon–Fri, 5:30–11 Sat–Sun.*

Bay State Cruise Company. Short jaunts around the Inner Harbor (including a sunset tour), to Georges Island in the Outer Harbor, and to Providence, R.I..... *Tel 617/723–*

7800. 67 Long Wharf, Aquarium T stop. May–mid Oct. Fee charged.

Boston Athenaeum. A private Beacon Hill club and refuge for Brahmins, this library was founded in 1807 and moved to this building, now a National Historic Site, in 1849. Try to take the tour so you can ask questions without feeling intrusive.... *Tel 617/227–0270. 10 Beacon St., Park Street T stop. Open Mon–Fri 9–5:30, Sat 9–4 (closed Sat in summer). Guided tours Tue and Thur at 3, by appointment. Admission free.*

Boston Beer Museum. Attached to the Samuel Adams brewery in an out-of-the-way neighborhood between Jamaica Plain and Roxbury.... *Tel 617/368–5080. 30 Germania St., Stony Brook T stop. Tours Thur–Fri at 2, Sat at noon, 1, and 2. Admission free ($1 donation requested; goes to local charities).*

Boston Duck Tours. 80-minute tours on renovated World War II amphibious trucks venture out into the Charles River (near the Museum of Science and up to the Hatch Shell); volunteers get a chance to steer. On the street portion, the elevated vehicles give a better view than the trolleys, particularly the rumble seats; in bad weather, though, you're more comfortable on a trolley.... *Tel 617/723–DUCK. Tours depart from the Prudential Center, 800 Boylston St., Prudential T stop. Go at 9am to get tickets for later in the day; only groups can reserve seats. Mid-April–fall. Admission charged.*

Boston Harbor Cruises. For whale-watching, sunset, and Inner and Outer Harbor cruises, as well as the shuttle to the Charlestown Navy Yard. Comedy, mystery, and dinner theater cruises are also available.... *Tel 617/227–4321. 1 Long Wharf, Aquarium T stop.*

Boston Public Library. One of Boston's most striking public buildings, and the first municipal library in the U.S.... *Tel 617/536–5400. 666 Boylston St., Copley T stop. Open Mon–Thur 9–9, Fri–Sat 9–5. Guided tours available (except Sat); call for hours. Admission free.*

Boston Tea Party Ship and Museum. Replica of one of the ships that patriots boarded in 1773.... *Tel 617/338–1773. Congress St. Bridge, South Station T stop. Open daily 9–6*

June–Aug; until 5 Mar–May and Sept–Nov; closed Dec–March. Admission charged.

Botanical Museum. See **Harvard University natural history museums.**

Brickbottom Artists Association. A group of artists who have turned a warehouse into living and work spaces, the Brickbottom gang hosts regular open houses.... *Tel 617/ 776–3410. 1 Fitchburg St., Somerville, Lechmere T stop. Admission free.*

Bulfinch Pavilion and Ether Dome. The last contribution to Boston by architect wunderkind Charles Bulfinch, and the site of the first public use of ether.... *Tel 617/726–2000. Massachusetts General Hospital, 55 Fruit St., Charles T stop. Open Mon–Fri 9–5, unless meetings are scheduled. Admission free.*

Bull and Finch. The real name of the Beacon Hill bar that the TV show "Cheers" was based on. It looks nothing like the TV set inside, as you can quickly see from the gift shop upstairs.... *Tel 617/227–9605. 84 Beacon St., Arlington T stop. Open 11am–1:30pm.*

Bunker Hill Monument. Obelisk commemorates Revolutionary battle in which greatly outnumbered colonials inflicted a stunning number of casualties on the British before defeat; National Park Service rangers give hourly chats in summer. The display cases on their own are a little dull, and the walk up the 294 steps not worth the effort (unless you're trying to tire out kids).... *Tel 617/242–5641. Monument Square, Charlestown. No nearby T stop. Open daily 9–5. Admission free.*

Bunker Hill Pavilion. A flashier telling of the Bunker Hill tale, downhill from the real thing, every half-hour.... *Tel 617/241–7575. 55 Constitution Rd., Charlestown Navy Yard. Open Apr–Nov, daily 9:30–4; July–Aug, until 5. Admission charged.*

Busch-Reisinger Collection. See **Harvard University art museums.**

Charles Riverboat Cruises. Narrated cruises up the Charles River, with departures from CambridgeSide Galleria and the

Esplanade. Schedule is heavily dependent on the weather; the season runs from mid-spring through mid-fall.... *Tel 617/621–3001. 100 CambridgeSide Place, Lechmere T stop. Call for schedule.*

Charlestown Navy Yard. To make the most of your visit to this sprawling, redeveloped complex, stop first at the visitor information center across from the USS *Constitution* and see what activities are available that day. Some tours, such as that of the 1805 Commandant's House, are scheduled Wed–Sun in summer, weekends only after Labor Day. It's free to tour the house, the USS *Cassin Young,* visiting ships, and the USS *Constitution* (tel 617/242–5670, open daily 9:30–3:50 for guided tours, 3:50–sunset for top deck only), but not to visit the privately operated USS *Constitution* Museum (tel 617/426–1812, open daily 9–5; 10–4 Dec–Feb) or Bunker Hill Pavilion (see above).... *Tel 617/242–5601. Constitution Rd. and Chelsea St., Charlestown. Water shuttle from Long Wharf/Aquarium T stop run by Boston Harbor Cruises (see above). Open daily 10–6 summer; 10–4 winter. Admission free.*

"Cheers." See **The Bull and Finch**.

Children's Museum. Large hands-on museum for kids, with several daily activities including crafts, music, and animal visits.... *Tel 617/426–8855. 300 Congress St., South Station T stop. Open Tue–Sun 10–5 (Fri also open 5–9, for only $1 admission); closed Mon except school vacations. Admission charged.*

Christian Science World Headquarters. Mary Baker Eddy established the First Church of Christ, Scientist, here in 1879, which I.M. Pei morphed into a megacomplex in 1973. The *Christian Science Monitor* is published here, and on weekdays you can see the Mapparium (tel 617/450–3790, 175 Huntington Ave.), a walk-through stained-glass globe in the Christian Science Publishing Society building.... *Tel 617/450–2000. Massachusetts and Huntington Avenues, Prudential T stop. Open Tue–Sat 9:30–4, Sun 11:15–2. Admission free.*

Church of the Covenant. Tons of Tiffany glass in the chapel, contemporary art in Gallery NAGA (tel 617/266–9060)....

Tel 617/266–7480. 67 Newbury St., Arlington T stop. Open Tue–Fri 9–noon. Admission free.

Commonwealth Brewing Company. Outpost for discriminating beer drinkers (and not so discriminating diners), in the desolate area around North Station.... *Tel 617/523–8383. 138 Portland St., North Station T stop.*

Computer Museum. Engaging museum, not for technophiles only.... *Tel 617/423–6758. 300 Congress St., South Station T stop. Open daily 10–6 mid-June–Labor Day; rest of year Tue–Sun (and Mon during grammar school and high school vacations) 10–5. Admission charged (half-price Sun 3–5).*

Copp's Hill Burying Ground. Freedom Trail cemetery, overlooking Charlestown.... *Hull and Snowhill St., North Station T stop. Open dawn–dusk. Admission free.*

Cybersmith. Coffee bar with computer stations for patrons; software, books, and computer accessories are also for sale.... *Tel 617/492–5857. 36 Church St., Cambridge, Harvard T stop.*

Faneuil Hall. Upstairs in this Freedom Trail site are a Charles Bulfinch–designed meeting hall, historical paintings, and artifacts of the first Massachusetts militia.... *Tel 617/635–3105. Dock Square, State T stop. Open daily 9–5. Admission free.*

Faneuil Hall Marketplace. Scenic shopping district also known as Quincy Market (after the large center building) is mediocre but mobbed.... *Tel 617/338–2323. Bounded by Commercial Ave. and Clinton, Congress, and Chatham Streets; State or Aquarium T stop. Shops open Mon–Sat 10–9, Sun 12–6; restaurants open 11am–2am.*

First and Second Church. Call ahead to see the modern interior rising from the ruined exterior of the church, which turned 100 in 1967 and burned in 1968.... *Tel 617/267–6730. Open Mon–Fri 9–5. 66 Marlborough St., Arlington T stop. Admission free.*

First Baptist Church. Back Bay church designed by Henry Hobson Richardson.... *Tel 617/267–3148. 110 Common-*

wealth Ave., Copley T stop. Open Mon–Fri 10–4. Admission free.

Fogg Art Museum. See **Harvard University art museums.**

Fort Point Artists' Community Gallery. A good launching pad to explore this artists' neighborhood, it also exhibits 10 curated shows of contemporary art a year.... *Tel 617/423–4299. 300 Summer St., South Station. Open Thur 12–5, Fri 12–6, Sat–Sun 1–5. Admission free.*

Franklin Park Zoo. Highlights of this mediocre zoo include a walk-through aviary, an African tropical forest pavilion, and a petting barn. Buses run from the Forest Hills and Andrew T stops to the park.... *Tel 617/442–2002, 442–4896. Blue Hill Ave. and Seaver St., Dorchester. Open Apr–Oct daily 9–5; Nov–Mar till 4:30. Admission charged.*

Frederick Law Olmsted National Historic Site. National Park Service rangers give hourly tours of Fairsted, the ivy-covered house of America's most famous landscape architect and park planner. You can check out his designs for Central Park, West Point, Yosemite National Park, and many of Boston's green spaces. The 51 bus runs from Cleveland Circle and Reservoir on the Green Line's C and D spurs, respectively, across Warren Street.... *Tel 617/566–1689, ext. 221. 99 Warren St., Brookline. Open Fri–Sun 10–4:30. Admission free.*

Isabella Stewart Gardner Museum. Gardner's fascinating collection of European and American art has been displayed "as is" since 1924.... *Tel 617/566–1401. 280 The Fenway, Museum T stop. Open Tue–Sun 11–5 (and most Mon holidays). Admission charged.*

Gibson House. Get a glimpse of Boston's "Upstairs, Downstairs" lifestyle in this Victorian house museum in the Back Bay.... *Tel 617/267–6338. 137 Beacon St., Arlington T stop. Tours at 1, 2, and 3, Wed–Sun May–Oct; Sat–Sun Nov–April. Admission charged.*

Globe Corner Bookstore. See **Old Corner Bookstore**.

Hard Rock Cafe. Those who buy T-shirts at "Cheers" are often seen buying more here, the self-dubbed "Massachusetts Institute of Rock." It's loud inside, and the food unexceptional.... *Tel 617/424–7625. 131 Clarendon St., Back Bay Station.*

Harvard University. The Information Office in Holyoke Center is the place to hook up with free guided tours of the fabled campus.... *Tel 617/495–1573. Harvard T stop. Weekdays at 10 and 2, Saturday at 2.*

Harvard University art museums. Included are the **Fogg**, the **Busch-Reisinger**, and the **Sackler** museums; one ticket gets you into all three.... *Tel 617/495–9400. Broadway and Quincy St., Harvard T stop. Open Mon–Sat 10–5, Sun 1–5.*

Harvard University natural history museums. Admission deal similar to the Harvard art museums—four for the price of one—applies here Included are the **Peabody Museum of Archaeology and Ethnology**, the **Museum of Comparative Geology**, the **Mineralogical and Geological Museum**, and the **Botanical Museum**.... *Tel 617/495–3045, 26 Oxford St., Harvard T stop. Open Mon–Sat 9–4:30, Sun 1–4:30.*

Institute of Contemporary Art. Modern art museum, not in the league of the MFA. Docents lead tours weekends at 1 and 3.... *Tel 617/266–5152. 955 Boylston St., Hynes Convention Center T stop. Open Wed–Sun 12–5, Thur till 9. Admission charged.*

John F. Kennedy Library and Museum. Exhibits tell about the life and times of JFK. Free shuttle buses run frequently from the T stop.... *Tel 617/929–4523. Columbia Point, Dorchester, JFK/UMass T stop. Open daily 9–5. Admission charged.*

John F. Kennedy National Historic Site. JFK's earliest home.... *Tel 617/566–7937. 83 Beals St., Coolidge Corner T stop. Open mid-May–mid-Oct, Wed–Sun 10–4:30. Admission charged.*

John Hancock Observatory. Besides awesome views, there are narrated exhibits, coin-operated telescopes, computer quizzes, and more. A cheesy gift shop rounds out the fun.... *Tel 617/572–6429. St. James Ave. and Clarendon St., Copley T stop. Open Mon–Sat 9am–11pm; also on Sun 10am–11pm (May–Oct) and noon–11 (Nov–Apr). Admission charged.*

King's Chapel. Former Anglican bastion on the Freedom Trail, offering weekly music events and Sunday Unitarian services. The burying ground next door is open daylight hours year-round. Its tombstones have been shifted over the years, so you can't be sure whom you're standing over.... *Tel 617/ 227–2155. Tremont and School Sts., State T stop. Open Mon–Sat 9:30–4, Sun 12–4, June–Oct; call for off-season hours. Admission free.*

Longfellow National Historic Site. George Washington and Henry Wadsworth Longfellow slept here, although not together. The latter wrote "The Song of Hiawatha" here, among other works discussed on the guided tour....*Tel 617/ 876–4491. 105 Brattle St., Cambridge, Harvard T stop. Open daily 10–4:30. Admission charged.*

***Make Way for Ducklings* Tour.** Book-based tour takes children and their adult companions through Beacon Hill and the Public Garden. Reservations necessary.... *Tel 617/426– 1885. Tours run Sat late spring; Thur–Sat, July 4–Labor Day.*

Massachusetts Bay Lines. Daytime harbor cruises for kids, and evening blues and reggae cruises for grown-ups. There's also a $2 lunchtime harbor cruise.... *Tel 617/542–8000. 60 Rowes Wharf, Aquarium T stop.*

Massachusetts Institute of Technology (MIT). Free tours weekdays at 10 and 2, starting at the Information Center, point out the sprawling campus's outstanding modern art and architecture.... *Tel 617/253–4795. 77 Massachusetts Ave., Kendall T stop. Open Mon–Fri 9–5.*

Massachusetts State House. Take a free guided tour (weekdays 10–4), pick up a map for a self-guided tour, or just wander through the maze of the Bulfinch original building and modern additions. There are cheap eats in the small fourth-floor cafeteria.... *Tel 617/727–3676. Beacon and Park Sts., Park Street T stop. Open Mon–Fri 9–5. Admission free.*

Mineralogical and Geological Museum. See **Harvard University natural history museums.**

Mount Auburn Cemetery. From the T, take either the #71 or #73 bus to this favorite haven of both the dead and the quick.... *Tel 617/547–7105. 580 Mt. Auburn St., Cam-*

BOSTON | DIVERSIONS

bridge, Harvard T stop. Open daily 8–7 summer; 8–5 winter. Admission free.

MuSEAm Ferry. Buy an all-day or a one-way ticket for this ferry, which shuttles from the Museum of Science to the USS *Constitution*, the Old North Church (actually to Lincoln Wharf nearby), the New England Aquarium, and the Children's and Computer Museums.... *Tel 617/422–0392.*

Museum of Afro American History. Part of the Black Heritage Trail on Beacon Hill, this low-key museum occupies the buildings which housed the first city school for black children and the African Meeting House (behind the school).... *Tel 617/742–1854. 46 Joy St., Charles St. or Park St. T stop. Open weekdays 10–4. Admission free.*

Museum of Comparative Zoology. See **Harvard University natural history museums**.

Museum of Fine Arts. Plan to spend at least half a day here; mummies and Monets are the big draws, but there are many more masterpieces and curiosities. The West Wing hosts special exhibitions.... *Tel 617/267–9300. 465 Huntington Ave., Museum T stop. Open Tue–Sat 10–4:45 (Wed till 9:45, Sun till 5:45), West Wing open Thur–Fri till 9:45. Admission charged; free Wed 4–9:45.*

Museum of Science. A planetarium and super-wide-screen theater supplement the 450-plus interactive exhibits and separate children's activities.... *Tel 617/723–2500. Science Park, Science Park T stop. Open daily 9–5 (Fri till 9); 9–7 July 5–Labor Day. Admission charged.*

New England Aquarium. Several levels of fish tanks and exhibits spiral around a huge, wonderful central tank at this superb facility, which also offers performing sea mammal shows and great whale-watching cruises.... *Tel 617/973–5200 (973–5277 for whale-watching info). Central Wharf, Aquarium T stop. Open weekdays 9–5 (Thur till 8), weekends and most holidays 9–6. Admission charged.*

New Old South Church. An 1875 church that's a National Historic Landmark.... *Tel 617/536–1970. 645 Boylston St., Copley T stop. Open weekdays 8:30–6, Sat 9–4. Admission free.*

Nichols House Museum. Art-filled 1804 town house on Beacon Hill, designed by Bulfinch, is open for tours. Administered by the Society for the Preservation of New England Antiquities.... *Tel 617/227–6993. 55 Mount Vernon St., Park Street T stop. Tours hourly 12–5, Tue–Sat May–Oct; Mon, Wed, Sat rest of year (closed Jan). Admission charged.*

Old Corner Book Store. Also known as the Globe Corner Book Store, the historic house/publishing site is a convenient place to get further travel reading.... *Tel 617/523–6658. Washington and School Sts., State T stop. Admission free.*

Old Granary Burying Ground. Freedom Trail graveyard where such patriots as Paul Revere and Sam Adams rest in peace.... *By Park Street Church, Park and Tremont Sts., Part Street T stop. Open year-round, dawn–dusk.*

Old North Church (Christ Church). North End church where the "two if by sea" lanterns were hung to warn Charlestown patriots of British movements. Frequent, brief tours are given; donations solicited for upkeep. The gift shop next door also serves as a museum.... *Tel 617/523–6676. 193 Salem St., Haymarket T stop. Open daily 9–5. Admission free.*

Old South Meeting House. The Freedom Trail landmark is expected to reopen in 1997, after extensive structural renovation and exhibit remodeling.... *Tel 617/482–6439. 310 Washington St., Downtown Crossing T stop. Normally open daily 9:30–5; weekdays 10–4 and weekends 10–5, Nov–March. Admission charged.*

Old State House. Dwarfed by downtown Boston, the charming museum has a permanent exhibit focusing on the Revolution, and a second-floor exhibit on more modern themes.... *Tel 617/720–3290. 206 Washington St., State T stop. Open daily 9:30–5. Admission charged.*

Orchard House. Guided tours lead you through the house where Louisa May Alcott lived. Take Route 2 west through Lexington to Route 2A, turn right, and make an immediate left on Lexington Road. The house is on your right just before the road merges with the Cambridge Turnpike.... *Tel 508/369–4118. 399 Lexington Rd., Concord. Open Mon–Sat 10–4:30, Sun 1–4:30, Apr–Oct; weekdays 11–3, Sat*

10–4:30, Sun 1–4:30, Nov–Mar. Closed Jan 1–15. Admission charged.

Harrison Gray Otis House. Hourly tours are given at this brick mansion designed by Charles Bulfinch. Two-hour neighborhood walking tours (Sat June–Oct) begin here with a slide show.... *Tel 617/227-3956. 141 Cambridge St., Charles or Bowdoin T stop. Open Tue–Fri 12–5, Sat 10–5. Admission charged.*

Park Street Church. Guided tours of the Congregational landmark offered Tue–Sat in summer. Otherwise, content yourself with browsing the more interesting Old Granary Burying Ground next door.... *Tel 617/523-3383. Park and Tremont Sts., Park Street T stop. Admission free.*

Paul Revere House. This frame house was almost 100 years old when the patriot moved in; the restored interior has furnishings from Revere's time and earlier.... *Tel 617/523-1676. 19 North Sq., Haymarket T stop. Open daily 9:30–4:15 (closed Mon, Jan–Mar). Admission charged.*

Peabody Museum of Archaeology and Ethnology. See **Harvard University natural history museums**.

Pierce-Hichborn House. Next door to Paul Revere's house, this larger brick one was owned by his cousin.... *Tel 617/523-1676. 29 North Sq., Haymarket T stop. Tours daily 12:30 and 2:30 (closed Mon, Jan–Mar). Admission charged.*

Plimoth Plantation. Historical re-creation of Pilgrim settlement, with costumed interpreters. Take I-93/Route 3 south to Braintree, follow Route 3 to Exit 4 in Plymouth, and follow the signs.... *Tel 508/746-1622. Route 3A, Plymouth. Outdoor exhibits open daily 9–5, Apr–Nov; indoor exhibits open 9–4 daily except Mar. Admission charged.*

Prudential Center Skywalk. The city's other observatory has fine views, but less compelling displays than the John Hancock.... *Tel 617/236-3318. 800 Boylston St., Prudential T stop. Open Mon–Sat 10–10; Sun noon–10. Admission charged.*

Sackler Museum. See **Harvard University art museums**.

St. Stephen's Church. Bulfinch gem in the North End, across the Prado from Old North.... *Tel 617/523–1230. 401 Hanover St., Haymarket T stop. Open daily 8:30–5. Admission free.*

South End Artists Association. Call to find out about open studios in the half-seedy, half-splendid Victorian neighborhood.... *Tel 617/338–8903. 46 Waltham St., Back Bay Station T stop.*

Sports Museum of New England. Exhibit on the first floor of the CambridgeSide Galleria includes memorabilia of Boston sports heroes, plus some hands–on stuff.... *Tel 617/57–SPORT. 100 CambridgeSide Place, Cambridge, Lechmere T. Open Mon–Sat 10–9:30, Sun 11–7. Admission charged.*

Swan Boats. Pedal-powered barges traverse the Public Garden lagoon Apr–Labor Day.... *Tel 617/725–4505. Public Garden, Arlington T stop. Admission charged.*

Trinity Church. Guided tours are by appointment only, but don't hesitate to duck in yourself and soak in the glory of the 1877 edifice.... *Tel 617/536–0944. 206 Clarendon St., Copley T stop. Open daily 8–6. Admission free.*

BOSTON | DIVERSIONS

Boston Diversions

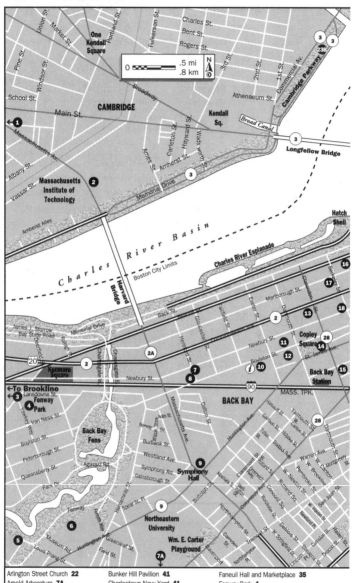

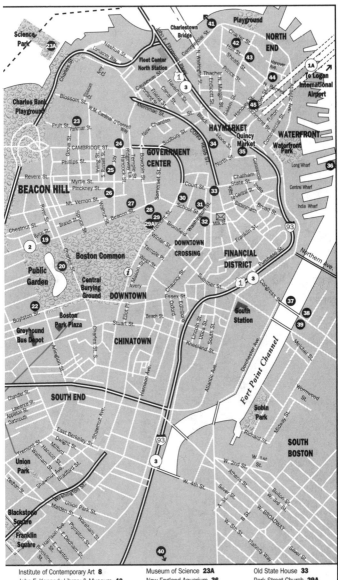

Institute of Contemporary Art **8**	Museum of Science **23A**	Old State House **33**
John F. Kennedy Library & Museum **40**	New England Aquarium **36**	Park Street Church **29A**
John F. Kennedy National Historic Site **3**	New England Holocaust	Paul Revere House **45**
King's Chapel **30**	Memorial **34**	Pierce-Hichborn House **45**
Longfellow National Historic Site **1**	New Old South Church **11**	Prudential Center Skywalk **10**
Massachusetts State House **27**	Nichols House Museum **26**	St. Stephen's Church **44**
MIT Information Office **2**	Old Corner Book Store **31**	Sports Museum
Mount Auburn Cemetery **1**	Old Granary Burying Ground **28**	of New England **23B**
Museum of Afro American History **25**	Old North Church **43**	Swan Boats **20**
Museum of Fine Arts, Boston **6**	Old South Meeting House **32**	Trinity Church **14**

getting

4

outside

When it comes
to recreation,
Bostonians go to
the river. Along
the Charles on
the Esplanade and
on a narrower

trail on the Cambridge side, runners, walkers, cyclists, and
Rollerbladers weave perilously in and out of each other's way.
Those in sailboats and sculls on the river claim higher moral
ground; plus they've only got to dodge the occasional Duck
Tour amphibious vehicle. Assuming the rowers are not oblivi-
ous to the entire world except the coxswain, they get a great
view of both shores. Crew, like running, is extremely competitive in Beantown. You only have to visit the great preppie
mating ritual—Harvard's annual Head of the Charles
Regatta, in late October—to understand how deep rowing's
roots go here.

The Lowdown

Parks to get lost in... You don't have to run, bike, or
blade your way through Boston to enjoy the city's green-
ery (or winter snow country). Each of the baubles on
Olmsted's Emerald Necklace—Back Bay Fens, Muddy
River Improvement, Jamaica Park, Arnold Arboretum,
and Franklin Park—is a quick escape from urban din and
density. The first two in the Fenway area near Kenmore
Square attract people from the urban neighborhood: college students and gay residents (some of whom use the
tall reeds to screen intimate activity). The larger grounds
around Jamaica Pond draw an ethnically diverse crowd of
grandparents and grandchildren, Caribbean fishermen,
and excercising yuppies. The ostensibly educational
Arnold Arboretum provides quiet bowers for romantic
strolls, while rough-hewn Franklin Park gets hikers, family runover from the zoo, and golfers who can't afford the
country clubs. Frisbee players and in-line skaters tend to
hew to both sides of the Charles. In spring and summer,
students also like to sunbathe on the docks of the
Esplanade, while part of Memorial Drive in Cambridge
becomes one long in-line skating rink on Sundays. Like
city parks everywhere, including the **Common** and
Public Garden to which they connect, they should be
avoided after dark. They can be navigated by foot and
bicycle, with the exception of the Public Garden:
although there are few rangers to enforce this, you're supposed to walk your bike through the Public Garden. The
running trails (see "Run for your life," below) are favorites
of walkers, too. You can find out about other activities in

these urban oases by calling the **Parks and Recreation Department** (tel 617/635–4006).

The islands you never heard of... The overlooked gem of outdoor getaways lies just offshore: the **Boston Harbor Islands State Park.** From May through early October, you start by taking the **Bay State Cruises** ferry (tel 617/ 723–1800; $7) from Long Wharf to 30-acre **Georges Island.** It's home of the remains of 19th-century **Fort Warren,** which served as a prison for Confederate soldiers during the Civil War, and of the park's only concessions (very important to remember, since there's no fresh water). From July through Labor Day, you can hop a free water taxi from there to **Bumpkin, Gallops, Grape, Lovells, and Peddocks Islands**; others are accessible only by private boat. You can picnic on Georges and the other islands with taxi service, and camp (somewhat primitively) on four of them. **Peddocks** is the largest, at 185 acres; rangers give guided tours of the ruins of Fort Andrews, built in 1900. On 60-acre **Lovells Island,** you can hike through woods and meadows and around World War II installations, as well as swim (although wading might be a better idea thanks to the improved but still-gross harbor pollution). To camp on Lovells or Peddocks, contact the **Metropolitan District Commission** (tel 617/727–5290). **Grape,** also about 60 acres, is perfect for bird-watching, while its Hingham Bay neighbor, the 35-acre **Bumpkin,** has quiet trails and stone ruins. To camp on either of these, contact the **Department of Environmental Management** (tel 617/740–1605). In the center of it all, 16-acre **Gallops** has World War II remnants and sweeping views of the harbor. Before you get too excited about these idyllic outer-bay retreats, remember that you need to lug your own water, that poison ivy abounds, and that Logan International flight paths are conveniently routed directly overhead. If you can ignore the roar of jet engines, Boston and its troubles will seem far away indeed.

On Walden Pond... When he wasn't sulking in jails over taxes, Henry David Thoreau liked to commune with his bean patch at Walden Pond (tel 508/369–3254, Rte. 126, Concord; open 5am to sunset year-round; $2 per car in July and August; no pets). The pater hippie's rustic retreat is now a reservation open for hiking, swimming, and boating (no gas engines). What's more, it's just a half-hour drive from the city. Formed by glaciers (like Jamaica Pond), Walden Pond is 100 feet deep at points, with 62 acres of water that's warmest in July and August, when a lifeguard is on duty. If you don't feel like taking a dip, you can tackle the 1.7-mile walking trail around the pond; there are lots of roots and rocks to clamber over, so wear appropriate shoes. In the summer, on holiday weekends, and at peak fall foliage times, you'll want to arrive before 10am, when the parking lot usually fills up.

Run for your life... The **Charles River** and the **Emerald Necklace** parks are certainly good places to run, but it doesn't quite explain why running is such a mania in Boston. Could it be the Puritan view that life is suffering, so why not add a little more? Or the fact that the minimal equipment required to jog appeals to parsimonious Yankees? In any case, the New England tradition of marathoners like Joan Benoit Samuelson and Bill Rodgers inspires members of Boston's numerous competitive running clubs and solo striders. Although many hotels can give their guests maps for popular running routes, it's easiest just to head to the Charles and pick two bridges to loop around. The longest route, about 17 miles, would take you from the Science Museum Bridge (Monsignor O'Brien Hwy.) to Watertown Bridge and back. The shortest loops, all under a mile, connect Allston (on the Boston side) with Harvard University. Start at either the Anderson or Western Avenue Bridges and loop back at the John Weeks footbridge for these short courses. If you're going for distance, keep in mind that above the Harvard Bridge the stretch along the Cambridge side is more scenic—narrow stretches in Allston and Brighton on the Boston side occasionally pass by industrial-looking areas. You'll also want to carry water with you—the few fountains close to the trail are near Community Boating and the Hatch Shell on the Esplanade (which also has public restrooms), and even those are turned off in winter. The trail is often very windy. The Cambridge side is a little more protected than the Boston side, so plan your route accordingly and pack enough wind gear in winter.

The best midsize running route may be between the Longfellow and Harvard Bridges. Just under three miles, the loop goes from the foot of Beacon Hill past the Hatch Shell onto a lagoon-dotted stretch of the Esplanade that hugs the Back Bay, with the Charles sitting to your right. You cross the river at its widest point on the Harvard Bridge, where painted "Smoot increments" mark your progress (see You Probably Didn't Know). On the Cambridge side, you'll pass stately college buildings and get a sweeping view of the Boston skyline on the way to the "Salt and Pepper" Longfellow Bridge—so called because the ornamental posts at either end look like salt and pepper shakers. To the north, the predominantly red-brick hotels and offices of Cambridge square off against the glassy towers of the Massachusetts General Hospital (MGH) complex in Boston's old West End. Of course, you can start anywhere along the loop; it's easily accessed from the Esplanade and Cambridge. The two-mile loop around the Science Museum and Longfellow Bridges is less picturesque, but also has less foot traffic to dodge.

Experienced Boston runners seeking a change of pace navigate the winding courses from the Fens to Jamaica Pond, or from there to Arnold Arboretum—it's best to consult a map for these two. The **Southwest Corridor** is an easier-to-follow paved trail alongside the Orange Line tracks, going from Back Bay Station to Forest Hills, near the Arnold Arboretum. Don't run the Corridor or the Fens at night, though. Those looking for a hill workout should head to **Beacon Hill.** For the longest, highest trek, start at Charles Street and go up Mount Vernon, which has the stateliest homes. Any number of other, narrower streets are good too. For track workouts, the outdoor track at MIT in **Steinbrenner Stadium** (on Vassar Street in Cambridge, near the Harvard Bridge) is home to several running clubs' weekly workouts—except in the coldest months. In season, show up Tuesday evenings at 6:30 if you want to pace yourself against them. The **YMCA** in Back Bay (see "The Club Scene," below) has an indoor track. Any other questions? Get advice from the knowledgeable staff at the **Bill Rodgers Running Center** in the North Market building of Faneuil Hall Marketplace (See Shopping).

The Marathon... Naturally, no discussion of local running would be complete without mentioning the **Boston Marathon,** even though plenty of Bostonians have only watched it on television like everyone else. It's held the third Monday in April, a state holiday known as Patriot's Day. Plan ahead if you don't want to visit the city when it's swarmed by casually dressed, physically fit tourists. Normally you must run a qualifying time at another marathon in order to be one of the 9,000 participants, but for the 100th running in 1996, the organizers added entrants by lottery to increase the field to about 30,000. The 26.2-mile course actually starts west of the city, at the town green in Hopkinton, and goes through Framingham, Ashland, Natick, Wellesley (the half-way point, traditionally the site for an enthusiastically cheering crowd of Wellesley students), Newton (home of Mile 21's Heartbreak Hill, the third in a series of major uphills where most runners begin to hit the wall), and Brookline, before winding up in Copley Square, jammed with spectators. A note to onlookers: Commonwealth Avenue at Kenmore Square has good views around the 25-mile mark, and people are many knees deep along the final quarter-mile on Boylston Street from Hereford to Dartmouth Streets. If you're thinking of entering, contact the Boston Athletic Association (tel 617/236–1652) for more details. If you just want to visit the scene of the crime, the finish line is usually visible on Boylston Street for months after the race. *The Tortoise and the Hare* sculpture near the fountains in Copley Square also commemorates the event, second in hoopla only to the Fourth of July.

Pedal pushers... Despite the occasional daredevils bent on running you over, most cyclists in Boston avoid city streets, with good reason. Cambridge has begun creating bike lanes, but local drivers have their own inimitable way of roaring the wrong way down one-way alleys, ignoring stoplights, and generally abusing speed limits. It's a Beantown specialty, if you haven't noticed. Consequently, the two nearest bike trails receive heavy use. The nearly 18 miles of the paved **Dr. Paul Dudley White Bikeway** overlap with running trails on both sides of the Charles River, from the Museum of Science Bridge to Watertown. (See "Run for your life," above). If you're on a bike, you're supposed to stay nearer to the road than the river—where runners, walkers, and Rollerbladers are already vying for space. But pedestrians and cyclists end up dodging each other anyway; don't plan on setting any speed records here. The 11-mile **Minuteman Bicycle Trail** follows an old railroad track from the Alewife T, at the end of the Red Line in North Cambridge, through the towns of Arlington, Lexington, and Bedford. It can be very busy with families on weekends.

So where to pick up your spokes? Each side of the Charles has an established rental shop. **Community Bicycle Supply** in the South End primarily rents mountain bikes (tel 617/542–8623; 496 Tremont St. at East Berkeley; rental hours are 9:30am to 7pm daily, April through the end of September; $20 a day, with credit card and picture ID). In Cambridge, the **Bicycle Workshop** rents 10-speeds and three-speeds (tel 617/876–6555; 259 Massachusetts Ave., near Windsor St. in Central Square; open 10 to 6 Monday through Saturday, and noon to 5pm Sunday; $15 a day, with credit card and picture ID). Both also sell or rent helmets and locks, and have new bikes and repairs.

Blade runners... Beantown has not escaped the urban scourge known as in-line skating (also called Rollerblading). Not only is it a great excuse to wear futuristic, skintight synthetic outfits in colors not found in nature, it's also great for showing off deft concrete versions of moves like the full gainer, and generally adding to the tranquil nature of Boston streets and sidewalks. Bladers are everywhere in the Hub, and universally lack tact; don't be surprised if you see seven-foot people next to you in the ice cream shop. If you like a good show, however, try the trick skating often going on by the **Hatch Shell** or in **Copley Square** at dusk, when pedestrian crowds have thinned. On Sundays from 11am till 7pm (May through October), bladers have a 1.5 mile swath of Cambridge's Memorial Drive all to themselves; it's closed to auto traffic from Western Avenue to the Eliot Bridge. For rentals, **Eric Flaim In-Motion Sports**, near Massachusetts Avenue in the Back Bay, is closest to the prime blading spots (tel 617/247–3284; 349 Newbury St.; open 10am to 7pm Sunday through Thursday, and 10 to 8 Friday and Saturday; $21 a day, with $200 credit-card deposit). The downstairs store offers a lesson and rental for $35 total, and free lesson with purchase. Instructors give you an hour plus on the Commonwealth Avenue mall near Kenmore

BOSTON | GETTING OUTSIDE

Square, training on smooth grass and cement (all rentals include full padding, by the way). The **Beacon Hill Skate Shop**—in Bay Village, not Beacon Hill—has in-line and ice skates for sale or rent, with padding, and also sells skateboards (tel 617/482–7400; 135 Charles St. South at Tremont St.; open 11am to 6pm Monday through Saturday, and noon to 5pm Sunday; $5 an hour, $15 a day, MasterCard or Visa required for security deposit).

Swimming holes in the concrete jungle... You can't swim in the Charles River, and Boston Harbor, though cleaner, isn't out of the (polluted) water yet. So it's either join the masses at North and South Shore beaches, take a dip in Thoreau's old swimming hole, Walden Pond, or hunt for a decent pool in the city. Sadly, they're in short supply. Of the hotels that do have pools, some are outdoors with a limited season, and many are too small to get much exercise in. The best hotel pool for lap swimming is the 25-yard affair at the **Hyatt Regency Cambridge.** It's above the parking garage and has windows on both sides, one of which gives you an inspiring view of the Charles River; alas, it's for guests only. The **Westin Hotel** (tel 617/262–9600; 10 Huntington Ave.) charges $10 a day to nonguests to use its 20-yard pool and health club, while the **YMCA** and the **Boston Athletic Club** (see "The club scene", below) have swimming pools and other facilities open to nonmembers for $10 and $20 a day, respectively. Two nothing-fancy public pools with separate wading areas for kids are within most tourists' reach, both just off the river with good views and cooling breezes. The city operates a pool in the **North End Playground** (Commercial and Foster Streets), with varying hours and admission fees; recently it's been free, open weekends in July and August. **Lee Pool** (tel 617/523–9746; in Charlesbank Park near Charles and Blossom Streets, across from the Massachusetts General Hospital complex) is generally open daily from Memorial Day through Labor Day, with free admission. It's one of 17 pools in the Greater Boston area managed by the **Metropolitan District Commission** (tel 617/727–9547). If you just want to get your toes wet (or your kids' toes), the **Frog Pond** on the Boston Common becomes a wading area from July 4 until the last weekend in August; it's open 10am to 6pm.

Like all parts of the Common, it has its share of street people napping on the sunny benches.

The club scene... If dodging traffic and trekking around the Freedom Trail doesn't give you enough of a workout, several health clubs have daily passes for visitors. Both the busy **YMCA** (tel 617/536–7800; 316 Huntington Ave.) and the smaller **YWCA** (tel 617/351–7600; 140 Clarendon St.) charge $10 a day to use the facilities, including a swimming pool at both locations and an indoor track at the YMCA. The YMCA also has four courts for handball or racquetball and four squash courts ($3 per game). Near South Station, the **Boston Athletic Club** (tel 617/269–4300; 653 Summer St.) charges $20 a day. It's got fitness equipment, a pool, seven tennis courts, two squash courts, and six racquetball courts—as well as a restaurant and lounge under construction. It's no wonder the fees are high enough to foster a slighter snootier scene.

Whatever floats your boat... In the middle of Jamaica Park in Jamaica Plain lies, you guessed it, **Jamaica Pond,** a 70-acre, 70-foot-deep pond (at high water) where you can rent rowboats and 15-foot Precision sailboats in season (tel 617/522–6258; rowboats April through mid-October; $6 an hour, $3 with state fishing license or for senior citizens; sailboats July through Labor Day; $10 an hour; season boating memberships range from $40 to $80). On hot days, this is a good place to practice the New England ethic of self-denial. There's no swimming—none whatsoever—the pond is a backup reservoir for the city.

    Community Boating (tel 617/523–1038), on the Esplanade between the Hatch Shell and the Longfellow Bridge, offers unlimited instruction and use of boats and sailboards to members, with proof of swimming ability and a checkout test. The 30-day adult membership is $65, not much more than the $50 two-day visitor membership. Ages 17 to 22 pay $50 for a 30-day membership; ages 10 to 17 can sail the whole summer for $1. The season runs from April through October from 1pm to sunset weekdays and 9am to sunset weekends and holidays. If you have the right sailing credentials, you can rent a boat from the **Boston Harbor Sailing Club** at Rowes Wharf (tel 617/523–2619; 200 High St., Aquarium T; open May–Oct). If you don't, and you're in town long enough, you can take

GETTING OUTSIDE | **BOSTON**

classes and become qualified. Or, if you want, just come to look at the club's fleet on Rowes Wharf.

Ice, ice, baby... One of winter in Boston's few redeeming features should be skating in the **Public Garden.** Unfortunately, it's an unpredictable affair due to the vagaries of weather and public funding. They can't change the temperature, but area philanthropists are working to make the finances more consistent. The Public Garden lagoon is usually divided into areas for figure skating and hockey skating, one on each side of the bridge. Hockey celebrities like Bobby Orr usually give free clinics one weekend a season; check the *Boston Globe*'s Calendar section on Thursdays and Weekend column on Saturdays for special events. Meanwhile, the city is planning to restore skating to the **Frog Pond** in Boston Common by winter 1996, with a new building in the works to house skate rentals, ice maintenance machines, and concessions. **The Metropolitan District Commission** (tel 617/727–9547) operates 20 other public rinks in the Greater Boston area, most of them in neighborhoods far out of most tourists' way. One exception is **Steriti Rink** in the North End (tel 617/523–9327; Commercial St. near Foster St.; fee charged on weekends, $3 for adults and $1 for children; open mid-November to mid-March, generally weekday mornings, Friday afternoons, and all day Saturday and Sunday), but just as at the Public Garden, Hans Brinkers should bring their own silver skates. You can try **Beacon Hill Skate Shop** in Bay Village (see "Blade runners," above), which rents and sells figure skates and hockey skates ($5 an hour, $15 a day, MasterCard or Visa deposit required). **Eric Flaim In-Motion Sports,** which in 1995 rented only Rollerblades and other in-line skates, has plans to offer the real thing by winter of 1996.

Hitting the beach... Believe it or not, some Southies cherish their beaches enough to have made them the site of Southern California–style "locals-only" turf wars. It's quieter there now; and until the harbor cleanup makes more progress, most sane people use city beaches for strolling and sunning only. You may feel more comfortable on one of the North or South Shore beaches. One easy way to do it is to take the commuter train from

North Station to the **Singing Beach** in Manchester (just
under an hour), or all the way to the end of the line at
Rockport, where you'll find cliffs and tide pools. The further north the beach, the more lock-jawed the beachgo-
ers. The first beach out of town, **Revere**, is a big-hair
scene, while Crane's Beach in **Ipswich** has a long swath of
sand, nice for family picnics. Or, you can always follow
half of Boston in the summer to **Cape Cod**, two hours
away by car.

Tee time... Unfortunately, this part of New England is
known more for its golf courses that *don't* let people play
than for the ones that do. Even in the early nineties, one
high-profile Jewish executive got so tired of waiting for a
membership in a prestigious club south of the city that he
bought his own (nondiscriminating) country club, the
Willowbend. Fortunately, there are more democratic
courses on the fringes of Boston and Cambridge. In
Dorchester's Franklin Park, the **William Devine Golf
Course** is 6,100 yards, par 70 (tel 617/265–4084; weekdays $9.50 for nine holes, $16 for 18; weekends $10.50
and $19). In Boston's southernmost neighborhood, Hyde
Park, across from Stony Brook Reservation, the **George
Wright Golf Course** has 18 holes open daily at dawn. The
par-70, 6,400-yard course is more difficult and more picturesque than Franklin Park's. It's tighter and more heavily treed, but crowded nonetheless (tel 617/361–8313; 420
West St.; weekdays $22, weekends $25; rental clubs, carts,
and lessons available). Trickier still is the 6,603-yard, par-
71, 18-hole course at **Putterham Meadows** in suburban
Brookline (tel 617/730–2079; weekdays $23, weekends
$26; cart and club rentals and private lessons available).
Across the river in Cambridge's tranquil Fresh Pond Park
is the **Thomas P. O'Neill Jr.** ("Tip" to you and me) **Golf
Course**, which has nine holes on its 3,161-yard, par-35
course (tel 617/349–6282; 691 Huron Ave.; weekdays $14
for 9 holes, $20 for 18; weekends and holidays $17 for 9
holes, $25 for 18). Can't get enough? Call the
Massachusetts Golf Association (tel 617/449–3000) for
more courses in the state.

ping

5

As the cradle of
New England
preppiedom,
Boston can be
tough going on
shoppers—you're
not supposed to

spend money on frippery here. Luckily, the ever shifting sea of university life brings new tastes and fashions to the Charles, so it is possible to buy more than a new kelly green blazer while you're in town. Used books and records are standbys, but Boston has learned to cater to many tastes. Thrifty Yankees, filthy-rich foreign students, Brahmin snobs, and Cambridge multiculturalists all have their own shopping haunts. What's more, diverse stores are often jumbled together in the same neighborhood—there's no uptown versus downtown here—making the real pleasure for Boston shoppers a pedestrian one (in the original sense of the word). Take a walk down brownstone-lined Newbury Street or around the eclectic architecture of Harvard Square, for example, and you'll find shops of all sorts—high- and low-brow, chain and boutique—squeezed into every possible cranny, with plenty of places to unload money on less durable favorites like ice cream and coffee. With the exception of Faneuil Hall Marketplace, Boston's great shopping districts haven't been homogenized into the equivalent of outdoor malls. You'll still see vestiges of city life like liquor stores, dry cleaners, pharmacies, and grocery stores, not to mention agencies that deal in the area's most sought-after commodity—apartments. Locals, tourists, and students blend easily in these areas, although if you take your cellular phone shopping with you, you must head directly to the cafe at Emporio Armani with the rest of the Euro set. If you're lonely for faceless, suburban shopping, try one of the three indoor malls nearby.

What to Buy

You'll have a hard time avoiding T-shirts, caps, and historic-site paperweights with "Boston" printed on them. Other than Boston baked beans (real or candied), however, there are very few gifts that really say Boston: the local crafts tend to be politics and parking, not handmade goods. The city has been around for more than 360 years, though, so antiques do good business. Thanks to the 200,000 or so college students in the area (not to mention their professors), there's a vast trade in new and used books, clothing, and music. When it comes to clothes, though, don't expect to find good deals; many designer boutiques rely on dipping into the deep pockets of international students. But their wares often end up at Filene's Basement anyway, so the label-conscious have several price options.

Target Zones

If you want to make one stop only, head for Boston's best shopping district—the eight blocks of **Newbury Street**, from the Public Garden to Massachusetts Avenue. Lined with picturesque town houses, its got everything from Cartier to comic books, and it's only one block over from **Boylston Street**, a somewhat less picturesque shopping stronghold. Newbury also has a smorgasbord of restaurants, cafes, and ice cream parlors—and you can't get lost on it. It's a straight Back Bay street with T stations bookending it and in the middle. Heading from Arlington Street to Mass. Ave., you start at the Ritz-Carlton Hotel and Burberry's, and end up at Tower Records and Urban Outfitters, with a lot of less common names in between. **Harvard Square** in Cambridge has more stores geared toward students, in a less easily navigated web of streets, but still has plenty of charm, not to mention traffic. Most tourists in Downtown Crossing's pedestrian zone are headed straight for Filene's Basement, but there are also pushcarts selling funky jewelry, cheap clothes, and ethnic food among the teen fashion and traditional jewelry stores. **Faneuil Hall Marketplace**, right on the **Freedom Trail**, draws hordes of tourists to its increasingly mundane collection of shops, pushcarts, restaurants, and food vendors. About the only reason to visit are the nicely restored buildings. It's more pleas-

Hey, what a market!

Cheek by jowl with the sanitized tourist shops of Faneuil Hall, the Haymarket—an enclave of pushcarts, trucks, and small butcher and cheese shops along Blackstone Street between Government Center and the North End, with its own T stop nearby—offers a taste of a Boston that's nearly gone. Touted by many as the place to buy produce in the city, this is the country's oldest market, harking back more than 200 years. For those who dare to wriggle between the carts and jump over puddles of dubious origin, the Haymarket makes for a great shopping experience. Here, Irish and Italian get along—at least as well as they do with anyone else. Someone's teenage son chases a supposed shoplifter, while a large, brusque man with a voice to match warns one customer off of squeezing the peaches and simultaneously assures another that the price is the best in town. The full market is open only Fridays and Saturdays, from about 7am to midafternoon. If the vendors don't know you, don't attempt to haggle; but at the end of the day, when the produce is past its peak, try making an offer for the entire watermelon or the last flat of strawberries.

BOSTON | SHOPPING

ant to window-shop at night, when the crowds have thinned and musicians have taken the place of jugglers and other street performers.

A few neighborhoods specialize in particular goods. **Charles Street** on **Beacon Hill** is the antique lover's dream, as long as the dream isn't on a budget. Dazzling and dusty artifacts fill storefronts from Beacon Street to Cambridge Street, with a few more antique shops around the corner on Chestnut and River Streets. Head to the **North End** for imported Italian and European food; you'll spot stores on Cross, Hanover, Salem, and Prince Streets, although they're overshadowed in number by the many cafes and restaurants. Foodies will want to combine the trip with a stop at the outdoor **Haymarket** on Fridays and Saturdays. **Chinatown** has more restaurants than shops, and it would be a better place to browse if it didn't overlap with the seedy **Combat Zone**, Boston's fading porn district.

As for malls, **Copley Place** is the only one in Boston proper, and quite a tony one at that, with Neiman Marcus, Tiffany, and Gucci in residence. Across from Back Bay Station, it hooks up via skywalks with the Prudential Center, an office and retail complex that includes Lord & Taylor and Saks Fifth Avenue. Copley Place is best for browsing on a cold or wet day, or before or after a movie in its multiplex. If weather permits, check out nearby Newbury Street. **CambridgeSide Galleria**, across the river, by the Lechmere T station, has been angling for a movie cinema but residents are currently opposed. The mall is clean but not particularly high-end; highlights for tourists are the Harley-Davidson store, the New England Sports Museum, and the paddleboats in the adjacent lagoon, where the Charles Riverboat cruise departs. The **Chestnut Hill Mall** on Route 9 in suburban Brookline boasts a Barneys New York, a Bloomingdales Home, and other fashionable stores, but is worth a special trip only if you're mall-deprived at home.

Bargain Hunting

Clothing deals can be summed up in four words: "the original **Filene's Basement**." It's important to distinguish the *real* one from the store's suburban incarnations which pale in comparison. At the Downtown Crossing location, clothes, women's shoes, accessories, and housewares are culled from such highfalutin stores as Neiman Marcus, Henri Bendel, and Barneys New York, as well as less elegant retailers. All price tags have a date stamped on the back, and the price drops precipitously as time passes. Boston is nothing if not a great book town, with Cambridge offering bargains on both the new and used fronts. The Hub's academic population ensures a good supply of secondhand books. If you're looking for cheap antiques, skip smug Charles Street (though **Upstairs, Downstairs** is worth checking out). You're more likely to sniff out a good buy in the warehouses off Cambridge's no-atmosphere Monsignor O'Brien Highway.

Hours of Business

Proving that Massachusetts is at least trying to free itself from the shackles of its Puritan heritage, blue laws restricting Sunday commerce were repealed in 1994, so many stores are open—believe it or not—seven days a week now, particularly those in the major shopping areas. Most stores do business at least from 10 to 6 Mondays through Saturdays and noon to 6 on Sundays, with many staying open till 8 on Thursdays, as on Charles Street. In general, the smaller the store, the more idiosyncratic its schedule. Hours are often extended during the winter holiday season, but if the weather's really terrible, store and restaurant owners sometimes close early. Call ahead if you're in doubt.

Sales Tax

The sales tax is a relatively low 5 percent and doesn't apply to items of clothing that cost less than $300 or to groceries. Only the amount above $300 is subject to the tax. So go ahead, go crazy for $299 or less.

The Lowdown

Shopping bags to show off... The fancy shopping bags that can be spotted as they are whisked from cabs into lobbies at the Four Seasons and the Ritz-Carlton Hotels often come from stores only a short walk away. Crass out-of-towners may be impressed by jewelry legends like **Tiffany & Co.** and **Cartier,** but Bostonians know to buy their bijous and bridal gifts from **Shreve, Crump & Low.** It sounds like a law firm, but it's the best place to wear white gloves while you shop for that sterling silver swan brooch you always wanted. The cream of current European designs can be bought straight from the sources, just as if you were in Milan or Paris. Try **Giorgio Armani Boutique,** the most haute in couture and price of the Italian designer's three Hub outlets. The less expensive

Emporio Armani is several blocks down the street, while the youthful **Armani Exchange** is in Copley Place, where the designer with the famous linked initials, **Gucci**, also has a mall boutique. Newbury Street's **Fiandaca** sells evening wear that has turned up on several First Ladies, Joan Collins, and Anita Baker, among others, but don't bother just looking—it's open by appointment only. The famous French saddle makers, **Hermès of Paris** do sell tack and saddles at their Arlington Street shop, but more likely purchases are their signature scarves. Facing each other on Newbury are **Joseph Abboud** and **Alan Bilzerian**, where Bostonians who equate service with discretion shop. Alan's fashions are trendier than Joseph's, and the selection smaller, though Joseph's is a good place for stargazing when Hollywood and Broadway actors are in town. Be forewarned that if you buy from Abboud's casual J.O.E. line, you'll get a more casual shopping bag, of recycled paper, which just doesn't have the cachet of the standard bag. Women can try Italian designer frocks (Moschino, Dolce & Gabbana) at nearby **Serenella**. If the staff at **Charles Sumner** can't help a lady find a designer dress, who can? It's a Boston institution. Another one, **Louis, Boston** prides itself on service, which may include the ability of sales personnel not to laugh at what you're paying. You won't get a bag from the Louis Café, at the rear of the handsome Back Bay landmark, but you'll still feel well served.

Clothes to make you feel young again... If baggy jeans, flannels, rubber vests, skateboard logos, and rave caps speak to you, **Urban Outfitters** and its locally based rival, **Allston Beat**, do their best to keep abreast of street fashions. While college kids are attracted by the moderate prices, anyone who lived through the seventies polyester kick the first time may feel like they're trapped in an expensive Salvation Army. **The Garment District** (a store, not a neighborhood) in Cambridge offers more of the same, but also has budget recycled clothing, sold by the pound. For fancier young women, **Betsey Johnson** sells flimsy little dresses in fun colors for serious money, while **Emporio Armani** clothes international students who like to hang out at its cafe. To tell the truth, the Italian designer's store looks an awfully lot like Next, the British store next door, which in turn is like an upscale Gap.

Clothes to make you feel grown-up... The conservative cut never goes out of style in Boston, hence the city's affinity with chains like Brooks Brothers for men and Talbots for women (or, for more "adventurous" women, Ann Taylor). The local heroes of this look are **Jos. A. Bank Clothiers** in Back Bay, a big store by Newbury standards and located, in a charming inversion of office hierarchy, directly underneath the Katherine Gibbs Secretarial School. If you need three new red-and-blue rep ties, look no further than Cambridge's **J. Press**, where you'll also find tweeds and fine wool coats for taking out the hounds. But if you're not an aspiring banker or country squire, don't despair. For women, **Settebello**'s owner travels frequently to Europe to buy exclusive suits, sportswear, and accessories from German and Italian designers. **Georgiou** has tailored dresses and separates each season in a limited number of colors and prints, usually in linen, wool, and silk. The advantage is that the limited choice means you can tell quickly if a given season's line will work for you or not. The quiet yet cutting-edge chic habiliments (mostly by American designers) at Cambridge's **Jasmine** are worth a look too. Men can try Jasmine's neighboring male counterpart, **Sola Men.**

Everything under one roof... OK, for full-fledged department stores, there are really only two, **Filene's** and **Macy's**, which conveniently face each other in Downtown Crossing. The former sits atop **Filene's Basement**, which was recently bought from Filene's and has become its own franchise with stores in other cities. This is the only Basement, however, with timed markdowns and consistent shipments of designer discards. Competition for some items—wedding gowns, Ferragamo shoes, lingerie—can be intense; go on weekdays (*not* at lunchtime) for less stressful shopping. Bostonians were stunned in 1996 when Macy's renamed their beloved Jordan Marsh, a department store that has been around a lot longer than its 1951 brick building suggests (right across from Filene's more graceful 1912 structure). At Christmas, Jordan Marsh was famous for its Enchanted Village, an extremely cute recreation of a New England hamlet. If you're still hungry for anonymous shopping after reckoning with these downtown dinosaurs, Boston has a few nonessential stops. Upscale **Lord & Taylor** presides over stylish but not particularly trendsetting clothes, while conservative **Saks Fifth Avenue** in the Prudential Center gets flashy every so often. In Copley Plaza, **Neiman Marcus**, the Texas chain known jokingly as "Needless Markups," has a style all its own, namely extravagance.

World-beat chic... Since the 1960s, imported Third World clothing, rugs, and crafts have provided cheap, colorful, vaguely political ways for college students to dress themselves and their dorm rooms. And in Boston time, the sixties are practically yesterday, so the trend shows no sign of slowing. **Serendipity** and **Nomad**, which both have branches on both sides of the Charles, troll the globe (Latin America, Africa, Middle East, Far East) for jewelry, crafts, clothes, and, at Nomad, home furnishings. **A Taste of Culture** near Harvard Square has a wild mix of African masks, South American crafts (the owner's Peruvian), and international gewgaws, at moderate prices. Though Chinatown is better known for its restaurants, you can also find imported clothes, shoes, crafts, and toys at places like **Oriental Gift and Design** (it's mostly schlock).

Well-heeled wares... Foot fetishists looking for the perfect cordovan-leather men's club shoe should try **Church's English Shoes**, or **Allen Edmonds**, which also has women's shoes, at the Public Garden end of Back Bay. At the other end of Newbury, but not a whole lot less expensive, **Thom Brown** has recently made a name for itself selling clunky shoes that look best in nightclubs. In nearby **John Fluevog**'s world of ironic footwear, look for variations on classics like the bowling shoe, at inflated prices.

100 percent leather... The **Harley-Davidson** store in CambridgeSide Galleria is one of the few family-oriented stores left where you can buy leather chaps. There's a certain art gallery quality to the sparse racks of jackets, skirts, and pants in tasteful hues at **Designers Leather Clothiers** on Charles Street. Just a few doors down, a lot of international tourists are drawn to **Helen's Leather Shop** for a boutique selection of Western boots (for padnuhs and fillies).

Obscure objects of desire... The inspiration of a bereaved couple who lost their favorite pet, Beacon Hill's

Angel Dog is split between stuff for the canine in your life and doggie-themed decorative items in everything from poodle to pit bull. Another nonantique store on Charles Street, **Black Ink** has a curious selection of rubber stamps made from old engravings (zeppelin, anyone?). The **Lannan Ship Model Gallery**, open by appointment only, is for nautical obsessives whose wallets have grown way beyond balsa-wood kits. If you want to look like you traveled back in time and swiped the dishes from the hotel you stayed at, **Loulou's Lost and Found** has Harvard Square and Newbury Street locations for replicas of vintage resort and restaurant housewares.

Pages on a budget... Bostonians are such avid readers—and students have to buy so many books—that national, regional, and local bookstores have managed to survive while offering competitive prices. **Barnes & Noble**, which has several branches in the city, has also recently begun to operate the massive Boston University bookstore and the formerly student-run **Coop** at Harvard and MIT. But of the many worthwhile stores selling new books, **WordsWorth** and **Buck a Book** stand out as both bargain bonanzas and scenes unto themselves. The first is a veritable hive in Harvard Square, with shoppers day and night swarming through several levels crammed with shelves of books, all discounted from list price. The second, which has a half-dozen area stores, sells mint-condition overstocked books, gift wrap, children's items, and stray videos and cassettes. Regulars drop in frequently to monitor the eclectic inventory. If you can't find something a friend will love, you usually can find something they'll hate, at a gag-gift price.

Pages with beverages... Boston knows that it's civilized to sample a book along with a drink and a nibble. In the Back Bay, **Trident Booksellers and Cafe** has been the more bohemian place to test-drive a book (new or used) with a snack. The mammoth **Waterstone's**, which may still be under renovations from a fire in summer 1995, is a more recent addition. In Cambridge's Porter Square, the **Bookcellar Cafe** has live music and poetry readings. Magazine and newspaper hounds can stock up at the landmark **Out-of-Town News** kiosk in Harvard Square, then head to the cafe of their choice. A three-floor **Borders** is opening in Downtown Crossing (tel 617/557–7188).

Previously read pages... Since Bostonians like to save money as much as they like to read, used-book stores are big here. **The Brattle Book Shop** on a dingy lane near Downtown Crossing is one revered source where you might find out-of-print books or obscure tomes on the annals of Boston or naval history. Funky **Avenue Victor Hugo** on Newbury Street is another; it's still open nightly till 10pm, with a diverse selection of books—sci-fi is particularly strong—and magazines. Although the top floor of the spacious **Harvard Book Store** is devoted to new books, the popular bottom floor carries used and remaindered titles. When money is no object (but perhaps an important subject), **David O'Neal Antiquarian Booksellers** in Back Bay may have just the hallowed tome for you.

Very particular pages... Book specialists in Boston are as varied as the sand by the sea; a few have special totemic value. **Spenser's Mystery Books** pays tribute to Robert Parker's Boston gumshoe-cum-gourmet whose office was also in the Back Bay. The **Globe Corner Bookstore**, also known as the Old Corner Bookstore, was restored in the early 1960s to its 18th-century appearance; this building where publishers of the *Atlantic Monthly* used to work is now a travel bookstore. **We Think the World of You** mixes travel with gay and lesbian fare in the South End, heart of Boston's gay community. Across the river, Cambridge boasts New England's biggest women's bookstore, **New Words**, which covers the gamut on the lesbian, multiculti front. The **Lucy Parsons Center** keeps alive the spirit of May 1968 with far-left critiques of just about everything. Yes, they still read books at MIT, as the high-tech center known as **Quantum Books** attests.

Music meccas... Among local record chains, **Newbury Comics** has a hallowed, cultish status on the alternative rock circuit. Of the half-dozen used record and CD stores between Newbury Street's Massachussetts Avenue end and Kenmore Square, **CD Spins** is a clean, well-lighted place, focusing on rock and dance music with a sprinkling of everything else. Unique among the rock-heavy Kenmore Square stores, **Orpheus** is a three-room circus of records, sheet music, and ephemera in classical, opera, and jazz. It's even got 78s. Vinyl purists will want to take the T's Red Line to **Cheapo Records** in Cambridge's Central Square, for used R&B and rock LPs. **Disc Diggers** in Somerville's Davis Square has the area's largest selection of used CDs, plus some records and tapes. A shrine for audiophiles, **Cambridge Soundworks** sells nationally regarded speaker systems and has a very hip, equally low-key staff.

Home beautiful... French Provincial textiles and furnishings, along with a few antiques, create a cozy home at **Pierre Deux** in the Back Bay. On Beacon Hill, **Sfoggio** introduces the bright patterns of Italian majolica into Charles Street's subdued antique merchandise, while **Linen on the Hill** is a nook for imported kitchen, bed, and bath linens, with a smattering of decorative tchotchkes.

Art for art's sake... Although the Fort Point area is where a lot of cutting-edge artists live, work, and display their works, it's not the best area for strolling. Newbury Street (between Arlington and Berkeley Streets and a few blocks down, between Clarendon and Exeter Streets) is where the city's high-profile galleries are clustered. Traditionalists go to **Vose Galleries of Boston**, where art stops in the early 20th century, or to **The Copley Society of Boston** (a nonprofit society named for Colonial Boston's favorite portraitist) for slightly more adventurous fare from contemporary artists. **Pucker Gallery** shows contemporary work that's not too far out, like sculpture, paintings, and prints, while the **Barbara Krakow Gallery** trades in minimalist and conceptual pieces—your hipness factor rises upon entering.

Art for your sake... All the area museums have intriguing gift shops, even when they're squeezed into small spaces like the one at the Isabella Stewart Gardner Museum (see Diversions). Outside of their lofty environs, you can find aesthetically redeeming yet functional handmade goods at several spots: **Artsmart** specializes in nice but affordable jewelry. **The Society of Arts and Crafts** (Boston is really into societies) has more high-flown ceramic and carved wood objets along with baskets and vases, while the **Cambridge Artists' Cooperative** changes stock often but is a good bet for bowls, scarves, or other clothes.

Precious old stuff... Antiques shops selling top items at top prices crowd Charles Street; but the largest purveyor of fine furniture and decorative items is the cooperative **Boston Antiques Center**, close to North Station. Of the Beacon Hill dealers, two specialists are worth noting. At **Eugene Galleries**, maps and prints from every far-flung corner of the world—but especially that strange region called New England—are neatly hung or filed in a tiny square room. By contrast, entering the serenely spare interior of the **Edo Gallery of Asian Art** is like visiting a rock garden, an appropriate setting for its museum-quality Japanese rarities. Much less expensive, and staunchly eclectic, is Charles Street's **Upstairs, Downstairs** (actually downstairs), which sells furniture and objets that are not always in top condition.

Funky old stuff... The Fort Point artists area is packed with shops trafficking in vintage stuff from this century, such as the fifties-oriented **Cousin Bill's**, where you can find kitschy, functional items like toasters and coffee tables. On Congress and Summer Streets, there are more stores of the same ilk. Newbury Street's **Nostalgia Factory** has thousands of movie posters, old advertisements, and political ephemera, while Charles Street tastefully enters the 20th century at the appropriately named **Twentieth Century Limited**, which has elegant costume jewelry from the twenties and fantastic Deco artifacts. Out in Cambridge near Lechmere it's not cute like Charles Street, but dusty warehouses like the **Cambridge Antiques Center** have lower prices and everything from furniture to vintage clothing, not to mention free parking.

Kid stuff... Parents can take out two birds with one stone on Newbury Street. Near Arlington Street, the **Oilily** boutique makes Gap Kids look like Kmart. At **F.A.O. Schwarz**, it's not surprising that there are just as many adults as kids; it's a great place for office workers to spend their lunch hour trying out new electronic games. Little girls and connoisseurs of camp love the Barbie Boutique, which has its own entrance. The inexplicably chic Hello Kitty toys, pencils, and barrettes can be found at Chinatown's **The Yes! Station.** More of a place for the inner child than real children, **Eric Fuchs,**

near Government Center, stocks models, trains, and Dungeons and Dragons stuff, as well as dollhouse miniatures. Always worth a pilgrimage is **Learning-smith**, an incredible educational toy store just off Harvard Square. It's got everything from make-your-own chewing gum kits for kids to books on teaching and learning creativity.

Adult stuff... With the softening of the adult-entertainment business in Boston's Combat Zone, the jokey Newbury Street boutique called **Condom World** is the only sex shop worth noting, if just for its safer-sex motto: "Protect and Serve."

Little pretty things... The golden swan above the gilt-flecked entrance to the historic **Women's Educational and Industrial Union** in Back Bay lets you know you're in for a charming display of gifts (scarves, ceramics, jewelry, toys). Sales benefit womens charities. On Beacon Hill, squeezed between musty antiques shops, are the newfangled **J. Oliver's** and **Blackstone's of Beacon Hill**, the kind of places where you can buy tasteful stationery, Christmas ornaments, and Boston knickknacks.

Incredible edibles... You'll find specialty stores with cheese, candy, wines, and deli meats in the densely packed commercial blocks of the North End. Local cooks shop at the **Salumeria Italiana** on Prince Street. Moving beyond Italian wares into Continental and American cuisine, two tempting gourmet shops are busy: **Cardullo's** in Harvard Square, and shoe-box-sized **Savenor's** on Beacon Hill. For the some who like it hot, **Le Saucier** in Faneuil Hall Marketplace has a blistering variety of salsas and other peppery condiments.

The sporting life... If you insist on dressing in style for the great outdoors, Newbury Street's **Patagonia** has the latest in pastel mountain-chic—at least it's well made. Serious runners gravitate to the **Bill Rodgers Running Center**, where they generally won't find their guru but they may get a good deal on shoes. Similarly speed skater Eric Flaim has lent his name to **Eric Flaim In-Motion Sports**, though the off-ice version of his footwear—a k a in-line skates—are the main attraction here.

The Index

Alan Bilzerian. Au courant fashions for both sexes in a small, two-floor store. Great seasonal clearance sales.... *Tel 617/ 266–4200. 37 Newbury St., Arlington T stop.*

Allen Edmonds. High-end men's shoes. Many sizes, many widths, casual and dress. Women have to make do with equally pricey footwear from Bally and others.... *Tel 617/ 247–3363. 37 Newbury St., Arlington T stop.*

Allston Beat. A local study in street hip. Synthetic minishirts, shiny miniskirts, very big shoes.... *Tel 617/421–9555. 348 Newbury St., Hynes Convention Center T. Tel 617/868– 0316. 36 J F K St., Cambridge, Harvard T stop.*

Angel Dog. Gives new meaning to "going to the dogs." Burberry doggie coats, Italian and Swiss leather collars, watches with dog faces, and custom-made items depicting you-know-who.... *Tel 617/742–6435. 131 Charles St., Charles T stop.*

A/X Armani Exchange. This is where you get very, very fancy jeans and t-shirts. *Tel 617/927–0451. 100 Huntington Ave., Copley Place, Copley T stop.*

Artsmart. American artisans of jewelry and home objets. Two locations.... *Tel 617/695–0151. 272 Congress St., South Station T. Tel 617/497–9472. 1352 Massachusetts Ave., Cambridge, Harvard T stop.*

Avenue Victor Hugo. The used-book store with shelves stacked high hasn't changed in years.... *Tel 617/262– 0880. 339 Newbury St., Hynes Convention Center T stop.*

Barbara Krakow Gallery. Minimalist, conceptual, and other- wise extremely contemporary art gets a classy showcase. *Tel 617/262–4490. 10 Newbury St., Arlington T stop.*

Barnes & Noble at Boston University. You can get BU text books as well as the usual superstore selections, complete with a ground-level cafe. *Tel 617/267–8484. 660 Beacon St., Kenmore Square T stop.*

Betsey Johnson. A neon designer even when she's working in pastels, Betsey Johnson is the antithesis of the Boston preppie look, which probably explains her appeal to young women.... *Tel 617/236–7072, 201 Newbury St., Copley T stop.*

Betsys. Whoever Betsy is, and whatever her cutsey reason is for dropping the apostrophe, you can't gripe about the romantic, thirties-accented women's clothing and accessories. Comfy hand-knit sweaters and other items are made locally.... *Tel 617/536–1050. 201 Newbury St., Copley T stop.*

Bill Rodgers Running Center. A road-runners' must-visit. There are some T-shirts for the tourists upstairs.... *Tel 617/723–5612. North Market, Quincy Marketplace, State T stop.*

Black Ink. Probably the foremost store in the nation for rubber stamps of antique engraved images. If that's not your cup of tea, it also has cool paper, stationery, soap, and gift items made from recycled junk like glass, tires, and circuit boards.... *Tel 617/723–3883. 101 Charles St., Charles T stop.*

Blackstone's of Beacon Hill. It's cute and cluttered. It has pewter, glassware, porcelain, frames, prints, children's items and a whole mess of ornamental objects.... *Tel 617/227–4646. 46A Charles St., Charles T stop.*

Bookcellar Cafe. Like its affiliate, Avenue Victor Hugo, the store is 90 percent used books, 10 percent new. On-site coffee. *Tel 617/864–9625. 1971 Massachusetts Ave., Cambridge, Porter T stop.*

Boston Antiques Center. Posh stuff from the past. Along with a bounty of furniture in the four-story restored warehouse, there are elegant decorative items. A ground-floor restuarant serves *nuevo* American food.... *Tel 617/742–1400. 54 Canal St., North Station T stop. Closed Sun and Mon.*

The Brattle Book Shop. Used and rare books. A family-run business, established in 1825.... *Tel 617/542–0210. 9 West St., Park Street T stop.*

Buck a Book. Locations downtown and in Cambridge at Harvard and Davis Squares. Look for the tacky green and white sign.... *Tel 617/266–0019. 647 Boylston St., Copley T. Tel 617/357–1919. 125 Tremont St., Park Street T stop.*

Cambridge Antiques Center. The 150 dealers have four floors of furniture, art, china, jewelry, vintage clothing, and junk.... *Tel 617/868–9655. 269 Msgr. O'Brien Highway, Cambridge, Lechmere T stop. Closed Mon.*

Cambridge Artists' Cooperative. Affordable housewares by local artisans, in fabric, wood, metal, and glass.... *Tel 617/868–4434. 59A Church St., Cambridge, Harvard T stop.*

Cambridge Soundworks. Henry Kloss designs the nationally renowned speakers and systems sold by a pleasantly pressure-free staff.... *Tel 617/225–3900. CambridgeSide Galleria, Cambridge, Lechmere T stop.*

Cardullo's. Imported foods, mostly European, and a deli counter are a welcome sight in food-desolate Harvard Square.... *Tel 617/491–8888. 6 Brattle St., Cambridge, Harvard T stop.*

Cartier. Leather bags, scarves, clocks, watches, and jewelry from the famous firm, with prices not nearly as understated as the elegance. *Tel 617/262–3300. 40 Newbury St., Arlington T stop.*

CD Spins. Cheap used compact discs (also some new but marked down). Conveniently near a Tower Records and Newbury Comics.... *Tel 617/267–5955. 324 Newbury St., Hynes Convention Center T stop.*

Charles Sumner. A Boston standby for women's designer clothes.... *Tel 617/536–6225. 16 Newbury St., Arlington T stop.*

Cheapo Records. One of the last great bastions of vinyl. Two long, narrow floors of used jazz, rock, soul, and R&B albums and singles. Also has several handfuls of compact discs. *Tel 617/354–4455. 645 Massachusetts Ave., Cambridge, Central T stop.*

Church's English Shoes. Male shoe-seekers are seated in thronelike leather chairs and treated royally here.... *Tel 617/ 424–1077, 383 Boylston St., Arlington T stop.*

Condom World. It's somehow reminiscent of a magic and novelty shop. Prophylactic devices of every stripe (literally), gag gifts, and adult toys in a downstairs space. *Tel 617/267– 7233. 332 Newbury St., Hynes Convention Center T stop.*

The Coop. In 1995, Barnes & Noble took over the cooperative founded by Harvard students in 1882. Less emphasis on music, clothing, and campus logos, and more on books, is the new game plan.... *Tel 617/499–2000. 1400 Massachusetts Ave., Cambridge, Harvard T. Tel 617/499–3200. 3 Cambridge Center, Cambridge, Kendall T stop.*

Copley Society of Boston. Contemporary art, mainly by New England artists at various levels in their careers.... *Tel 617/ 536–5049. 158 Newbury St., Copley T stop.*

Cousin Bill's. Streamlined stuff from the 1950s, most of which is still functional. *Tel 617/695–2924. 283 Summer St., South Station T stop.*

David O'Neal Antiquarian Booksellers. The Back Bay source for rare volumes and first editions.... *Tel 617/266–5790. 234 Clarendon St., Copley T stop.*

The Designers Leather Clothiers. Alterations, custom orders, and repairs are specialties of the Beacon Hill boutique.... *Tel 617/720–3967, 106 Charles St., Charles T stop.*

Disc Diggers. A short walk from Davis Square, this eclectic, well-stocked store sells used and new compact discs at low prices, plus plenty of vinyl for record collectors. The displays are crowded but remarkably organized, and the staff is very hip.... *Tel 617/776–7560, 401 Highland Ave., Somerville, Davis T stop.*

Edo Gallery of Asian Art. Choice art and crafts from 16th-through 19th-century Japan.... *Tel 617/523–5211. 65 Chestnut St., Charles T stop.*

Emporio Armani. It's fun to window-shop the trendy cafe denizens here.... *Tel 617/536–1050, 201 Newbury St., Copley T stop.*

Eric Flaim In-Motion Sports. In-line skaters are like cock-roaches in Boston—they multiply and infest. If you feel compelled to join the fun, come here.... *Tel 617/247–3284. 349 Newbury St., Hynes Convention Center T stop.*

Eric Fuchs. Hobbies for adults with a lot of free time on their hands.... *Tel 617/227–7935. 28 Tremont St., Government Center T stop.*

Eugene Galleries. A small treasure chest for antique maps and prints.... *Tel 617/227–3062, 76 Charles St., Charles T stop.*

F.A.O. Schwarz. The toy mecca from New York. Look for the big bronze teddy bear outside, or rather the clumps of people getting their photo taken next to it.... *Tel 617/266–5101. 440 Boylston St., Arlington T stop.*

Fiandaca. A full line of women's clothes fit for the ruling class, as well as handbags, gloves, belts, and exclusive jewelry. On the second floor, above the clothing store Hooloomooloo, near Emporio Armani, it's open by appointment only. *Tel 617/859–8202. 222 Newbury St., Copley T stop.*

Filene's. All the normal department-store wares are attractive-ly displayed on the downtown building's six floors, with the usual jewelry-and-perfume gauntlet on the ground floor and Ralph Lauren and Laura Ashley boutiques on the top. The CambridgeSide mall version is more compact. *Tel 617/357–2100. 426 Washington St., Downtown Crossing T. Tel 617/621–3800. 100 CambridgeSide Place, Cambridge, Lechmere T stop.*

Filene's Basement. If your new evening gown hasn't been snatched up after four weeks, you'll get 75 percent off. Frequent sales often lop off another 10 to 25 percent. Naturally, there's a temptation to try to hide the good things, and a storewide effort to thwart it. (And if the date is missing, an item is considered to have been put on sale that day.) A large overhead chart explains the famous pro-gressive-discount system. An automatic teller machine sup-plies additional cash (although major credit cards are accepted), and an in-store Dunkin' Donuts supplies addi-tional energy. You can enter from the Downtown Crossing T stop or by a separate entrance from Filene's on Summer

Street. *Tel 617/542–2011. 426 Washington St., Downtown Crossing T stop.*

The Garment District. Students and short-on-cash types like to pick through the dollar-a-pound clothes, though you can also find trendy and practical new stuff, priced accordingly.... *Tel 617/876–5230. 200 Broadway, Cambridge, Kendall T stop.*

Georgiou. An oasis of taste in gimmicky Faneuil Hall. Bargains are upstairs.... *Tel 617/723–7540. North Market, Faneuil Hall, State T stop.*

Giorgio Armani Boutique. The most haute in couture and price of the Italian designer's three Boston retail outlets.... *Tel 617/267–3200. 22 Newbury St., Arlington T stop.*

Globe Corner Bookstore. The historic School Street building dates back to 1718, but all three locations sell the latest in travel books and maps.... *Tel 617/523–5870. 1 School St., State T. Tel 617/859–8008. 500 Boylston St., Copley T stop. Tel 617/497–6277, 49 Palmer St., Cambridge, Harvard T stop.*

Gucci. Luggage, leather goods, menswear and a small amount of women's clothing.... *Tel 617/247–3000. Copley Place, 100 Huntington Ave., Back Bay Station.*

Harley-Davidson Motor Clothes & Collectibles. The name pretty much says it all.... *Tel 617/225–9999, Cambridge-Side Galleria, Cambridge, Lechmere T stop.*

Harvard Book Store. A robust selection.... *Tel 617/661–1515. 1256 Massachusetts Ave., Cambridge, Harvard T stop.*

Helen's Leather Shop. Slick Western boots for men and women, as well as motorcycle and bomber jackets.... *Tel 617/723–6328. 110 Charles St., Charles T stop.*

Hermès of Paris. If your riding apparel is complete, don't fear, you can also buy men's and women's clothing, towels, porcelain, blankets, fragrances, haberdashery, watches, and stationery. Closed Sundays. *Tel 617/482–8707. 22 Arlington St., Arlington T stop.*

Jasmine. No wild, ethnic prints, prefab grunge, Army surplus, or other student staples here: just chic tailored clothes and accessories for women. *Tel 617/354–6043, 37A Brattle St., Cambridge, Harvard T stop.*

John Fluevog. Where shoes aspire to be an artform. Clear-plastic pumps, retro lace-up and go-go boots, and something called the roller clog.... *Tel 617/266–1079. 302 Newbury St., Hynes Convention Center T stop.*

J. Oliver's. Chockablock with tasteful gifts and stationery, the store also has a sly side, with funky vintage items.... *Tel 617/ 227–4646. 38 Charles St., Charles T stop.*

Jos. A. Bank Clothiers. Where to dress for corporate warfare.... *Tel 617/536–5050. 122 Newbury St., Copley T stop.*

Joseph Abboud. Three stories of stylish clothing for men and women, with prices to match the posh interior.... *Tel 617/ 266–4200. 37 Newbury St., Arlington T stop.*

J. Press. The Ivy League look has been defined for nearly a century at this traditional Cambridge clothier. You can buy off the rack or made to measure.... *Tel 617/547–9886. 82 Mt. Auburn St., Cambridge, Harvard T stop.*

Lannan Ship Model Gallery. If you build model ships, make an appointment. Otherwise, sneak a peek from the sidewalk. Lannan also sells nautical antiques and paintings.... *Tel 617/451–2650, 540 Atlantic Ave., South Station T stop.*

Learningsmith. A Cambridge gem. Kids will find brew-your-own root beer kits, while Mom and Dad bone up on gardening with huge starter sets. *Tel 617/661-6008. 25 Brattle St. Harvard Square T stop.*

Linen on the Hill. A slice of a storefront that's attractively stocked with imported bed and table linens and pretty objects that strike the owner's fancy.... *Tel 617/227–1255. 52 Charles St., Charles T stop.*

Lord & Taylor. An upscale department store, with clothes for men, women, and children, mostly by American designers.... *Tel 617/262–6000. 760 Boylston, Copley T stop.*

Louis, Boston. Stands serenely alone among Back Bay row houses and modern office buildings, in an 1862 brick mansion. The Boston leader in pricey menswear also has a floor for women's apparel, plus a gourmet cafe for lunch and dinner.... *Tel 617/262–6100. 234 Berkeley St., Arlington T stop.*

Loulou's Lost and Found. Retro housewares.... *Tel 617/859–8593. 121 Newbury St., Copley T. Tel 617/441–0077. 0 Brattle St., Cambridge, Harvard T stop.*

Lucy Parsons Center. Who says that class warfare is dead? New and used books and magazines, weighted to the left of center.... *Tel 617/497–9934. 3 Central Square, Cambridge, Central T stop.*

Macy's. Formerly Jordan Marsh, one of Boston's stalwarts, and still a full-scale department store. It's got everything from shoes to Super Mario Brothers, plus a furniture-clearance basement. Rebecca's Cafe on the ground-floor discounts its pastries late in the day. *Tel 617/357–3000. 450 Washington St., Downtown Crossing T stop.*

Neiman Marcus. Like a glamorous lobby, the three-story emporium sets the tone for the rest of Copley Place. *Tel 617/536–3660. Copley Place, 100 Huntington Ave., Back Bay Station T stop.*

Newbury Comics. It's got a corner on the college market. Strong alternative rock inventory, frequent sales.... *Tel 617/236–4930. 332 Newbury St., Hynes Convention Center T. Tel 617/491–0337. 36 JFK St. (in a small indoor mall called The Garage), Cambridge, Harvard T stop.*

New Words. Probably the biggest women's bookstore in the Northeast Corridor. It also has an international feel-good vibe, kids books, stationery, and gifts.... *Tel 617/876–5310, 186 Hampshire St., Cambridge, Central T stop.*

Nomad. If you like funky, multiculti, Third World pants that look like wall hangings, look no further. Even if prep school hippie isn't your thing, you can't argue with the prices on jewelry and crafts.... *Tel 617/267–9677. 279 Newbury St., Hynes Convention Center T stop. Tel 617/497–6677. 1736 Massachusetts Ave., Cambridge, Porter T stop.*

The Nostalgia Factory. This store stocks more than 5,000 movie posters.... *Tel 617/236–8754. 336 Newbury St., Hynes Convention Center T stop.*

Oilily. For the aspiring clotheshorse in the family. Kids fashions from the Continent, in bright fabrics and prints, with prices to keep away pretenders. *Tel 617/247–9299. 31 Newbury St., Arlington T stop.*

Oriental Gift and Design. A few steals can be found among the eminently browsable shelves of Chinese toys, stationery, shoes, decorations, and jewelry.... *Tel 617/482–0827. 72 Harrison Ave., Chinatown T stop.*

Orpheus. Records, sheet music, and ephemera in jazz, opera, and classical music. It also stocks vintage movie memorabilia.... *Tel 617/247–7200. 362 Commonwealth Ave., Kenmore T stop.*

Out-of-Town News. As the address notes, this is where you zero in on Harvard Square in all its ragtag, bustling glory. Newspapers and magazines from across the globe are on sale from 6am until midnight.... *Tel 617/354–7777. 0 Harvard Square, Cambridge, Harvard T stop.*

Patagonia. Good-looking outdoor clothes and gear that you'd hate to get dirty. The store attempts to resemble a lofty-ceilinged cabin. *Tel 617/424–1776. 346 Newbury St., Hynes Convention Center T stop.*

Pierre Deux. French Provincial fabrics and housewares for genteel renegades from the early American look.... *Tel 617/536–6364. 111 Newbury St., Copley T stop.*

Pucker Gallery. The downstairs gallery has a peaceful fountain.... *Tel 617/267–9743. 171 Newbury St., Copley T stop.*

Quantum Books. MITers, Harvard wonks, and other techies keep up with the latest in their field at this large store in the Marriott complex. *Tel 617/494–5042. 4 Cambridge Ctr., Cambridge, Kendall T stop.*

Saks Fifth Avenue. Top designers, foreign and domestic.... *Tel 617/262–8500. Prudential Center, Ring Rd., Prudential T stop.*

BOSTON | SHOPPING

Salumeria Italiana. A high-quality deli, free of tourist traffic.... *Tel 617/523–8743. 151 Richmond St., Haymarket T stop.*

Savenor's. Game for game? In addition to an adventurous meat and seafood counter, this small specialty-food store has fresh gourmet breads and pastries, pricey but perfect produce, and highfalutin ice creams and sorbets.... *Tel 617/723–6328, 160 Charles St., Charles T stop.*

Serendipity. Global chic for women who get their makeup, if they wear any, at The Body Shop.... *Tel 617/437–1850. 229 Newbury St., Copley T stop. Tel 617/661–7143. 1312 Massachusetts Ave., Cambridge, Harvard T stop.*

Serenella. Airy women's boutique in the heart of Newbury Street.... *Tel 617/262–5568. 134 Newbury St., Copley T stop.* ·

Settebello. For those students who can afford the clothes, Settebello often carries them into their careers and beyond.... *Tel 617/864–2440. 52C Brattle St., Cambridge, Harvard T stop.*

Sfoggio. Perhaps the brightest spot on Beacon Hill, this store is devoted to hand-painted ceramics, mostly from Italy.... *Tel 617/ 742–6435, 103 Charles St., Charles T stop.*

Shreve, Crump & Low. The quintessential Boston store did service in fall '95 as a movie set (for a Ricki Lake vehicle, with Shirley Maclaine, named *Mrs. Winterbourne*), but the focus is still on attentive service, with two floors of jewelry, china, silver, porcelain, crystal, and other giftware. *Tel 617/267–9100. 330 Boylston St., Arlington T stop.*

The Society of Arts and Crafts. A small exhibition space, its shelves brim with jewelry and other artsy-craftsy goods. Price signs on the shelves help shoppers, indicating ranges for each artisan's work.... *Tel 617/266–1810. 175 Newbury St., Copley T. Tel 617/345–0033. 101 Arch St. (second story), Downtown Crossing T stop.*

Sola Men. This is the male version of the neighboring Jasmine and Sola boutiques for women. Chic, nonstudent-oriented apparel by U.S. designers. *Tel 617/354–6043, 37A Brattle St., Cambridge, Harvard T stop.*

Spenser's Mystery Book. Welcome to the world of who-dunits, both new titles and rarities.... *Tel 617/262–0880. 314 Newbury St., Hynes Convention Center T stop.*

A Taste of Culture. Away from the high-rent heart of Harvard Square, this store has lots of little crafts from South America and Africa to pore over.... *Tel 617/868–0389. 1160 Massachusetts Ave., Cambridge, Harvard T stop.*

Thom Brown. The shoe store will no doubt change its style to keep attracting young trendsetters. Also has leather bags and backpacks.... *Tel 617/266–8722. 331 Newbury St., Hynes Convention Center T stop.*

Tiffany & Co. Though it's not quite the same as the New York mother ship, Boston's outpost of the famed jeweler has all the requisite fine china, perfume, crystal, and silver.... *Tel 617/353–0222. Copley Place, 100 Huntington Ave., Back Bay Station.*

Trident Booksellers and Cafe. As much a hangout as a bookstore.... *Tel 617/267–8688. 338 Newbury St., Hynes Convention Center T stop.*

Twentieth Century Limited. An upstairs store for tasteful jewelry and decorative items from the recent past.... *Tel 617/742–1031, 89 Charles St., Charles T stop.*

Upstairs, Downstairs. Antiques don't have time to gather dust before they're sold here—maybe because the prices are always reasonable.... *Tel 617/ 367–1950. 93 Charles St., Charles T stop.*

Urban Outfitters. If you wanna dress like a teenager, fine, but the best bargains here are the funky household furnishings, often made from recycled or natural materials.... *Tel 617/236–0088. 361 Newbury St., Hynes Convention Center T stop. Tel 617/864–0070. 11 JFK St., Cambridge, Harvard T stop.*

Vose Galleries of Boston. American art from the 17th through early 20th centuries, with some Barbizon School paintings is the raison d'être of this family-run Boston institution.... *Tel 617/ 536–6176. 238 Newbury St., Copley T stop.*

Waterstone's. Former home to one of New England's obscure religious movements, the Spiritualist's 1884 stone temple was turned into a movie theater, then a bookstore, which had smoke and water damage from a nearby fire in the fall of 1995. But owners of the three-story goliath that carried 150,000 titles plan to reopen, and may have a Faneuil Hall branch soon.... *Tel 617/ 859–7300. Newbury and Exeter Streets, Copley T stop.*

We Think the World of You. A compact South End bookstore for travelers and gay and lesbian readers. You can also find out about gay-community events or buy tickets to some shows here.... *Tel 617/423–1965, 540 Tremont St., Back Bay Station.*

Women's Educational and Industrial Union. Lots of little pretty things, children's clothes and toys, stationery, and needlework downstairs; upstairs, a high-class thrift shop for antiques.... *Tel 617/536-5651. 356 Boylston St., Arlington T stop.*

WordsWorth. Getting lost in the busy, warrenlike store with more than 100,000 titles is half the experience here. The other is getting a discount on everything except textbooks.... *Tel 617/354–5201. 30 Brattle St., Cambridge, Harvard T stop.*

The Yes! Station. If you know who Hello Kitty (and her friends) are, then you know what this store is largely about. In addition to the Sanrio stuff for kids (stationery, jewelry, school supplies, toys), the store also sells Hong Kong–produced CDs and comic books.... *Tel 617/482-1022. 28 Kneeland St., Chinatown T stop.*

nigh

6

tlife

Boston nightclubs
roll up their red
carpets when
other cities are
laying theirs
down—last call
lights flicker at

1:45am. With less time to collect cover charges and hawk overpriced drinks, club impresarios in Beantown work extra hard to make their dance floor the place to be. The target audience: college kids, grunge victims, and yuppies. From one week to the next, the hippest, most hyper scene will move— Hub night crawlers are nothing if not nomadic, though on any given night they'll probably visit only one hot spot.

For younger party hounds, Boston might close early, but there is a frenzy in those dancing hours, an urgency to have fun before being shuffled out of the clubs at 2am. Then there is the ever-exciting scramble to get invited to the after-hours scene lurking in some loft apartments and alcohol-free clubs.

Getting to nightclubs in Boston is easy—it's getting home that poses a problem, even if you have really only had a couple. Most of Boston's clubs are accessible by public transportation, but for some reason known only to city officials and cabbies' unions, the MBTA stops running around 12:45, with at least an hour left to drink and dance. Rest assured: There are plenty of surly taxi drivers around after hours, and Boston is generally a safe city to walk in—even in the wee hours if you observe the simple precautions of taking well-lighted streets and maybe someone with you. For more mature night owls, you can expect to be back in your nest by midnight, since the elegant hotel bars and rooms with a view that cater to you tend to close even earlier.

Remember, Boston is a college town, so most clubs cater to the hordes of baseball-cap-sporting fraternity brats and wealthy international students. But don't assume that all clubs do: There are also nightspots devoted to drag queens, kink freaks, the idle rich, and recovering addicts, and some dance clubs change their focus on a nightly basis to attract a rotating clientele. Call before you go, or check local listings to verify that a given night's theme is up your alley (unless you're into discovering the road not taken).

Liqour Laws and Drinking Hours

The drinking age in the Hub is 21, and most nightclubs employ burly bouncers to scrutinize IDs. So the underaged have a scant chance of sneaking in—unless, of course, they are part of the city's wealthy foreign-student royalty, who push hundred-dollar bills into the hands of doormen causing them suddenly to read 21 on a passport that says 19. The 2am closing is strictly observed by all established clubs, although covert drinking often continues in Chinatown, where some restaurants, catering to the cravings of night owls, stay open until 4am.

Sources

To find out the latest news on where nightclub mavens are traveling in droves, pick up the weekly *Boston Phoenix* for its Arts section, or the *Boston Globe*'s Calendar section, both published on Thursdays, or the *Boston Herald*'s Scene guide on Fridays. The clubs run more detailed ads in the oh-so-hip *Phoenix*, while the *Globe* has longer write-ups on just a few clubs each week. *Stuff* magazine, a free paper found littering Newbury Street haunts, is another nightlife source, tailored to the young and affluent. Gay and lesbian travelers should look for a copy of *Bay Windows* (free in stores, 50¢ at newsstands) for more extensive, frank coverage of the same-sex circuit (both full- and part-time gay clubs); the *Phoenix* also writes convincingly about the scene in a monthly One in Ten supplement.

The Lowdown

Where the Eurobrats play... You'll see them around town, perfectly coiffed, elegantly Armani'd, and armed with gold cards and overseas stipends. They're the ones seated first at trendy eateries like the **Armani Cafe** (tel 617/262–7300, 210 Newbury St.) and **Sonsie** (tel 617/351–2500, 327 Newbury St.); they have access to private tables at the best restaurants in town. And they dance every night of the week, making their rounds to all the right spots on all the right nights. "They" are the international students who have infiltrated Boston's nightclubs and upscale stores. Usually dubbed "Eurobrats" or "Eurotrash" by the natives, they have breathed new life into the Hub's clubs and have mapped out their own nightly club migration.

Recently revamped **Joy** apes a club by the same name in Spain. It's hot, hot, hot. You'll find the jet set here, swathed in designer ensembles, impatiently tapping their Italian shoes while waiting in a line that stretches down Washington Street. Inside, two floors of Beautiful People grind to acid jazz and pumping techno. Joy is located in the Theater District, so there is plenty of parking here, but most of the Euroelite valet park their luxury cars at the curb. Next to the **Paradise** rock club, another Euroscene, **M80**, is a bit more stuffy than Joy and filled with Middle Eastern royalty who are in town pretending to study at Boston's universities. Self-proclaimed decadent internationals sip overpriced champagne, grin smarmily at singles, and feign cell phone conversations over the drone of music. A chic crowd, slightly more down-to-earth, dances the night away at **The Roxy** on Tremont Street, which is predominantly multinational on Friday nights. A largely Asian scene, including loads of gorgeous women, dances at **Europa**, usually alongside hopeful American men. On Thursday nights, **Avalon** in Kenmore Square rivals the United Nations for its international crowd. Avalon used to be the best Eurobar until Joy moved into town. On Sunday nights downtown, **Il Panino**, a five-story trattoria-cum-disco, turns into a multigear Eurohaven. Usually, the crowd's just the city's Italian elite and executive Bostonians.

For the facially pierced... Boston's live-music scene is brilliant, with many local guitar bashers going on to to bigger success. But when the grunge look hit the Hub, it never left, so there are scores of modern primitives still sporting tattooed bodies, necks, and faces, with pierced noses, navels, and nipples. Some rockers are poseurs, and recognizable by their overpriced retro outfits put together at chain stores that cater to the cool crowd. Appearance aside, this crowd knows how to party but still retain their smug composure (and liquor). **The Middle East** in Cambridge has the hottest scene going, with a hang out bar upstairs for scoping and scooping, and live music in three rooms. It books the best local bands and occasional national acts. Formerly the ultra hip Spit, **Axis**, along the Lansdowne Street strip, tries really hard to be as cool as its counterparts. But it seems to attract MTV-obsessed college students from middle America who think they are cool if they put green streaks in their hair and wear fashionable sneakers. Axis does have sexy servers and pectoral-dominant doormen, who may make it worth a visit. Thursday nights, club kids flock here in packs for the hippest, hottest dance scene in Beantown. **The Causeway**, a tiny, dingy bar near North Station, has the most authentic rocker crowd around. This is where white go-go boots really belong, because you know the drag queen wearing them has had them since the sixties. Local bar bands who do mostly covers play at the Causeway; bands with ambition, and their own material, are more likely to play Kenmore Square's **Rathskeller**. Dubbed "the Rat" by locals, it's been around for generations and is the last bastion of punk rock. The bar upstairs—which serves good pub grub—is full of dour-faced, but fun, people; downstairs in the cellar, the bands play.

If you like Sinatra... Hotel lounges are still the best bet for the well-heeled older crowd who like piano bars, jazz trios, and dry martinis. Nothing is sacred, though: the Lenox Hotel recently converted its popular Diamond Jim's piano bar into a Samuel Adams brewpub. Surely that will never be the fate of the Copley Plaza Hotel's stately **Plaza Bar**, a high-ceilinged, carved-wood, nose-in-the-air cubbyhole. If the cocktail music from the pianist in the corner is too intrusive, you can rub elbows with the graying men in suits at **Copley's** just down the plushly carpeted hall. A large, dark wood bar divides the room into two sections, with celebrity caricatures hanging on the walls. Other hotel lounges in which to luxuriate: the Bostonian's airy **Atrium Lounge**, where on Saturdays a cabaret vocalist joins the nightly pianist; the Westin's **Turner Fisheries Bar**, a posh, modern-art corner with jazz combos Thursdays through Saturdays and a pianist otherwise; and the expensive, sedate bars at the **Ritz-Carlton** and **Boston Harbor Hotel**. (See Accomodations for hotel listings.) Two sophisticated rooms with fabulous views, hushed conversations, and marked-up food and drink are the 52nd-floor **Top of the Hub** in the Prudential Center and the 33rd-floor **Bay Tower Room**. The former recently renovated to include a marble entryway and elegant light-wood furnishings in its restaurant and lounge areas. The latter is a private club by day that opens up to the well-dressed public at night; a swing quartet plays Fridays and Saturdays, and you can dine other nights to a jazz pianist.

If you see a shamrock, it's not a real Irish bar...
Boston is a city full of the Irish—need we mention the Kennedys? Scores of umpteenth-generation Bostonians with Irish surnames tattoo Notre Dame fighting-Irish lepechauns on their arms and sport shamrocks on their shirts. And there are almost a hundred Irish bars in Boston. But there is a definite distinction between a down-home Irish pub, where banter is tinged with musical brogues and Guinness is served, and the bars with a luminous shamrock in the window, where the wannabes

swill Schlitz. All the authentic Irish bars look the same: dark wood bars and booths, stained glass, smoke drifting to the ceiling. Only the crowd varies a little from pub to pub. **Mr. Dooley's Tavern** and **The Green Dragon** are two Irish-run downtown pubs (read: tourists and business types) where Guinesss beer and chicken curries imported from Dublin are the mainstays. The manager of these bars, Michael Sherlock, has a brogue as thick as the pubs' pea soup, and has managed to attract Irish natives into the bars partly with Celtic bands crooning traditional ballads but mostly because of his charisma. **The Druid**, a neighborhood, Irish-catered bar, is the perfect place for a couple of black and tans and a chat with some young locals in Cambridge's Inman Square. Another great Guinness-quaffing bar, **Brendan Behan** in Jamaica Plain attracts a diverse, young, arty crowd. **The Kells** in Allston-Brighton reflects its neighborhood, where a huge number of recent Irish immigrants live and work, particularly during summers when Emerald Isle schools are out. **Ned Kelly's** in Dorchester has only the rare American visitor; most of its regulars are Irish born and bred. A classy neighborhood joint, it serves up fantastic food, a great pint, and good conversation. Ned Kelly's is packed weekends, as is **The Eire Pub** down the road, where the mostly male, somewhat older revelers swap fibs over pints of stout. **The Irish Embassy** in the North Station area is another gritty pub where Americans rub elbows with Irish natives. It sometimes books Celtic bands and is always crowded weekends or after games at the nearby FleetCenter. Young Irish travelers and college students also make use of its hostel accommodations.

If you're curious about the dozens of fake Irish bars around town, peek into **The Purple Shamrock** or **The Black Rose**, but be leery of fanny-pack-sporting tourists trying to do Irish jigs on the tables. Both of these Faneuil Hall clubs are teeming all weekend, but usually with a drunken American crowd who wait in line and pay a big cover to hear mediocre Irish bands. Near North Station, **The Harp** might be great for a beer after a game at the FleetCenter—but not for a homey get-together with your mates.

What about South Boston and Charlestown, the city's traditional Irish American enclaves? Well, Southies define a neighborhood bar as just that: a bar for the neighborhood. You may not get thrown out, but you won't exactly be welcomed with open arms either. The decor at such locals-only watering holes tends to be barebones, and the tinny music recorded. Head instead to the pubs where patrons don't aspire to public housing.

Where the kinks play... Boston's reputation as the place that put the Puritan into "puritanical" precedes it. Just look at history: When one of Salem's wives wanted to stray, the story goes, her husband had her branded a witch and burned at the stake. So, it is safe to say, the sex scene here, well, sucks. Some clubs try to hold fetish nights and welcome the latex-bound to whip each other into a frenzy, but these nights are frequently dominated only by the pathetic. That's not to say there aren't Bostonians searching for debauchery; it's just that the lascivious keep themselves, and their sex lives, underground. The best place to find like-minded kinky fellows is in the *Boston Phoenix*'s pullout Variations section. There are hundreds of ads from spankers, hookers, couples, and the curious all looking for a memorable night of X-rated excitement. (*Bay Windows* also has fairly explicit personals for men seeking men and women seeking women.) One of the few clubs in town for S&M fiends and silk-panty worshippers is **Man Ray**, in Cambridge. The scene here is likely to be composed of voluptuous secretaries who have traded their white socks and sneakers for a leather bodysuit in hopes of a Friday-night tryst. (The other nights are kinky too, but not devoted to bondage and domination.) The men here are no better—drooling pervs who line up to be whipped during the stage shows held hourly here. The techno-music at Man Ray is some of the best in town, though, so it's worth a visit just to dance and crowd-watch. One of the more authentic kink clubs is **Jacques,** a two-floor bar tucked away in Bay Village, a predominantly gay neighborhood downtown. Here transvestites blend in so well with the fag hags that even if you want to pick up a man, you might just go home with a woman by mistake. The Thursday floor show is a delight, with breeders and non-cross-dressers welcome.

Esprit de hard core... There aren't too many places left for low-life losers and sex addicts in Boston. Once full of seedy sex shops and dirty-movie houses, the Combat Zone is being squeezed out of its Washington Street wedge between downtown and Chinatown. The building that housed the ironically named Pilgrim Theater and the remaining stripper club, the **Naked i**, was slated to be demolished by early 1996, although the Naked i had plans to reopen in the area. The club may reek of stale beer and rank self-performed sex, but it has an air of authenticity, right down to the girthful biker bouncer at the door. No one quite knows what really happens in the leather room at **Ramrod**, where only leather-clad or shirtless men are welcome. Judging by the whips and dog collars adorning most of the visitors, it is probably a bit of cheek-smacking fun. But the main bar has a diverse assortment of men, either playing pool, chatting with their pals, or making eye contact with the local talent. During the summer, motorcycles line the curb, and their spike-wearing riders swagger into the unmarked doors of the Ramrod. In the winter, the same crowd travels by cab.

College cheer... There are thousands of college students in this intellectual mecca and dozens of clubs that cater to them. Strangely, there's no real Cambridge college nightclub scene—meaning that Cambridge kids may grab a bite to eat in Harvard Square, then head to Boston hot spots. Near Fenway Park in Kenmore Square, an entire street of nightclubs has cornered the college market. The first club on Lansdowne Street is **Avalon**, where Friday and Saturday nights are dedicated to students who have to study during the week. Avalon's weekend crowd—which includes suburban big hairs—dances to Top 40 hits and sips drinks titled "Sex on the Beach" or "Screaming Orgasm," ordering the expensive concoctions with a giggle and a wistful look at the cute guy or girl nearby. The next club, **Mama Kin**, is partly owned by local bad boys made good, Aerosmith. Celebrity spotting is a good fallback here when the local band downstairs in the Gothic glitz bar strains your patience. National acts play upstairs in the Playhouse less occasionally—and A-smith has been known to drop in and kick out the jams, as they say. **Venus de Milo** may be the best club on the block, with gorgeous girls writhing in cages and sexy men dancing with their rippling bulges accented in tight clothes and muscle T-shirts. **Axis** attracts the teenaged, angst-ridden crowd of misunderstood youth. On weekends, Axis is home to X-girls and skateboard rats with multicolored hair. Thursday night is prime dance time, with techno-tunes blaring downstairs and alterna-funk upstairs. **Bill's Bar** is the No. 1 place to chill out on Lansdowne Street. Soap opera fanatics descend Monday nights to watch "Melrose Place" on a wide-screen television. The crowd is otherwise down-to-earth, the scene laid back, and the staff upbeat. The best part is the music, chosen by the clientele from a jukebox chock-full of current hits and underground classics. On Sundays, live reggae bands heat up the tiny, booth-filled pub. Boylston Street near Mass. Ave. is another student hangout. Patrons of **Dad's Beantown Diner** may look underage, but a bouncer explains their youthful glow by saying Dad's is where "the well-kept rich chicks go." Definitely a place for ostentatious yet American children of privilege, Dad's is packed all weekend. Its jukebox plays dance mixes, unlike that of the **The Pour House** next door, which has more alternative rock. Another student meeting spot, The Pour House clientele look just as fresh-faced as the Dad's crowd.

One-stop hopping... For the same sort of one-stop club hopping you find on Lansdowne Street, try "The Alley" downtown, a strip of clubs along the pedestrian zone at 1 Boylston Place. If you're on the scope for explosive hairdos and leopard-skin spandex ensembles, **Zanzibar** is the place to be—the Alley's club for serious partyers. Those nostaligic for the heyday of John Travolta in *Saturday Night Fever* should come here—the guys slick back their hair with gel and bathe in Polo cologne, and the women have a penchant for snapping gum while teetering on white patent-leather pumps. Proper dress is required; gold lamé suffices as formal wear here. **The Alley Cat Lounge** attracts a baseball-cap, no-fringe crowd of preppies who drink beers and try to dance in Docksiders. Across the alley at **Avenue C**, a fantastic disc jockey plays eighties punk tunes from the Clash and the Cure along with other Brit band favorites. This scene attracts the cool, composed students in Boston from the West Coast, who know the "real" grunge scene and pull it off without body odor. The staff, however, includes some of the rudest (sorry, I mean "most authentic") people in town.

Where the jocks flex their muscles... Professional sports players have to party too, so they have carved out their own spots in town. **Daisy Buchanan's** is a Newbury

Street basement-level bar where baseball and basketball players, and the occasional football giant, hang out in nondescript wooden booths, play pinball machines, and scarf up free hot dogs on weekends. Famous for its bar-room brawls, Daisy's is still a popular haunt. Sometimes our sports heroes spread out to the chain restaurant and bar around the corner, **Whiskey's**, which is just a larger version of Daisy's. **The Roxy** on Tremont Street is another pro-athlete haunt, especially during its Thursday "rhythm and soul" nights, although it too has hosted some high-profile altercations. Sports stars usually hang in the club's VIP room upstairs, but the guards for the VIPs are easily charmed into giving access.

Where the girls are... While there is only a smattering of dedicated lesbian spots, there are dozens of gay-friendly scenes for girl-meets-girl scoping (see "Where the boys are" below). **Coco's** is the last women-only bar, located in an isolated part of the city, on Massachusetts Avenue near Roxbury, but the chicks here are worth the hike. You won't find their diversity, or their numbers, anywhere else. The patrons range from lipstick lesbians to diesel dykes. Sunday nights, lesbians of all sartorial stripes can opt for **Esmé** at the swanky **Mercury Bar** in the Theater District, or head to Inman Square in Cambridge for a tea dance (a euphemism inspired by blue laws—the usual dance music and booze are served) at **Ryles Jazz Club**, which also holds **Fusion**, a sapphic dance party on Saturdays. Upstairs is dark and neon; downstairs, wooden tables look out onto a busy street. Jamaica Plain, Hyde Park, and Cambridge's Central and Inman Squares are neighborhoods where the coffee bars are often percolating with women seeking women.

Where the boys are... Gay clubs have the best dance floors in Boston—no ifs, ands, or buts. **Chaps**, a Back Bay oasis halfway between the Fenway and downtown clusters of clubs, has the most interesting scene going. Most of its patrons are sculpted, bare-chested heart-throbs wearing the latest fishnet or metal fashions. The dancing here is phenomenal. A great pickup place for bisexuals, Chap's is also popular with straights, thanks to its throbbing techno beat and vintage dance tracks. A four-floor nightlife emporium with a roof-deck bar in the summer, Back Bay's **Quest** is a perfect spot for lipstick lesbians and stern dykes alike, who dance cheek to chic with an "in" crowd of boy toys. **Club Cafe** in the South End is part eatery, part nightclub, all gay. It's an upscale spot where couples compete with their friends over whose date has the best biceps. It's a favorite for first dates or special occasions. **The Paradise** in Cambridge (not to be confused with the rock club of the same name in Boston) is popular with closeted gays because of its darkened windows and dimly lit entrance. The Paradise has the most diverse clientele in town, and plays good music. On Thursdays Central Square's **Man Ray** has its "campus" night, which is rife with pretty boys and their manly, S&M-crazed counterparts. **The Safari Club** in the South End is the last of the gay bath houses, where men can frolic in a gym and showers. The crowd at the Safari Club is diverse in age and size; you don't need to be a member, you just need to have one (i.e., men only). **The Boston Eagle**, a dark, dank hangout for an older crowd on Tremont Street, is one of the friendliest spots for strangers—the bartenders always recognize new faces and will introduce you to regulars. **Luxor**, a video bar for a mostly male crowd in Bay Village, has pub grub downstairs and MTV-like videos blaring from TV screens in the rooms upstairs. One room is full of older queens, one is reserved for muscle-shirted young men, and another is strictly for scoping potential significant others. The biggest gay scene around is at **Avalon** in Kenmore Square on Sunday nights, which attracts so many outrageous divas that they have extended the dance floor into the club next door, **Axis.** The oldest gay club in Boston, as the campy decor attests, is **Playland** in Chinatown—it embraces the piano bar and other clichés with relish.

Nonclub cruising... If you're not the club type but definitely want to same-sex cruise, take a walk through the South End neighborhood. The cafes here are an escape from smoky, sweaty discos, but still have people to pick up. **Mildred's** and **Francesca's**, both on Tremont Street, have the best coffees, and the best crowds for cruisings. Most of the eateries in the South End have hot wait staffs as well, like **Moka Cafe** around the corner, more a funky West Coast hangout than East Coast cafe. People congregate here for cookies and cappuccinos before launching into clubland. The Fenway is another neighborhood with a high pickup potential, from cafes to the reeds in the park.

Clubs for weekend warriors... On Saturday nights, Boston nightclubs are notably devoid of urban dwellers due to the suburban weekend warriors. These people have one purpose for coming into the big city: to party. And they take up all the space usually occupied by city people. Among these clubs is the Theater District's **Mercury Bar**, one of the few in town where suits are required. The Mercury Bar's bar stools are full of impeccably coiffed people, and the dance floor packed with clumsy white people, but it's still a fun place to see and be seen. (To be heard is another matter—the music can be ear-poundingly loud.) At **Il Panino** in the Financial District, a five-floor entertainment emporium, the crowd is upscale—sometimes older divorcees or young women looking for a generous older gentleman. The food is exquisite (and expensive) in both establishments.

In the neighborhood... Boston has always had an inferiority complex about its clubs. Residents are incessant whiners, complaining about the 2am curfew and the lack of really wild nightlife. But there is one thing that Boston can boast about, and that's the abundance of great neighborhood bars. These neighborhood spots are small, some too tiny to handle crowds, but there are some that welcome strangers, such as **The Cantab Lounge** in Cambridge's Central Square. From the outside, the Cantab looks dark and dreary—a neon light flickers halfheartedly in front—though the nightlife inside is anything but drab. More than a club, it's a community, the kind of place where everyone knows your name after a single visit. The Cantab is Boston's real "Cheers," but instead of bantering about sports, the regulars discuss politics and academics or check out poetry slams downstairs. There is live music every night, sometimes folk, sometimes blues, but on weekends regulars know they will hear the ever-popular crooning of Little Joe Cook and the Thrillers, who have headlined at the Cantab for 15 years. **Wally's** boasts one of the few integrated working-class crowds around. It's a South End hangout for Berklee music students and neighborhood old-timers, who squish themselves into the tight space to hear local jazz or the occasional big-name act. **Grendel's Den** in Harvard Square is a haven for nostalgic hippies and beatniks. Its cellar bar comes complete with a working fireplace and flannel-wearing crowd.

You'll find stimulating conversation and good brews. At **The Delux Cafe** in the South End, Elvis busts and knick-knacks from the sixties and seventies clutter the walls. The crowd of rockers and barflies is gay and straight, working-class and white-collar, and always friendly.

Clubbing al fresco... Although it's a dance club year-round, **Quest** in Back Bay attracts large crowds in summer to its roof deck, above a video bar and two levels of dancing (house and disco). Straight nights are Tuesdays, Wednesdays, Fridays, and Sundays, although there's some crossover on the remaining gay nights. **The Rattlesnake Bar and Grill** near the Public Garden has a long line of students and young office workers snaking out of it in summer, waiting to drink beer and maybe eat cheap Tex-Mex food on the roof deck or at the noisy, brightly colored bar.

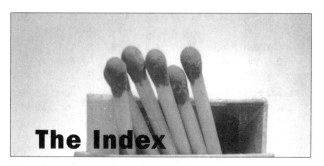

The Index

Alley Cat Lounge. Part of an alley of nightclubs at 1 Boylston Place, this has the most casual dress and basic pub grub. Lines on weekends, but it's big enough to move around inside.... *Tel 617/351–2510. 1 Boylston Place. Boylston T stop. Cover.*

Avalon. The biggest nightclub in Boston, squeezing in 1,500. An eclectic schedule of entertainment includes alternative and college-radio favorites (see Entertainment). Adjacent to the dance club Axis.... *Tel 617/262–2424. 15 Lansdowne St. Kenmore T stop. Cover.*

Avenue C. This club is for early Cure fans, or anyone else who longs for the days of eighties punk and real alternative rock.... *Tel 617/423–3832. 5 Boylston Place. Boylston T stop. Cover.*

Axis. Axis books local bands and the occasional big-name act, and has packed dance parties.... *Tel 617/262–2437. 13 Lansdowne St. Kenmore T stop. Cover.*

Bay Tower Room. Leave the jeans and denim jacket in your hotel room; spiff up for dinner and cocktail music high above Boston's downtown and waterfront.... *Tel 617/723–1666. 60 State St. State or Government Center T stops. Cover charge after 9 pm.*

Bill's Bar. Tiny, friendly, packed with booths, and a choice jukebox. What more do you need?.... *Tel 617/421–9678. 5 ½ Lansdowne St. Kenmore T stop. Cover.*

The Black Rose. Despite the Celtic fiddler and some great local Irish bands, it's hard to ignore the Faneuil Hall crowd. If the tourists don't get you, the beer nuts will.... *Tel 617/742–2286. 160 State St. State or Government Center T stops. Cover most nights.*

The Boston Eagle. The friendliest gay bar in town.... *Tel 617/542–4494. 520 Tremont St. Back Bay Station.*

The Brendan Behan. A proven Irish pub, this Jamaica Plain watering hole is perfect for a taste of local flavor....*Tel 617/522–5386. 378 Centre St. Stony Brook T stop. Cover some nights.*

Cantab Lounge. A local bar for the bohemian set.... *Tel 617/354–2685. 738 Massachusetts Ave., Cambridge. Central T stop. Cover some nights.*

The Causeway. The tiny room is barely recognizable from the street; look for the burly bouncer outside who will lead the way upstairs.... *Tel 617/367–4958. 65 Causeway St. North Station T stop. Cover some nights.*

Chaps. The hottest gay dance club in town.... *Tel 617/266–7778. 27 Huntington Ave. Prudential T stop. Cover.*

Club Cafe. A trendy spot for gays and lesbians. The food served in the front is pricey (but tasty); the video bar in the back is a prime place for same-sex singles to meet.... *Tel 617/536–0966. 209 Columbus Ave. Back Bay Station.*

Coco's. The sole women-only club in Boston has two floors offering eclectic dance and live music.... *Tel 617/427–7807. 965 Massachusetts Ave. No T access; valet parking available. Cover.*

Dad's Beantown Diner. The closest thing to a teenybopper hangout in Boston.... *Tel 617/296–3237. 911 Boylston St. Hynes Convention Center T stop. Cover.*

Daisy Buchanan's. A basement bar on oh-so-trendy Newbury Street; great for spotting local sports celebs....*Tel 617/247–8516. 240A Newbury St. Copley T stop.*

The Delux Cafe. A local bar and eatery in the South End. Designated drivers get free sodas.... *Tel 617/338–5258. 100 Chandler St. Back Bay Station.*

The Druid. A tiny, thriving neighborhood joint, the Druid is Inman Square's after-work hangout bar.... *Tel 617/497–0965. 1357 Cambridge St., Cambridge. Central T stop. No cover most nights.*

The Eire Pub. An authentic Irish pub in a largely Irish-immigrant-populated section of Dorchester. No telephone number listed—the pub has a pay phone. *379 Dorchester Ave. Adams Corner T stop.*

Esmé. Sunday-night lesbian dance party at the opulent, wooded Mercury Bar.... *Tel 617/482–7799. 3 Boylston Place. Boylston T stop. Cover.*

Europa. This club tries hard to live up to its name. It's big with a huge crowd of sophisticated Asians, some from nearby Chinatown.... *Tel 617/482–3939. 51 Stuart St., Chinatown T stop. Cover.*

Francesca's. A cozy South End espresso bar and cafe, Francesca's is a good staging ground for gay club crawling. If you don't have a date, feel free to read or hang out with the wait staff.... *Tel 617/482–9026. 564 Tremont St. Back Bay Station.*

Fusion. The comfy Ryles Jazz Club in Inman Square turns one floor into a club for lesbians Saturday and Sunday nights....

Tel 617/876–9330. 212 Hampshire St., Cambridge. Central T stop. Cover.

The Green Dragon Tavern. One of Faneuil Hall's best bars. A real Irish scene....Tel 617/367–0055. 11 Marshall St. Government Center T stop. Cover some nights.

Grendel's Den. With an eclectic menu, perfect hot apple cider, and no cover, Grendel's Den is packed almost every night.... Tel 617/491–1160. 89 Winthrop St., Cambridge. Harvard T stop.

The Harp. The Harp sometimes books overseas bands, like Ireland's Commitments. Expect throngs....Tel 617/742–1010. 85 Causeway St. North Station. Cover.

Il Panino. No, really, it's classy. The first floor has an Italian bistro, the second offers highly recommended dining, the third floor is a deluxe jazz bar, and the fourth and fifth—what else?—a dance club. Boston's one-stop night on the town.... Tel 617/338–1000. 295 Franklin St. State T stop. No cover.

The Irish Embassy Pub. An Irish pub reminiscent of those on the Emerald Isle. There's usually a line to get in.... Tel 617/742–6618. 234 Friend St. North Station. Cover.

Jacques. Part nightclub, part pub, and always populated by divas and drag queens....Tel 617/426–8902. 79 Broadway. Boylston or New England Medical Center T stops. Cover some nights.

Joy. At this dance club, Daddy-subsidized gold cards are preferred.... Tel 617/338–6999. 533 Washington St. Downtown Crossing T stop. Cover.

The Kells. A hotspot on the weekends, this Boston Irish bar attracts Americans along with the Allston–Brighton locals.... Tel 617/782–9082. 161 Brighton Ave. Harvard Avenue T stop (Green Line, B spur). Cover some nights.

Luxor. A gay video bar in the Theater District. We'll assume the address and last four digits of the phone number are a coincidence.... Tel 617/423–6969. 69 Church St. Boylston or New England Medical Center T stops.

Mama Kin. A rock tourist destination to rival Hard Rock Cafe.... *Tel 617/536–2100. 36 Lansdowne St. Kenmore T stop. Cover.*

Man Ray. One of the best dance floors in town. On Thursday nights it's gay and called Campus. On Friday nights leather-and-lace-clad lonely hearts flock in for a sexual fetish night.... *Tel 617/864–0400, 21 Brookline St., Cambridge. Central T stop. Cover most nights.*

M80. Big with Eurotrash, M80 is so popular its owners just expanded the dance floor.... *Tel 617/562–8800. 969 Commonwealth Ave. Pleasant Street T stop (Green Line, B spur). Cover.*

The Mercury Bar. It lures after-work suits during the week and suburbanites on the weekends. Hoity-toity restaurant and tapas bar in the front.... *Tel 617/482–7799. 116 Boylston St. Boylston T stop.*

The Middle East. Boston's best club for live bands. Three stages named Upstairs, Downstairs, and the Bakery hold an eclectic mix of music, poetry slams, and fledgling theater. Belly dancing, often a feature upstairs in the Bakery, and the creditable Middle Eastern cuisine in the restaurant make it a bustling hangout.... *Tel 617/492–9181. 472 Massachusetts Ave., Cambridge. Central T stop. Cover in some rooms.*

Mildred's. Another South End cafe with tasty food and good coffee. Club crawlers meet here and then hit the town.... *Tel 617/426–0008. 552 Tremont St. Back Bay Station.*

Moka Cafe. The Moka Cafe has crunchy-granola eats but a trendy crowd.... *Tel 617/424–7768. 130 Dartmouth St., Back Bay Station.*

Mr. Dooley's Tavern. A downtown pub populated by an authentic Irish set and run by a Dubliner.... *Tel 617/338–5656. 77 Broad St. State T stop.*

Naked i. Topless, bottomless, and frequented by scuzzy onlookers, the Naked i now represents Boston's entire red-light district—if it's found a new home by this printing.... *Tel. 617/426–7462. 666 Washington St., Chinatown T stop. Drink minimum.*

BOSTON | **NIGHTLIFE**

Ned Kelly's. A Dorchester pub, packed on weekends when it bills local Celtic acts.... *Tel 617/282–4708. 1236 Dorchester Ave. Fields Corner T stop.*

The Paradise. In the discreet darkness of this gay club, dancing to hard-core techno, strip shows, and frequent appearances by porn stars urge indiscretion.... *Tel 617/864–4130. 180 Massachusetts Ave., Cambridge. Central T stop. Cover.*

Playland. An old-style, campy gay club, it has a reputation as a "wrinkle room," but young explorers can be found among the kitsch.... *Tel 617/338–7254. 21 Essex St., Chinatown T stop.*

The Pour House. Avoid this bar if you don't want to have a drunken freshman hitting on you. Go there if you do.... *Tel 617/236–1767. 909 Boylston St. Hynes Convention Center T stop. Cover some nights.*

The Purple Shamrock. If you want to see a barroom brawl, to the sounds of a mediocre Irish band, you might get lucky here.... *Tel 617/227–2060. 1 Union Street. Government Center T stop. Cover.*

Quest. Quest has a fantastic dance floor, a live rock basement, a roof deck, and a video bar all in one building. Its crowd is postmodern eclectic—gay, lesbian, straight, and everything in between.... *Tel 617/424–7747. 1270 Boylston St. Kenmore T stop. Cover some nights.*

Ramrod. From the outside, Ramrod looks like a mean biker bar thanks to the line of motorcycles parked outside, even in the off-season. But the bikers here are studded, leatherized, and cute—this is a bar for S&M leathermen.... *Tel 617/266–2986. 1254 Boylston St. Kenmore T stop. No cover most nights.*

The Rathskeller. The Rat is the last punk scene in Boston. Listen to bands downstairs, upstairs....*Tel 617/536–2750. 528 Commonwealth Ave. Kenmore T stop. Cover for cellar.*

The Rattlesnake Bar and Grill. A noisy, after-work Tex-Mex bar with many types of margaritas, and many young Bostonians waiting to get in. In summer the roof deck adds to its popularity.... *Tel 617/859–8555. 382 Boylston St. Arlington T stop.*

The Roxy. One of the most popular and biggest nightclubs in town. On Thursday nights, the scene is mostly hip-hop; on Friday nights, the club is dedicated to the international crowd. Saturday nights are known for the sports stars and celebrities who congregate in the VIP room upstairs.... *Tel 617/338–7699. 279 Tremont St. Boylston T stop. Cover.*

Ryles Jazz Club. Two stories, two stages in Inman Square. Contemporary jazz acts, lesbian dance parties (See Entertainment for more information).... *Tel 617/876–9330. 212 Hampshire St., Cambridge. No nearby T stop.*

The Safari Club. The last gay bathhouse in town heavily promotes safer sex; condoms are abundant.... *Tel 617/292–0011. 90 Wareham St., Back Bay Station. Cover.*

Top of the Hub. The view from above, not the lite–jazz music, is the point here. After you've had a few, the elevator ride down from the 52nd floor may be less fun than it was coming up. Jackets and ties recommended for men; collared shirts required. The tables in the restaurant have a $12 minimum, but there's no cover for the lounge.... *Tel 617/536–1775. Prudential Center, Prudential T.*

Venus de Milo. A Lansdowne Street hotspot, Venus de Milo is a great spot to people watch and dance.... *Tel 617/421–9678. 11 Lansdowne St. Kenmore T stop. Cover.*

Wally's. A Beantown favorite. Some of the best live jazz and blues in town.... *Tel 617/424–1408. 427 Massachusetts Ave. Massachusetts Avenue T stop.*

Whiskey's. Cheap eats and draft beers. On weekends, students line up to hang out.... *Tel 617/262–5551. 885 Boylston St. Copley T stop.*

Zanzibar. On the weekends the dance floor and the upstairs pool bar are packed full of suburban gals, their hairdos, and the cologne-drenched men who love them. On Tuesday nights Zanzibar has a European scene.... *Tel 617/231–2560. 1 Boylston Place. Boylston T stop. Cover.*

enterta

7

inment

There's a great
joke in the movie
Spinal Tap when
the manager of
the eponymous
heavy-metal band
tells the hapless

musicians they won't be playing Boston. Not to worry, he assures them: "It's not a big college town." Of course, the 50-plus institutions of higher learning in the area have long fueled a thriving rock scene. Not only has the Hub spawned such Stone Age hit-makers as Aerosmith, Boston, and The Cars—its indie scene also gave us underground demigods Mission of Burma and the Pixies. More recently, we have Boston to thank for Juliana Hatfield, Letters to Cleo, and the Lemonheads.

Despite the tradition of dueling guitars, Boston's musical engine really runs on classical gas, thanks again to the schools of music and conservatories, and to Brahmin tradition, which has always sniffed at anything new—and savored anything cheap, like a free recital. Even if you have to pay for your listening pleasure, the acoustics and ambience of the city's concert halls can help ensure that you get your money's worth. And who can overlook the flagship of city orchestras, the frequently televised Boston Pops? Fans of other musical genres—not just rock, but also jazz, blues,and folk—are equally loyal and numerous, meaning hopes for last-minute tickets are often dashed. Where jazz scenes have calcified in other cities, the presence of the Berklee School of Music keeps Boston's relatively young. Blues and folk audiences tend to be out of college, although many have yet to realize it 20 years later.

With so much slavish devotion to music, duly reflected in local media, Boston's homegrown theater and dance scene have suffered somewhat by comparative neglect; the fact that Boston doesn't provide funds means shoestring budgets are very tightly laced, and there's an attitude that New York City, four hours away, must have siphoned off many of the best talents. Huntington Theatre Company, one of the two leading regional theaters, does its casting in New York. But despite their lower profile within the city, many of the artists who do make their living in Boston—at places like the Boston Ballet and the American Repertory Theatre in Cambridge—are accomplished on a national scale and worth checking out, particularly if you can score half-price tickets. (The lack of arts funding means generally higher ticket prices than in other parts of the country; see "Getting Tickets," below.) The scruffy Boston Center for the Arts in the South End is a burgeoning off-off-Broadway venue for adventurous and experimental drama where the tickets are always cheap. And the Theater District still lives up to its name, hosting road shows and pre-Broadway touring tryouts of everything from Andrew Lloyd Webber to *Angels in America*, and dance troupes from Martha Graham's to Bill T. Jones'.

Sources

The *Boston Globe*'s Thursday Calendar and Sunday Arts sections have extensive entertainment listings for Boston and a large area beyond; the *Globe*'s Friday Music section offers lightly opinionated Critics' Tips for the week ahead in classical, rock, jazz, and alternative rock. The local contrarian weekly, the *Boston Phoenix*, published on Thursdays, provides complete urban listings and more ads with concert announcements than the *Globe*. **WFNX** (101.7 FM), the *Phoenix*'s radio station, is a good source of alternative rock concert updates; it also stages free summer concerts by bands such as Green Day. **WBOS** (92.9 FM) provides a wider-ranging rock concert hotline (tel 617/787–0929). For theater, if you're curious about a show that's already been reviewed in the *Globe*, check the *Phoenix*'s convenient Play by Play summaries. The critics, some of whom have drifted among the *Globe*, the *Phoenix*, and other local papers, tend not to be overly kind to either touring or local productions. Not so for the entertainment critics on Boston's incredibly provincial television stations, who seem to have a good time wherever they go.

How out of date is the MTA song?

Contrary to the folk singer's chestnut "The MTA," Boston's subway system is run by MBTA and is known as the T. Charlie, the song's hero who had "to ride forever beneath the streets of Boston" after the subway fare was raised, would find that more than the name of the T has changed. You may remember that he paid 10 cents to get on at Kendall Square, wanted to transfer to Jamaica Plain, but was a nickel short. Stuck on the train, he was thrown sandwiches by his wife at the Scollay Square station.... Well, sorry Charlie. These days he'd have to pay 85 cents for a token to board the T at the Red Line's Kendall Station. His route would change too. For starters, seedy Scollay Square was torn down in the 1960s to create the architectural wasteland known as Government Center. And as far as that sandwich goes, his wife would be more likely to throw him a pastry from the ubiquitous Dunkin' Donuts subway kiosks. (Visitors from Washington, D.C., San Francisco, and other cities with modern subways are often surprised to learn that eating and drinking is still permitted on the T. How else could we feed the mice that scurry along the Red Line tracks at Park Street?)

BOSTON | ENTERTAINMENT

Getting Tickets

BosTix (tel 617/723–5181) offers same-day, half-price, cash-only tickets to performances of music, theater, dance, and opera; it also has information on and advance tickets for other events, including sports. The BosTix kiosks are at Faneuil Hall (Tue–Sat 11–6, Sun noon–4) and Copley Square near Boylston and Dartmouth Streets (Mon–Sat 10–6, Sun 11–4). They're also outlets for **Ticketmaster** (tel 617/931–2000); despite hefty service charges, it's the best way to guarantee tickets to a concert since many box offices have limited hours or may not sell any seats until the day of the show, when a sellout is already likely. When desperate, try your hotel's concierge. Scalpers exist, of course, as they do everywhere. Check the classifieds in the *Globe* or the ads in the *Yellow Pages* under "Ticket brokers," businesses who pay people to stand in line at the 130 or so Ticketmaster outlets. Their prices are inflated enough that one local promoter has announced plans to create a rival ticket agency that will challenge Ticketmaster and make scalping more difficult. If you do buy tickets from a scalper on-site, above all be discreet—one property owner may look the other way, another may bar the door.

The Lowdown

I hear a symphony... Rarely staid Seiji Ozawa conducts the Boston Symphony Orchestra in—where else?—**Symphony Hall**, autumn through spring. In late spring (overlapping with the BSO) and summer, the hall's outstanding acoustics reverberate with the sound of the Boston Pops, now led by even less staid Keith Lockhart. BSO tickets can range from $20 to $70, but the sound is still fine in the cheaper second balcony seats, where you sit underneath the Renaissance-style statues set in niches near the elaborately paneled ceiling. A limited number of these seats are also available as same-day rush tickets at the box office on Tuesdays, Thursdays, and Fridays for under $10. Be aware that subscribers have generally held the best seats for generations, but at least theirs won't be anymore comfortable than yours. Pops tickets, which often sell out weeks in advance, don't have rush discounts but are much cheaper to start: in the mid-$30 range for tables and chairs near the front, down to the low teens for the second balcony. The Pops tradition of a week of free outdoor shows in summer, including its famous Fourth of July concert with fireworks, continues at the **Hatch Shell** on the Charles River Esplanade. The Pops's Independence Day crowd starts swarming that morning; if you're more into the music than the pyrotechnics, go to the rehearsal the evening of July 3. If you're more into fireworks, consider the Community Boating boathouse on the Esplanade, where you hear the performance via speakers but have a spectacular view of the fireworks afterward. The boathouse (tel 617/523-1038) sells advance tickets, which include a picnic dinner for this fund-raiser, and usually also has same-day tickets. The less renowned Boston Philharmonic, conducted by Benjamin Zander, has the advantage of playing in the New England Conservatory's smaller but acoustically perfect **Jordan Hall**, a 1903 gem that underwent large-scale restoration in 1995. Like Symphony Hall, it has a magnificent pipe organ at the rear of the stage, while Jordan's warmer interior has jade green walls with gilded accents and an off-white ceiling. The Philharmonic also plays in the Gothic, dark-wood Sanders Theatre in Harvard University's Memorial Hall, another place that oozes tradition. Since the Philharmonic doesn't have the international cachet of Ozawa and the celebrity soloists who join him or the TV glow of the Pops and telegenic Lockhart, tickets are cheaper and easier to get. Like the BSO, the programs include modern classical music as well as warhorses.

Chamber stars... The venerable Handel & Haydn Society, founded in 1815, performs instrumental and vocal works at **Symphony Hall**, as do subsets of the BSO and the Bank of Boston celebrity series, which brings in your Itzhak Perlmans, your Vienna Choir Boys, your sexy young violinists du jour. Gisèle Ben-Dor conducts the well-respected Pro Arte Chamber Orchestra at **Sanders Theatre**, a charming Gothic Revival auditorium in Harvard's ornate Memorial Hall. Campus halls and museums are another font of moderately priced, high-quality music in attractive settings. In Cambridge you'll find MIT's modern **Kresge Auditorium**, Sanders and Longy School of Music's intimate **Pickman Recital Hall**. Popular Boston venues include the Museum of Fine Arts's **Remis Auditorium** and

ENTERTAINMENT | BOSTON

Boston University's **Tsai Performance Center**, home to contemporary-music specialists Boston Musica Viva. A quintessential Boston tradition is weekend concerts in the rather somber **Tapestry Room** at the Isabella Stewart Gardner mansion (now a museum).

The line on choruses... Boston Cecilia has made its voices heard since 1875; it performs at **Jordan Hall**. Chorus Pro Musica performs with local orchestras at their regular venues, and stages independent programs of new and established choral works directed by Jeffrey Rink. For an offbeat option, get yourself to **Emmanuel Church** in Back Bay on time: It presents a Bach cantata every Sunday.

What's opera, doc?... It's a conundrum how a city that brims with music and theater can be so lacking in theater-with-music, a k a opera. At press time, Sarah Caldwell's Opera Company of Boston was restoring its **Opera House** after a period of insolvency, but breaths were not being held for a full season in 1996. In this climate of deprivation, the Boston Lyric Opera seems like a bounty. Its short runs at the partially restored **Emerson Majestic Theatre** sell out quickly; you can always try calling for returned tickets.

In (rock) concert... Let's face it, if they're really big, they probably won't play Boston in the summer—they'll be at Great Woods, closer to Providence, Rhode Island, although that could change now that the new Boston Garden, the **FleetCenter**, has air conditioning. But groups humble enough for 4,800 fans tops and who don't need stage dives or mosh pits for inspiration might play **Harborlights**, a beautiful white tent on the waterfront. Indoors, the less staid, 2,800-seat **Orpheum Theatre** has hosted the Cranberries, Chris Isaak, Sheryl Crow and other acts from the white side of Top 40. The 1,400-seat **Berklee Performance Center** brings in top-flight jazz artists and world-music artists to edify students at the Berklee School of Music and to entertain the rest of us. Local radio stations often mount free rock shows in summer at the **Hatch Shell**; check the newspaper for announcements. The 900-seat **Somerville Theater**, just off the Red Line, frequently rolls up its movie screen to present world- and folk-music artists. Ticketmaster handles virtually all advance sales. On the more intimate and musically adventurous club front, a few players dominate. At a capacity of 1,500, the cutting-edge **Avalon** is the biggest. The light and sound equipment is first-rate, but you'll still want to bring earplugs if you value your hearing. A balcony provides mosh-free viewing, and the long bars on the lower level are also safe hangouts. Tickets are only sold here on the day of the show; otherwise, use Ticketmaster. Down the Green Line in Boston University territory, **Paradise** is big on alternative acts and cult stars; like Avalon, it is attached to a dance club and tends toward early show times to make room for dance madness later at night (for more on both clubs, see Nightlife). Grungy, bare-bones **Local 186** in Allston features local rock and reggae acts, with occasional just-breaking national bands (when they're all still packed in one tour van).

All that jazz (and blues)... For jazz clubs, Cambridge is the front-runner with the two-story **Ryles** in Inman Square (see Nightlife) and the Charles Hotel's elegantly spare but pricey **Regattabar**. In Boston's Brighton area, away from the tourist sites, the newly expanded, comfortable **Scullers** also books nationally recognized acts. If you're feeling blue, you can always try down-to-earth **Harper's Ferry** in Allston, but the best bet is to head to Cambridge's **House of Blues**, part of an L.A.-based chain cofounded by Dan Aykroyd and a Hard Rock Cafe tycoon. **Johnny D's**, convenient to the T in Somerville, has a quiet brunch but swings in the evenings; cover charges are often low.

Just plain folk... The ratio of folk singers to folk clubs is lopsided in the Hub: **Club Passim** in Harvard Square is about it, and it almost closed in 1995. Volunteers now help operate the small smoke- and alcohol-free club, with a nightly lineup of national, regional, and local folkies, plus poets and storytellers.

Broadway babies... Boston is no longer the premier Broadway tryout town, but now and then a production still tests its wings in the old Theater District, almost always at the opulent **Colonial Theatre**. Though the interior of this 1900 playhouse has been lavishly restored, long-legged types will want to avoid the cramped balcony. The Colonial also shelters touring shows that soared on the Great White Way, such as *Angels in America* and *Kiss of the Spider Woman*. The even more opulent and cavernous **Wang Center for the Performing Arts** is a glamorous nest for hoary Broadway revivals such as *Grease* and *Jesus Christ Superstar*. The **Shubert Theatre** across the street has been dark more often than not recently; it's seen *Jelly's Last Jam* and other Broadway musicals on its stage. For all three, prepare to pay from $35 to $60 a seat; a few tickets may show up at BosTix.

High drama... A Boston standby, Peter Altman's sedate yet accomplished Huntington Theatre Company is in residence at the slightly worn but still elegant **Boston University Theatre** near Symphony Hall. Robert Brustein's American Repertory Theatre, across the river at Harvard's **Loeb Drama Center**, is nationally know for its weird takes on classics and elaborate no-holds-barred designs. Shows are in fall, late spring, and summer; its wintertime New Stages series moves to the **Hasty Pudding** and elsewhere. Both companies are highly regarded; both frequently make half-price tickets available to BosTix—take advantage or pony up as much as $40 a seat. Or you can check out the Theater District's **Charles Playhouse**, an off-Broadway-size house recently remodeled by the performance-art wild boys known as Blue Man Group for their eponymous show. The smaller **Lyric Stage** in the Back Bay also offers good value for the money (under $20 a ticket) with a company heavy into British comedy—Shaw, Wilde, Coward, etc. Both also use BosTix.

The next stage... The **Boston Center for the Arts** in the South End is where you'll find the bold and the budget-minded among Boston's smaller companies performing in three venues: the 140-seat BCA Theatre, the 90-seat Black Box Theatre, and the 40-seat Leland Center (a real hole in the wall). Notable presenters include Centastage (professional, community-minded), Speak-Easy Stage Company (musicals and comedies), Sugan Theatre (Irish and Irish American works), and the earnestly political Theater Offensive (gay, lesbian, bisexual, and "transgender" agitprop). Triangle Theatre is the more mainstream gay and lesbian company, also performing in the South End in the upstairs **Paramount Penthouse Theater**. If you enjoy watching ranting conceptual artists accompanied by TV screens, check out **Mobius** near Fort Point Channel, where a burgeoning art scene has taken hold.

Dinner and a show... Don't feel obligated, but restaurant-and-hotel package deals abound for the long-running *Shear Madness* at the **Charles Playhouse**—a crash course in Boston stereotypes. It's equally unessential to attend the various mock Italian weddings and Irish wakes staged around town. Instead, if it's summer, pack a picnic, hail a cab, and head outdoors to the **Publick Theatre** on the Charles River in Brighton. Though the productions vary in quality—there's one Shakespeare play and a raft of musicals like *Sweeney Todd* and *Anything Goes* every year—the theater kindly provides bug spray and sells a few refreshments.

Men in tights... The Boston Ballet produces a lavish, beloved *Nutcracker* and more ambitious fare at the **Wang Center**, where big-name visiting companies also perform. Jose Mateo's Ballet Theatre of Boston, smaller but adventurous, takes the stage at the **Emerson Majestic Theatre**, also a stage for other local and touring companies. Among modern dancers, Beth Soll and Company stand out, performing at a variety of Boston and Cambridge venues—including MIT's **Kresge Auditorium**—all year round.

Comedy tonight... Well-known comedians such as Rosie O'Donnell, Judy Tenuta, and Kevin Meaney come to the **Comedy Connection** in tourist central, a k a Faneuil Hall Marketplace. The summertime **Boston Harbor Comedy Cruises** find another way for comedians to make waves.

The silver screen... Get your tickets early to avoid disappointment at the movies in Boston and Cambridge; there are a lot more cineasts than cinemas. On the Boston side of the river, you'll find foreign and indepen-

ENTERTAINMENT | BOSTON

dent films at the **Sony Nickelodeon**, the Museum of Fine Arts' **Remis Auditorium** and (in T-accessible Brookline) the Hub's only nonprofit, independent movie house, **Coolidge Corner Theater**. Cambridge has the **Sony Harvard Square** multiplex and the **Harvard Film Archive**. The restored landmark (but still shabby) **Brattle Theatre** offers ever-changing double bills of art movies. For first-run megaplex fare, try Harvard Square or Boston's **Sony Copley Place**. In summer, the outdoor **Hatch Shell** has free movies on Friday nights; bring something to sit on. Or just luxuriate indoors at the **Wang Center**, which, harkening back to the theater's original function, offers a classic-film series. For movie listings, the best is the *Globe*.

Virtual playtime... **Jillian's Boston**, at the corner of low-rent, loud-music Lansdowne and Ipswich Streets, used to be an upscale billiards club. Now it's a virtual-reality play-room for regressive adults, with high-tech simulations of car racing, golf, and, yes, a pinball machine—as experienced from the inside. Unlike other arcades, children are allowed only on weekend afternoons and must be accompanied by an adult.

The big game... You're too late to see the Celtics on the parquet or the Bruins on the ice of the beloved, battered Boston Garden, torn down in 1995, but just a few feet away is the new **FleetCenter**, which promises to offer air-conditioning but no less fanatic spectators for basketball, hockey, and the occasional "Disney on Ice"-style entertainment (don't forget, this is Nancy Kerrigan country). There's talk about building a new domed stadium downtown; for now, you can still see the Red Sox play baseball day and night in outdoor **Fenway Park** (home of the home-run defeating Green Monster in left field) and the New England Patriots pass the pigskin 45 minutes south in **Foxboro Stadium**. The FleetCenter and Fenway Park are on the T; you'll have to drive to Foxboro Stadium, where the fans are said to be more aggressive than the players.

The Index

Berklee Performance Center. A long, multitiered hall. The world's best jazz, world-beat, and every other kind of player show their chops.... *Tel 617/266–1400, ext. 261 (box office), 617/266–7455 (recorded concert info). 136 Massachusetts Ave. Hynes Convention Center/ICA T stop. Box office open 10–6, closed Sun.*

Boston Center for the Arts. This brick complex in the South End houses three small theaters and the large-domed Cyclorama, originally built to house a circular mural. Local theater companies vie for residencies but may also rent performance space. Tickets are generally $15 or less, sold cash-only at the door and through BosTix.... *Tel 617/426–7700 (recorded events), 617/426–5000 (office). 539 Tremont St. Back Bay Station.*

Boston Harbor Comedy Cruises. The ship leaves Long Wharf on Thursday evenings in summer with stand-up comics on board and a cash bar.... *Tel 617/524–2500. 1 Long Wharf. Aquarium T stop.*

Boston University Theatre. The 850-seat Greek Revival theater is a little worn and the balcony (where BosTix seats tend to be) steep, but for the Huntington Theatre Company it's home.... *Tel 617/266–0800. 264 Huntington Ave. Symphony T stop. No summer season.*

Brattle Theatre. Opened in 1890, the downstairs theater served many purposes before becoming an art movie house in the Fifties. Comfort is not of the essence.... *Tel 617/876–6837 (recorded schedule), 617/876–6838 (office). 40 Brattle St. Harvard T stop.*

Charles Playhouse. Downstairs, pile in to watch the tourist-luring, murder-mystery farce *Shear Madness*. Upstairs is the less frequently used main stage, booked by touring companies and debuting productions.... *Tel 617/426–5225 (Shear Madness), 617/426–6912 (main stage). 74 Warrenton St. Boylston T stop.*

Club Passim. No smoking, no alcohol, and very sincere. A subterranean folk club, it's small and always packed when singers perform. Cover charges (cash only) vary but run cheap, as are the prices at the in-house cafe. Seats reserved by phone are held until show time.... *Tel 617/ 492–7679. 47 Palmer St., Cambridge. Harvard T stop.*

Colonial Theatre. Tucked into an office building is this 1,600-seat theater from 1900, which features Broadway tryouts and touring shows.... *Tel 617/426–9366 (office); for tickets call Ticketmaster, 617/931–2787. 106 Boylston St. Boylston T stop.*

Comedy Connection. Beantown's premier comedy house is on the second floor of Quincy Market, the middle of the three long buildings by Faneuil Hall. The cover ranges from less than $10 Sunday through Thursday to $20 for the Hollywood-approved headliners on Friday and Saturday nights.... *Tel 617/248–9700. Faneuil Hall Marketplace. Government Center T stop.*

Coolidge Corner Theater. Two screens; a sometimes tricky schedule of show times.... *Tel 617/734–2500 (recorded schedule) or 617/734–2501 (office). 290 Harvard St., Brookline. Coolidge Corner T stop.*

Emerson Majestic Theatre. Slowly being restored by Emerson College, the 859-seat theater built in 1903 is home to the Boston Lyric Opera (tel 617/248–8660), Jose Mateo's Ballet Theatre of Boston (tel 617/262–0961), and visiting performers.... *Tel 617/578–8727. 219 Tremont St. Boylston T stop.*

Emmanuel Church. The Lindsey Memorial Chapel is a beautiful Gothic Revival setting for free musical events, including a Bach cantata every Sunday.... *Tel 617/536–3355. 15 Newbury St. Arlington T stop.*

Fenway Park. Built in 1912, it's the oldest American ballpark, beloved by Red Sox fans and neighboring bars. The BoSox have not won a World Series since selling Babe Ruth's contract to New York in 1919.... *Tel 617/267–1700. 4 Yawkey Way. Kenmore T stop.*

FleetCenter. The air-conditioned replacement for the Boston Garden.... *Tel 617/227–3200 (recording). 150 Causeway St. North Station.*

Foxboro Stadium. The New England Patriots' increasing popularity meant regular-season football games sold out in 1995 before play even began.... *Tel 800/543–1776. Route 1. Foxboro. No nearby T stop.*

Harborlights. Great views of sunsets, skyscrapers, and ships under a billowy white tent make just about any pop concert here memorable, which the high ticket prices reflect.... *Tel 617/737–6100 (concert information), 617/443–0161 (box office). Fan Pier, Northern Ave. South Station.*

Harper's Ferry. In youthful Allston, a full-bodied blues tradition carries on.... *Tel 617/254–9743. 156 Brighton Ave. Harvard Avenue T stop (Blue Line).*

Harvard Film Archive. The museum-like setting gives film watching here an added intellectual air.... *Tel 617/495–4700. Carpenter Center for the Visual Arts, 24 Quincy St., Cambridge. Harvard T stop.*

Hasty Pudding. Off-Broadway-quality local and touring productions perform in this historic but drafty auditorium.... *Tel 617/496–8400 (box office/recording). 10 Holyoke St., Cambridge. Harvard T stop.*

Hatch Shell. The Art Deco treasure by the river hosts many free events besides the Boston Pops, including films and rock concerts.... *Tel 617/727–9548. Charles River Esplanade. Arlington T stop. Mid-April–Oct.*

House of Blues. An inconspicuous house in Harvard Square, it's part of a blues chain of the same ilk as Hard Rock Cafe—T-shirts and caps are available. The Sunday gospel brunch is popular, and you can always eat downstairs without paying extra for the concert you're overhearing (reservations strongly suggested).... *Tel 617/491–2583. 96 Winthrop St., Cambridge. Harvard T stop.*

Jillian's Boston. Virtual-reality computer and video games. Pay per game…. *Tel 617/437–0300. 145 Ipswich St. Kenmore T stop.*

Johnny D's Uptown. A wide, shallow room with good sound and a relatively healthy menu figure in this blues/folk club's success. Cajun dancing Monday nights…. *Tel 617/ 776–9667. 17 Holland St., Somerville. Davis T stop. No shows Mon.*

Jordan Hall. Home to the Boston Philharmonic, the acoustical-ly perfect hall also hosts the Boston Cecilia chorus (tel 617/232–4540), musicians on national tours, and numer-ous free concerts…. *Tel 617/536–2412. 30 Gainsborough St. Symphony T stop.*

Kresge Auditorium. Eero Saarinen's dramatically designed MIT hall presents a range of concerts and performances, many of them free. Dance faculty member Beth Soll and her company (tel 617/547–8771) might alight here…. *Tel 617/253–4003. 77 Massachusetts Ave., Cambridge. Kendall/MIT T stop.*

Local 186. Rock bands pump up the volume in this youth-packed Allston club…. *Tel 617/351–2680 (recorded concert info). 186 Harvard Ave. Harvard Avenue T stop (Blue Line).*

Loeb Drama Center. The modern 556-seat main theater houses the equally modern American Repertory Theatre (tel 617/547–8300). Student productions, often seen in the small experimental theater, take the main stage in spring, when ART's "New Stages" series heads to other local venues…. *Tel 617/495–2668. 64 Brattle St., Cambridge. Harvard T stop.*

Lyric Stage. On the second floor of the YWCA building, the res-ident company of this comfortable small theater is a reliable source of British comedies…. *Tel 617/437–7172. 140 Clarendon St. Copley T stop.*

Mobius. You never know what you'll find in this fifth-floor multi-media gallery and experimental theater space; the sched-ule changes virtually every week…. *Tel 617/542–7416. 354 Congress St. South Station.*

Opera House. Sarah Caldwell's Opera Company of Boston has restored some of this 1928 vaudeville house (vandalized and weather-beaten after the company's bankruptcy forced its closing in 1990), but no definite plans for reopening had been announced at press time.... *539 Washington St. Downtown Crossing T stop.*

Orpheum Theatre. The faded glory of this theater with sagging seats is largely unnoticed by patrons of its many rock concerts.... *Tel 617/482–0650. 1 Hamilton Place. Park Street T stop.*

Paradise. Multilevel balconies with good views and a large dance floor are reasons rock fans hope this club isn't swallowed up by the Eurodisco next door.... *Tel 617/254–3939. 967 Commonwealth Ave. Pleasant Street T stop.*

Paramount Penthouse Theater. Set design is a high point at the Triangle Theater company's gay- and lesbian-oriented fare.... *Tel 617/426–3550. 58 Berkeley St. Back Bay Station.*

Pickman Recital Hall. Avid classical music fans enjoy free recitals in this intimate space. Good acoustics.... *Tel 617/876–0956. Longy School of Music, 27 Garden St., Cambridge. Harvard T stop.*

Publick Theatre. The amphitheater on the banks of the Charles River has an appeal all its own, and it's not necessarily the acting.... *Tel 617/782–5425. Christian A. Herter Park, Soldiers Field Road. No nearby T stop. Jun–Sep.*

Regattabar. Hushed elegance greets the highly regarded jazz performers at this Charles Hotel nightclub, which often sells out in advance. There are waiting lists for the desperate.... *Tel 617/864–1200 (hotel), 617/876–7777 (tickets). 1 Bennett St. Harvard T stop.*

Remis Auditorium. This hall in the Museum of Fine Arts's West Wing has frequent classical music concerts, films, and lectures.... *Tel 617/369–3770. Museum of Fine Arts, 465 Huntington Ave. Museum T stop.*

Sanders Theatre. Concerts by the Pro Arte Chamber Orchestra (617/661–7067), the Philharmonic and others in Harvard's

ENTERTAINMENT | BOSTON

memorial hall.... *Tel 617/496–2222. 45 Quincy St., Cambridge. Harvard T stop.*

Scullers. The popular jazz club for local and national acts expanded its room in 1995 but not its pretensions, which are few.... *Tel 617/783–0811. DoubleTree Suites Hotel, 400 Soldiers Field Rd. No nearby T stop. No shows Sun–Mon.*

Shubert Theatre. The historic theater, built in 1910, may seat about the same as the Colonial with 1,680 seats, but in 1995 it was dark for more than half the year.... *Tel 617/426–4520. 265 Tremont St. Boylston T stop.*

Somerville Theater. The fraying cinema right by the T shows second-run movies in the evening at bargain prices when it doesn't have a folk, world-beat, or other concert.... *Tel 617/625–5700 (recorded schedule), 617/625–4088 (office). 55 Davis Sq., Somerville. Davis T stop.*

Sony Copley Place. A mall cinema with eight screens that vary greatly in size. Centrally located, sellouts are common.... *Tel 617/266–1300 (recording). 100 Huntington Ave. Copley T stop.*

Sony Harvard Square. The four-screen cinema, a few steps from the T, shows a mix of commercial and art-house movies.... *Tel 617/864–4580. 10 Church St., Cambridge. Harvard T stop.*

Sony Nickelodeon. The sign for this four-screen independent-movie outpost is on Commonwealth Avenue, but the theater is actually in the alley behind a Boston University building.... *Tel 617/424–1500 (recording). 606 Commonwealth Ave. Blanford St. T stop (Blue Line).*

Symphony Hall. The Boston Symphony Orchestra and the Boston Pops split the year in this 2,625-seat hall. When tables are brought in for the Pops's spring and summer concerts, fewer seats are available. The Handel & Haydn Society (tel 617/266–3605) also regularly performs here.... *Tel 800/274–8499 (out of area), 617/266–1492 (information), 617/266–1200 (charge by phone). 301 Massachusetts Ave. Symphony T stop.*

Tapestry Room. Reserve tickets in advance for the weekend chamber concerts, a quintessential Boston experience.... *Tel 617/566–1401 (recorded information). Gardner Museum, 280 The Fenway. Museum T stop. Sat–Sun at 1:30 except Jun–Aug.*

Tsai Performance Center. The 20th-century specialist Boston Musica Viva (tel 617/353–0566) performs in this Boston University hall, as do other classical and pop musicians. Free events are common.... *Tel 617/353–8724 (recorded schedule), 617/353–8725 (box office). Boston University, 685 Commonwealth Ave. B.U. East T stop (Blue Line).*

Wang Center for the Performing Arts. A sprawling monument of rococo restoration. With 3,800 seats, it's home to the Boston Ballet (tel 617/695–6950), touring companies, and a classic-film series. Check BosTix for theater and dance bargains.... *Tel 617/482–9393. 270 Tremont St. Boylston T stop.*

hotlines & other basics

Airports... **Logan International Airport** (tel 617/567–5400) on an island in Boston Harbor, is the largest airport in New England. It is served by 40 major U.S. and foreign carriers, and is currently undergoing a massive modernization program which will provide, among other things, much-needed extra parking. The five terminals (A–E) all have taxi stands (fare from the airport to downtown hotels is $12 to $15) and free airport buses. Shuttle-bus companies **Back Bay Coach** (tel 617/698-6188) and **City Transportation** (tel 617/561-9000) run directly from the airport to downtown for $7.50. The 22 and 33 buses from the airport stop at the subway (**the T**); the combined subway and bus fare is $1.45. Take the Blue Line T inbound and you'll be downtown within ten minutes. More scenic is the **Airport Water Shuttle** (tel 617/330–8680), which runs every 15 minutes on weekdays (6am–8pm), every half hour on weekends (Sat 10am–11pm, Sun 10am–8pm), and crosses Boston's inner harbor to the city waterfront in seven minutes. It costs $8 (seniors pay $4 and kids go free). Free buses connect the terminals with the Water Shuttle. For information on airport ground transportation, call 800/23–LOGAN.

Babysitters... **Personal Touch of Massachusetts** (tel 617/451–2052, fax 617/423–445) is an eight-year-old, bonded and insured organization whose employees will sit, walk, or whoop it up with your darlings at hotels throughout Boston, Cambridge, and Brookline. They charge $12 an hour for the first three children and $15 an hour for three to six kids. (More than six? Try the National Guard). There's a transportation fee to get the sitter home if you don't come back until after midnight.

Buses... The buses of the **Massachusetts Bay Transportation Authority** (MBTA) (tel 617/222–3200) complement the subway system, with over 150 routes. Bus fares are 60¢ for local buses and $1.50 to $2.25 for express buses. Buses are not frequently used in town, but mostly for jaunts to the outer suburbs. To transfer to the T, request a ticket from the driver when boarding the bus; to transfer back to a bus, take a ticket from the machine near the platform turnstile when exiting the T. **Peter Pan Bus Lines** (tel 800/343–9999), **Bonanza Bus Lines** (tel 800/556–3815), and **Greyhound** (tel 800/231–2222) provide wider-ranging regional and national services; all three lines stop at South Station.

Car rentals... All the big guys are here, and a few little ones as well. Call for locations: **AAA Wickers Motorhome Rental** (tel 508/887–7336, 800/890–2909, fax 508/887–0170), **Avis** (tel 617/561–3500, 617/534–1400, 800/831–2847, fax 617/561–3515), **Budget** (tel 617/497–1800, 800/527–0700, fax 617/437–7198), **Hertz** (tel 800/654–3131), **Thrifty** (tel 617/569–6500), **National** (tel 800/227–7368), **Rent-A-Wreck** (tel 617/576–3700).

Convention center... Hynes Convention Center has ballrooms, meeting rooms, five exhibition halls, and an auditorium which seats 4,000 (tel 617/954–2000, 900 Boylston St.).

Doctors and dentists... **Inn-House Doctor** (tel 617/859–1776, 24-hour hotline; or 617/558–3818) will bring pricey private health care (including pediatrics) into your Boston-area hotel room within one hour of your call, any time of the day or night. Inn-House also offers emergency dental care, as does **The New England Dental Center** (tel 617/266–2700). The **Beth Israel Hospital Health Information Line** (tel 617/667–5356) is staffed by nurses who will give free medical advice and make doctor referrals. Many other large hospitals offer referral services that are listed in the Yellow Pages. **AIDS Hotline** (tel 617/536–7733 or 800/235–2331), **AIDS Action Committee of Massachusetts** (tel 617/437–6200), **HIV**

testing and support, Fenway Community Health Center (tel 617/267–0159).

Driving around... This is not such a great idea in Boston, but if you have to, the roads are there—and so is the traffic. **I-95**, New England's major coastal route, bypasses Boston inland, but offshoot **I-93** (the "Central Artery") forges through the city center, becoming clogged at every hint of peak flow—this includes Sunday evenings. Although one local politician claimed it would be cheaper to raze the whole city than to bury the Central Artery, work is in progress to do the latter. Evidence of the "Big Dig" is everywhere; there's even a display about it at the Science Museum. Going west, **I-90** (the Massachusetts Turnpike, a toll road) links Boston with the Berkshire Mountains and then turns into the New York State Thruway, with connections to New York City, Vermont, and Canada. **Route 3** heads south from Boston to Cape Cod, and traffic backs up for miles every Friday evening, Memorial Day through Labor Day.

Emergencies... Police, fire, ambulance (tel 911), **AAA** (tel 800/222–4357), **Poison Control** (tel 617/232–2120), **Rape Crisis Center** (tel 617/492–8306), **Rape Crisis Hotline** (tel 617/492–7273), **State Police** (tel 617/523–1212), **Traveler's Aid** (tel 617/542–7286), **U.S. Coastguard** (tel 617/565–9200). The following hospitals have 24-hour emergency rooms **Children's Hospital** (tel 617/355–6611, 300 Longwood Ave.), **Massachusetts General Hospital** (tel 617/726–2000, 55 Fruit St.).

Events hotline... Citywide special-events information, City Hall (tel 617/635–3911).

Ferries... Realizing that ferries are far less stressful than cars, cabs, or even subways, Boston is trying to increase by-sea transportation. The airport shuttle and several commuter boats are already proving successful. In late 1995, the city started up **Boston by Boat: the MuSEAum Connection,** a water shuttle service linking five key tourist attractions: the Children's Museum, the Aquarium, the Museum of Science, the USS *Constitution,* and Burroughs Wharf in the North End. An all-day boat ticket costs $5 for adults and $4 for kids. It's a great deal and a great idea (though you'd never have time to take in all the attractions), but at present it's on trial, so watch for possible changes this year.

Festivals and special events...

January: **Martin Luther King Day** is celebrated with events citywide (tel 617/536–4100).

February: **Black History Month** (tel 617/742–1854) moti-
vates several events around town. **Chinese New Year** (tel
617/542–2574) is celebrated with dragon parades and
firecrackers in Chinatown.

March: **St. Patrick's Day Parade**, South Boston (tel 617/635–
3911) and **St. Patrick's Day Alternative Parade**, Cambridge (tel 617/349–4000)—we need two parades
because South Boston organizers won't allow gays and
lesbians to march unless they pretend they're straight
(controversy rages over the event every year); **New
England Flower Show**, Bayside Expo Center (tel 617/
536–9280), during the third week of March, is the oldest
annual flower show in the U.S.

April: **Red Sox Opening Day** (tel 617/267–8661) marks the
eternal optimism of BoSox fans; the **Swan Boats** return to
the Public Garden (tel 617/635–4505); the **Boston Marathon** (tel 617/236–1652) takes over city streets the third
Monday of the month; **Patriot's Day** in Lexington—also
celebrated on the closest Monday to April 19 (tel
617/862–1450)—is a major event including mock battles
in full uniform in Lexington and Concord, parades, and
horsemen representing William Dawes and Paul Revere.

May: **Lilac Sunday** is held at Arnold Arboretum in Jamaica
Plain (tel 617/524–1717); **Ducklings Day Parade,** in trib-
ute to the children's book *Make Way for Ducklings,* marches
through the Boston Public Garden (tel 617/426–1885);
The Boston Pops launch their May–August season in
Symphony Hall and the Hatch Shell (tel 617/266–1492).

June: **Harborlights Music Festival,** Fan Pier, Northern
Avenue (tel 617/547–0620) mounts a series of outdoor
concerts; **Concert Series at the Hatch Shell** (tel 617/
727–5251) presents free outdoor films and concerts all
summer, on the Esplanade beside the Charles River;
Boston Globe Jazz Festival hosts events citywide (tel
617/929–2649); **Gay Pride Day March** (tel 617/267–
0900) parades through town; on or around June 17, the
Bunker Hill Weekend and Parade commemorates the
Revolutionary War battle at Breed's Hill (tel 617/635–
3911); **Boston Harborfest** takes off in Boston Harbor,
late June–July 5 (tel 617/227–1528), with many waterfront activities, including the Boston Chowderfest con-
test and the annual turnaround of the USS *Constitution.*

July: **Independence Day Parade,** July 4 in City Hall Plaza
(tel 617/635–3911) celebrates the Fourth, while in the
evening the **Boston Pops Concert** ends with glorious fire-

works over the Hatch Shell on the Esplanade (tel 617/266–1492).

October: **Head of the Charles Regatta,** Charles River, Cambridge (tel 617/864–8415), is the biggest one-day crew race in the world.

November: **Thanksgiving** celebrations are commemorated at Plimouth Plantation (tel 508/746–1622).

December: **Boston Tea Party Reenactment** on the ersatz Tea Party Ship, by the Congress Street Bridge (tel 617/338–1773), is a lame, very touristy bit of historical playacting; **First Night** on December 31 (tel 617/542–1399) has been the alcohol-free way to ring in the New Year since 1976, with a day and night of citywide revelry—ice sculptures, art, dance, paper trumpets, theater, kids' events, and parades. A special button sold around the city gets you in to all performances; outdoor events are generally free (but lines can be long—dress warmly). It beats just getting drunk, although many residents manage to work that in, too.

Gay and lesbian hotlines... Gay and Lesbian Helpline (tel 617/267–9001), **Boston Alliance of Gay and Lesbian Youth** (BAGLY) (tel 800/422–2459), **Fenway Community Health Center** (tel 617/267–0900).

Newspapers... The *Boston Globe* is the liberal daily paper; The *Boston Herald* a less liberal daily tabloid. Check out the *Globe*'s Thursday Calendar section for extensive listings on nightlife, concerts, exhibitions, current events, and long lonely-hearts columns. The *Boston Phoenix* is a Thursday weekly that costs $1.50 and is strong on arts, entertainment, film and theater reviews, and more lonely hearts. Check out the monthly *Boston Parents' Paper* (free from children's stores, etc.) for kid-related listings and activities. *Bay Windows* and *in newsweekly* are free weekly gay newspapers, both with comprehensive gay-oriented listings. *Boston Magazine* is a monthly with high-quality, trendy-yuppie articles on the city; it spawns a plethora of "Best of Boston" awards, which you'll see displayed at pet stores, hair salons, and, most coveted of all, local restaurants.

Opening and closing times... Until November 1994, Boston's antiquated blue laws restricted store opening times, especially on Sundays. Since they were repealed however, the only remaining restrictions keep liquor stores closed on Sundays, and curtail some holiday hours. Despite the new laws, many stores and malls still open late and close by six on Sundays. Monday through

Saturday, most department stores downtown are open 9:30am–7pm; outlying malls are open 9am–9pm or 9:30pm. Museums generally open between 9 and 10am and close between 5 and 6pm; many are closed on Mondays. The subway stops running at 12:45am, starting up again at 5am weekdays, 6am on weekends.

Parking... Metered parking is available in the Back Bay and on downtown streets (25¢ for 15 minutes, one hour limit), but finding a meter is another question. Before lunch, you can usually find a spot at the two-hour meters on the far side of the Public Garden (near "Cheers" and the ducklings), and occasionally on Newbury Street as well. By late afternoon, though, it's almost impossible to find parking. Garages are generally expensive: the **Kinney System** lot at Government Center (tel 617/227–0385) charges $5.50 for the first hour, $8.75 for two hours, $10 for up to 10 hours, and $15.50 for 24 hours; the **Fitz Inn** in the Back Bay (tel 617/482–7740; 41 Stuart St.) charges $4 an hour; the **Pilgrim Parking** lot (tel 617/577-8466, 1 Memorial Dr., Cambridge) charges $2 an hour. The **Boston Common Garage** (tel 617/954–2096) underneath the Common reopened in 1995 after extensive renovations; it costs $4 for the first hour, $8 for two hours, $10 for 12 hours, and $18 for 24 hours, but overnight and weekend daytime rates are a bargain at $5. Valet parking can add an extra $20 per night to your hotel bill. Wherever you eat, sleep, or shop, the best bet is to check out validated parking options and save yourself a mint.

Pharmacies... In Cambridge, **CVS** at Porter Square (tel 617/876–5519) near the Porter Square T Stop is open 24 hours a day; most other CVS branches are open seven days a week until 8 or 10pm. For the **Walgreens** pharmacy closest to you, call 800/925–4773; the Walgreens at 757 Gallivan Boulevard., Dorchester (tel 617/282–5246) is open 24 hours a day.

Radio stations... Boston is one of the country's great radio towns. Try **WEEI** (590 AM) for sports, **WRKO** (680 AM) for talk and Red Sox games, **WGBH** Public Radio (89.7 FM) or **WCRB** (102.5 FM) for classical music, **WFNX** (101.7 FM) for alternative rock, **WBUR** (90.9 FM) for public-radio news, **WSSH** (99.5 FM) for easy listening, **WBCN** (104.1 FM) for rock, and **WODS** (103.3 FM) for oldies.

Restrooms... The most pleasant downtown facilities are in the lobbies of the **Marriott** and the **Westin** at Copley

Plaza mall. The more brave or desperate might risk the toilets downstairs at the **Boston Public Library** in Copley Square. At **Faneuil Hall** you'll find bathrooms beneath Quincy Market, and you can slip into the lobby at the **Marriott** on Long Wharf near the waterfront. Harvard Square is the worst place to pee. There's a woefully over-used facility on the second floor of the **Harvard Coop** (1400 Mass. Ave.); there's only one toilet per sex at **Au Bon Pain** (17 North Shad Building), and it always has a long line outside. **Pizzeria Uno** (22 JFK St.) has a decent facility (but don't tell them we sent you).

Smoking... European visitors won't even believe it: You can't even light up in the bars in the Boston suburb of Brookline, which has declared itself a "smoke-free" city. The no-smoking regulation applies to all Brookline-based businesses, including taxi cabs registered there. Increasing numbers of Boston establishments are following suit. Most big hotels have no-smoking floors, while restaurants must, by law, provide smoke-free seating.

Subways... The T, run by the MBTA (tel 617/222–3200) is the oldest subway in the nation. It operates from 5am to 12:45am weekdays (from 6am on weekends). In central Boston a one-way ticket costs 85¢, with fares of up to $2 on longer distances; you need a token to enter the system, which you buy from booths in each station. You can buy tourist passes for one day ($5), three days ($9), and seven days ($18) from Boston CVB Tourist Information Centers at the Park Street Station and at the Prudential Center. The MBTA **commuter rail** (the "Purple Line") runs 60 miles out of Boston to surrounding communities, connecting to the regular T at North Station, South Station, Porter Square, and Back Bay Station.

Taxes... Hotel room tax is 9.7 percent, meal tax is 5 percent, and gas tax is 10 percent. Sales tax on all goods except food, clothes, prescription drugs, and newspapers is 5 percent.

Taxis and limos... You'll find hundreds of cab companies in the Yellow Pages; we happen to like **Red and White Cab** (tel 617/242–0800), but it's purely a personal choice. You can either hail cabs from the street or call for them. Taxi drivers in New York, Chicago, and other big cities have a bad rap, but Boston cabbies are generally a friend-ly, trustworthy lot. Basic charge is $1.50 plus 20¢ for each $1/7$ mile thereafter. There is a 4 person maximum. Cabs from Logan cost $1 extra, plus the $1 tunnel toll. Call the Boston Police Department's **Hackney Hotline** (tel

617/536–8294) for info on specific services and lost property. For limos and private cars try **Carey Limousine** (tel 617/623–8700, fax 617/776–6500), **Commonwealth Limousine Service** (tel 617/787–5575, fax 617/787–0718), or **Fifth Avenue/DAV-EL Limousine of Boston** (tel 617/884–2600, fax 617/884–2707).

Telephones... The Boston area code is 617. Communities to the north and south use 508, and western Massachusetts is 413.

Tickets... You can buy day-of-show, half-price tickets to performing arts events at the bright, poster-covered **BosTix booths** (tel 617/723–8915) in Faneuil Hall Marketplace and Copley Square. The kiosks also serve as full-service ticket offices for theaters, museums, harbor cruises, trolley tours, sports events, and more. In Cambridge, **Out of Town Tickets** (tel 617/492–1900) in the Harvard Square T station also sells tickets to Boston shows and sporting events. **Ticketmaster** (tel 617/931–2000) takes ticket orders over the phone and adds a hefty surcharge for the privilege.

Time... Call 617/637–8687.

Travelers with disabilities... Contact the **Boston Guild for the Hard of Hearing** (TTY 617/267–3496, tel 617/267–4730), the **Information Center for Individuals with Disabilities** (tel 800/727–5540), or the state **Office of Handicapped Affairs** (tel 617/727–7440).

TV stations... Channel 2 is the local PBS station, Channel 4 is CBS, **Channel 5** carries ABC, and **Channel 7** is the NBC affiliate. Most hotels have cable and pay movie channels.

Visitor information... The **Boston Common Welcome Center** (tel 617/451–2227) is at 140 Tremont Street at West Street, by the Park Street T station. The **Greater Boston Convention and Visitors Bureau** (tel 800/374–7400 or 617/536–4100) has an information kiosk in the Prudential Center (800 Boylston St.) where you can pick up tourist brochures, trolley tickets (on the plaza outside), T passes, and Freedom Trail maps. Both are open daily, 8:30–5, except that the Welcome Center doesn't open until 9 on Sundays. The **Cambridge Discovery** kiosk at the Harvard Square entrance to the T also offers lots of maps, walking tours, and information.

Weather... Call 617/936–1234 for the weather forecast.